friend of liberal revolutions abroad, Lafayette was viewed as the agent of the American mission, carrying the example of republican government to oppressed peoples around the world.

Lafayette's "Triumphal Tour" of the United States in 1824–25 contributed to a revival of republicanism, a lessening of the factional and sectional strife which appeared to threaten the young nation's stability, and a renewed sense of the American mission.

After his return to France, Lafayette continued to exert an influence on American popular thought. His correspondence with friends in the United States reveals their concern with slavery, nullification, and other sectional issues, as well as their increasingly stereotyped reaction to revolutions, particularly the French Revolution of 1830.

The Marquis died in 1834, but his image was employed for nearly a century longer to arouse patriotic fervor and to unite Americans in what was viewed as an international mission to spread liberty and justice.

ANNE C. LOVELAND, Assistant Professor of History at Louisiana State University, has published articles and book reviews in various historical journals. She studied at the University of Rochester, where she was elected to Phi Beta Kappa, and Cornell University, where she received two fellowships and earned her M.A. and Ph.D. degrees. *Emblem of Liberty* is her first book.

EMBLEM OF LIBERTY

LAFAYETTE

Portrait by Samuel F. B. Morse — 1826

EMBLEM
OF
LIBERTY

The Image of Lafayette
in the American Mind

ANNE C. LOVELAND

LOUISIANA STATE UNIVERSITY PRESS/BATON ROUGE

68180

ISBN 0-8071-0804-9
Library of Congress Catalog Card Number 70-142336
Copyright © 1971 by Louisiana State University Press
All rights reserved
Manufactured in the United States of America
Printed by The TJM Corporation, Baton Rouge, Louisiana
Designed by Albert R. Crochet

To my mother and father

Acknowledgments

In the course of writing this book, I have incurred many debts. David Brion Davis supervised my early work on the image of Lafayette and offered much helpful criticism. I am also grateful for the example he provided of precision and clarity in the writing of intellectual history, an example which I have attempted to follow in my own work.

T. Harry Williams made a number of constructive suggestions; his friendly interest in this study has been an important source of encouragement over the past several years. Lewis Simpson and Merrill Peterson read the final manuscript and made several valuable comments and suggestions. I should also like to thank James D. Hardy, Jr., for elucidating the complexities of late eighteenth- and early nineteenth-century French history.

The staffs of the Cornell University Library and its Rare Book Room, as well as of the Louisiana State University Library, particularly the interlibrary loan department, greatly facilitated my research in nineteenth- and early twentieth-century sources. The LSU Council on Research provided financial support in the form of a faculty fellowship for the summer of 1968.

A number of persons helped in still other ways. In Ithaca, the warm friendship of Virginia Cronin Halebsky, J. William Forgie, and David L. Ammerman provided an intellectual stimulus as well as an inexhaustible fund of encouragement upon which I drew many times. In Baton Rouge, I owe a special debt to J. Kenneth Edmiston, without whom the writing of this book would have been a very lonely task indeed.

Contents

EMBLEM OF LIBERTY

1 The Nation's Guest

Of the many foreign travelers who visited the United States in the early nineteenth century, none was more enthusiastically received than the Marquis de Lafayette. Unlike the others, Lafayette had been issued a formal invitation, voted by the Congress in January, 1824, and transmitted by President James Monroe with the assurance that "the whole nation . . . ardently desires to see you again among them." [1] If the invitation testified to Lafayette's unique stature, so did the popular response that greeted his "Triumphal Tour." His visit was the occasion for what contemporary observers called a "jubilee of liberty."

Lafayette arrived in the Port of New York on August 15, 1824, accompanied by his son, George Washington Lafayette, and his secretary, Auguste Levasseur. Though he had originally planned to visit only the original thirteen states, he eventually traveled to every one of the twenty-four states in the union. The entire tour lasted over a year and included a pilgrimage to Mount Vernon and the tomb of Washington, as well as participation in the anniversary celebration of the Battle

[1] Quoted in Edgar Ewing Brandon (comp.), *Lafayette, Guest of the Nation* (Oxford, Ohio, 1950–57), I, 28.

of Yorktown.[2] When Lafayette departed from Washington on September 7, 1825, President John Quincy Adams bade "a reluctant and affectionate farewell" to the man who had been feted and celebrated as "the Nation's Guest."[3]

Lafayette's visit of 1824–25 was the high point of a long and affectionate relationship with his "adopted country." In portraying that relationship I have been concerned not with the flesh-and-blood Lafayette, but with the romanticized and idealized personage found in American mythology and, even more, with what it reveals about the people who created it. Lafayette's youth, his dramatic participation in the American Revolution, his intimate relationship with Washington and other Founding Fathers, and later, his role in the French Revolution and the "struggle for liberty" generally—all had conspired to make a legendary figure of him even before 1824. Thus the Lafayette of this study is largely a product of American thought and imagination—an image rather than a real person.

The image of Lafayette may be defined as a representation of the historical figure and the events, ideas, virtues, and principles associated with him. Not the work of a single mind, the image represents the collective American response to Lafayette and his career over three centuries. It is a combination of myth and fact, emotion and intellect. Of course, it would be impossible to say what all Americans thought about Lafayette. Probably a great many had never heard of him, and some who had were indifferent to him. I have necessarily been concerned with the response of articulate Americans—political leaders, public speakers, writers, and an amazing number of persons, most of them ordinary citizens, who corresponded with Lafayette. Their speeches and writings exhibit enough similarity of con-

[2] For the itinerary, see J. Bennett Nolan, *Lafayette in America Day by Day* (Baltimore, 1934).

[3] Quoted in *Niles' Weekly Register* (Baltimore), September 17, 1825, p. 42.

cept and feeling to suggest that an image of Lafayette did exist. Indeed, once it had crystallized in the 1820's, the image remained fairly static throughout its long history, varying only slightly as Americans molded it in accordance with contemporary events and issues. I should also add that I have not been concerned with the accuracy of the image—with its truth or falsity as a portrait of Lafayette—but with its capacity to illuminate the thinking of Americans at different periods in their history.

The image of Lafayette provides a key to the attitudes of Americans toward themselves and their country. On the one hand, since Lafayette was identified with the Revolution and the founding of the nation, his image reveals much about American concern for the republican experiment. On the other hand, as an emissary of liberty, Lafayette was identified in many Americans' minds with their own mission to spread republican principles throughout the world. Beginning with his first arrival in the United States and long after his death in 1834—but particularly in 1824–25 when he toured the country as "the Nation's Guest"—Lafayette served as a focus for discussion of these two concerns, the republican experiment and the American mission.

2 The Making of an Image

Welcome! Freedom's favorite son,
Welcome! friend of Washington;
For though his sun in glory's set,
His spirit welcomes La Fayette.

Welcome! Friend in adverse hours,
Welcome! to fair Freedom's *Bower;*
Thy deeds her sons will ne'er forget,
Ten millions welcome La Fayette.[1]

Visiting America in 1824–25, the Marquis de Lafayette was totally unprepared for the spectacular reception accorded him. The enthusiastic and sustained greeting of his American friends puzzled the aging warrior, who claimed he had not expected "anything more than a generous and quiet welcome." He confessed to the editor of the *New Hampshire Statesman* that he could not fully understand "how services rendered nearly half a century before, disinterested and patriotic as they might be, should cause such an enthusiastic display by a people, generally, strangers to him and in the heat of an excited canvass for the election of a President of the United States." Lafayette said that "he did not feel himself worthy of so much homage. Nor could he claim or appropriate all the honors to himself, but must attribute much to the cause he advocated, and the great love of liberty which characterized the American people." [2]

---

[1] Newark *Eagle,* September 24, 1824, quoted in Brandon (comp.), *Lafayette, Guest of the Nation,* II, 23.

[2] A[mos] A[ndrew] Parker, Esq., *Recollections of General Lafayette on His Visit to the United States, in 1824 and 1825* (Keene, N.H., 1879), 59. In Worcester, Massachusetts, Lafayette described the attentions he was receiving as "'the homage the people pay to the *principles* of the government, rather than to myself.'" [Samuel Lorenzo Knapp], *Memoirs of General La-*

As Lafayette suspected, his enthusiastic reception in the United States was largely a response to his symbolic role. The parades, balls, and banquets, the banners and songs, the delirious crowds lining his route through the twenty-four states of the union—all celebrated not an ordinary individual but a hero of the American Revolution and the apostle of liberty in two hemispheres. The Nation's Guest toured America as a symbol of the Revolution and a model of faithful adherence to republican principles. "To most of those who passed," James Fenimore Cooper observed, "his form must have worn the air of some image drawn from the pages of history. Half a century had carried nearly all of his contemporary actors of the Revolution into the great abyss of time, and he now stood like an imposing column that had been reared to commemorate deeds and principles that a whole people had been taught to reverence." [3]

For Americans, Lafayette functioned as one of the hero-symbols comprising the American pantheon. Standing apart from ordinary men, such figures were personages of idealized virtues who served as models of exemplary behavior. Their primary function was to symbolize and perpetuate collective values, particularly in periods of rapid change and social reorientation. An important part of any national ideology, such hero-symbols served in America as substitutes for the symbols, heraldry, inherited titles, and traditions to which older cultures looked for values and continuity.[4] Like George Washington,

---

fayette (Boston, 1824), 198. Cf. *United States Gazette*, September 28, 1824, quoted in Brandon (comp.), *Lafayette, Guest of the Nation*, II, 104.

[3] [James Fenimore Cooper], *Notions of the Americans: Picked Up by a Travelling Bachelor* (London, 1828), I, 61.

[4] P. Meadows, "Some Notes on the Social Psychology of the Hero," *Southwestern Social Science Quarterly*, XXVI (1945), 244–45, 247; Marshall W. Fishwick, "Giants on the Land," *Social Education*, XIV (1950), 16, 18, 20; Orrin E. Klapp, "Creation of Popular Heroes," *American Journal of Sociology*, LIV (1948), 135; Orrin E. Klapp, "Hero Worship in America," *American Sociological Review*, XIV (1949), 53, 60–62; Orrin E. Klapp, "Heroes,

Thomas Jefferson, Andrew Jackson, and Abraham Lincoln, Lafayette was elevated to the status of hero-symbol because he exemplified a behavior and character that seemed peculiarly relevant to Americans of the eighteenth and nineteenth centuries.

I

The image of Lafayette which provoked such an enthusiastic reception in 1824–25 had its origins in the circumstances surrounding the participation of the Marquis in the American Revolution. Lafayette's arrival in 1777 elicited an immediate response from the American people, who translated the rather prosaic actions of a young aristocrat seeking rank and glory into one of the most dramatic episodes of the Revolution. Lafayette was universally seen as a young nobleman who had left family, friends, and fortune, sacrificing the luxury and ease of courtly life to engage, at his own expense, in the cause of America and liberty.[5]

Americans were fascinated by Lafayette's motives in joining the Revolution. In contrast to those who came to America to serve their own interests, Lafayette appeared to have come to serve the interests of America. Other foreigners did not conceal their preoccupation with money and rank.[6] But the Mar-

Villains and Fools, as Agents of Social Control," *American Sociological Review*, XIX (1954), 57, 61–62.

[5] See, for example, the resolution of Congress awarding Lafayette an honorary commission in the army, in Worthington Chauncey Ford (ed.), *Journals of the Continental Congress, 1774–1789* (Washington, 1904–37), VIII, 592–93; General Nathanael Greene to his wife, November 20, 1777, quoted in George Washington Greene, *The Life of Nathanael Greene, Major General in the Army of the Revolution* (New York, 1867–71), I, 514; Samuel Adams to Samuel Phillips Savage, September 14, 1778, in Harry Alonzo Cushing (ed.), *The Writings of Samuel Adams* (New York, 1907), IV, 61; "Extract of a Letter from Paris to a Gentleman in Pennsylvania, Dated April 10, 1777," in *Pennsylvania Gazette* (Philadelphia), August 20, 1777.

[6] George Washington to Gouverneur Morris, July 24, 1778, in John C.

quis asked only two "favors" of Congress: "One is to serve at my own expense, the other is to begin my service as a volunteer." From the beginning of his career, he encouraged the belief that his sole motive in coming to the United States had been to support the American cause. "The moment I heard of America, I lov'd her," he wrote to Henry Laurens, president of Congress. "The moment I knew she was fighting for freedom, I burnt with the desire of bleeding for her." [7]

If Lafayette's motives seemed to contrast sharply with those of other foreigners, they also differed from those of American patriots. As a "volunteer of Liberty in a foreign country," the Marquis seemed to embody a higher patriotism, transcending the natural attachment to a particular country. Thus Samuel Adams viewed Lafayette's participation in the American Revolution as "an Instance of a young Nobleman 'of Rank & fortune foregoing the pleasures of Enjoyment of domestick Life and exposing himself to the Hardships and Dangers of a Camp' not in *his own* but a foreign Country, 'in the glorious Cause of freedom.' " [8] Adams' inference, that because Lafayette fought "not in *his own* but a foreign Country," he therefore fought "in the glorious cause of freedom," was shared by other Americans and probably lay behind the popular notion of Lafayette's "disinterestedness" and exalted patriotism—a patriotism serving no particular country but rather the universal cause of mankind. As a result, Lafayette was elevated to the status of a model patriot, whose love of liberty and man-

Fitzpatrick (ed.), *The Writings of George Washington from the Original Manuscript Sources, 1745–1799* (Washington, 1931–44), XII, 226–28; Greene, *Nathanael Greene*, I, 548.

[7] Quoted in Louis Gottschalk, *Lafayette Joins the American Army* (Chicago, 1937), 22, 276. Lafayette's letter to Laurens was published in the *South Carolina and American General Gazette* (Charleston), January 28, 1779. See also Lafayette's letter to Congress, accepting his commission, quoted in Gottschalk, *Lafayette Joins the American Army*, 34.

[8] S. Adams to Savage, September 14, 1778, in Cushing (ed.), *Writings of Samuel Adams*, IV, 61.

kind was untainted by parochialism or self-interest. "Uncon-
nected with us by religion and manners as well as country, it
was enough for him that Liberty was in distress." [9]

The characteristics that Americans ascribed to Lafayette
were the classic aristocratic virtues. Disinterested, persever-
ing, amiable, humane, honorable, he was the embodiment of the
"natural aristocrat" as defined by Thomas Jefferson and John
Adams.[10] Indeed, the virtues Lafayette personified were those
which had brought the new republic into being and on which
its continued existence seemed to depend.[11] During the Revolution and afterwards, Lafayette would frequently be cited
as an example of true patriotism, an embodiment of the virtues
necessary to sustain the republican experiment.

But while the popular image of Lafayette emphasized his
disinterestedness and patriotism, Americans who knew the
Marquis personally formed a somewhat different picture of
him. John Adams was highly critical of Lafayette's "unlimited
ambition," [12] and James Madison and Thomas Jefferson were

[9] "Oration, Upon the Character of a TRUE Hero," *South Carolina and
American General Gazette*, December 3, 1779. See also the Reverend Israel
Evans, quoted in Louis R. Gottschalk, *Lafayette and the Close of the Ameri-
can Revolution* (Chicago, 1942), 327; Resolutions of Congress: September 9,
October 21, 1778, May 16, 1780, in Ford (ed.), *Journals of the Continental
Congress*, XII, 894, 1034–35, XVII, 432; *Pennsylvania Journal and Weekly
Advertiser* (Philadelphia), August 14, 21, September 11, October 30, 1784;
Maryland Gazette, August 26, 1784, quoted in Louis R. Gottschalk, *Lafayette
Between the American and the French Revolution, 1783–1789* (Chicago,
1950), 144; *Connecticut Courant* (Hartford), August 24, 1784.

[10] Thomas Jefferson to John Adams, October 28, 1813, J. Adams to Jef-
ferson, November 15, 1813, in Lester J. Cappon (ed.), *The Adams-Jefferson
Letters: The Complete Correspondence Between Thomas Jefferson and
Abigail and John Adams* (Chapel Hill, N.C., 1959), II, 388–89, 397–98.

[11] H. Trevor Colbourn quotes Samuel Adams' assertion that "no State
can long preserve its Liberty where Virtue is not supremely honored," a view
shared by other Americans. According to Colbourn, Americans considered
virtue "as important to the body politic as virginity to a young maiden." H.
Trevor Colbourn, *The Lamp of Experience: Whig History and the Intellectual Origins of the American Revolution* (Chapel Hill, N.C., 1965), 76–77,
187, and see also 25, 40–53, 67, 96–97, 131.

[12] Lyman Butterfield (ed.), *Diary and Autobiography of John Adams*

also distressed by the young Frenchman's obvious desire for glory and popularity. Had not Montesquieu warned that "ambition is pernicious in a republic"? [13] In America, a young nation whose founding and continued existence appeared to depend on public virtue, the contrast between Lafayette's genuine ambition and apparent disinterestedness inevitably raised certain questions about the nature of patriotism in a republic, particularly the relation of individual self-interest to the national welfare.

Such questions, and their answers, are suggested in a dialogue between Madison and Jefferson concerning their mutual friend Lafayette. Having just accompanied Lafayette during his visit to America in 1784, Madison reported to Jefferson the young Frenchman's "strong thirst of praise and popularity." Jefferson's response indicated agreement with his fellow Virginian's appraisal. "Your character of the M. Fayette is precisely agreeable to the idea I had formed of him," he wrote. "I take him to be of unmeasured ambition but that the means he uses are virtuous." The implication of Jefferson's remarks was that ambition or self-interest was not necessarily evil, but that its valuation depended on a favorable balance of ends and means. Taking a second look at Lafayette's character, Madison revised his original estimate. He wrote to Jefferson, "Though his foibles did not disappear all the favorable traits presented themselves in stronger light. On closer inspection he certainly possesses talents which might figure in any line. If he is ambitious it is rather of the praise which virtue dedicates to merit than

---

(Cambridge, Mass., 1961), III, 71; J. Adams to James Warren, April 16, 1783, quoted in Gottschalk, *Lafayette and the Close of the American Revolution*, 423–24. See also Greene to Washington, August 28, 1778, in Greene, *Nathanael Greene*, II, 127; Alexander Hamilton to Lafayette, November 3, 1782, in Harold C. Syrett (ed.), *The Papers of Alexander Hamilton* (New York, 1961–), III, 192–93.

[13] Baron de Montesquieu, *The Spirit of the Laws*, trans. Thomas Nugent (New York, 1949), 25, 21, and see also 19–24.

of the homage which fear renders to power. His disposition is naturally warm and affectionate and his attachment to the United States unquestionable. Unless I am grossly deceived you will find his zeal sincere and useful wherever it can be employed in behalf of the United States without opposition [to] the essential interests of France." [14]

Madison and Jefferson viewed and resolved the question of Lafayette's ambition within the intellectual framework of the American Enlightenment, a synthesis of utilitarianism and the moral sense philosophy. Accepting self-interest or ambition as a basic element of human nature, they placed their faith in the existence of certain checks against its unrestrained pursuit. On the one hand, the moral sense planted by the Creator in all men served as a curb on self-interest. Few Americans would deny that Lafayette possessed a large share of the natural virtue implanted in all men.[15] Madison himself had admitted that Lafayette was ambitious of praise, not homage, and that he hoped to win it through merit rather than power. The concept of national interest, which measured individual actions in terms of the happiness or well-being of others ("the greatest good for the greatest number") also served as a check on self-interest. Along with the inner check of virtue, the outer check of national interest insured "social health through restrained self-interest." [16] Thus both Jefferson and Madison were confident that Lafayette's "affection" for and "attachment" to America guaranteed that his actions in pursuit of glory or

[14] James Madison to Jefferson, October 17, 1784, Jefferson to Madison, March 18, 1785, Madison to Jefferson, August 20, 1785, in Julian P. Boyd (ed.), *The Papers of Thomas Jefferson* (Princeton, N.J., 1950–), VII, 446, VIII, 39, 414–15.

[15] See, for example, R. H. Lee to Arthur Lee, October 27, 1778, in James Curtis Ballagh (ed.), *The Letters of Richard Henry Lee* (New York, 1911), I, 445.

[16] For a discussion of the intellectual framework of the American Enlightenment, see Daniel J. Boorstin, *The Lost World of Thomas Jefferson* (Boston, 1960), 140–45, 163–65; Adrienne Koch, *The Philosophy of Thomas Jefferson* (New York, 1943), 15–18, 20, 41–43, 116.

popularity could not but serve the best interests of the United States.[17]

II

If Madison and Jefferson were unable to accept the image of Lafayette as a model patriot, their dialogue demonstrates that they did share the popular view of him as servant and benefactor of America, an image which Lafayette himself did much to perpetuate. Requesting a furlough to return to France, he declared his desire that "I shall always be considered as a man who is deeply interested in the welfare of these United States." [18] Even John Adams conceded Lafayette's zeal in behalf of American interests, and Benjamin Franklin, writing from France, consistently pictured the Marquis as "our firm and constant Friend." [19]

In the role of servant of America, Lafayette seemed endowed with a dual citizenship. As a Frenchman who had joined the American Revolution, he personified the Franco-American alliance. Dr. Samuel Cooper recognized Lafayette's function as agent and symbol of Franco-American unity, writing that his "whole conduct, both public and private, appears to me to have been most happily adapted to serve the great purpose of the alliance, and cement the two nations." [20] In France, Lafayette's

[17] Cf. Washington to the Secretary for Foreign Affairs, April 16, 1783, in Fitzpatrick (ed.), *Writings of Washington*, XXVI, 326–27; Hamilton to James Duane, May 14, 1780, and Duane's reply, May 23, 1780, in Syrett (ed.), *Papers of Hamilton*, II, 321–22, 329.

[18] Lafayette to President Henry Laurens, October 13, 1778, in Jared Sparks (ed.), *The Writings of George Washington* (Charleston, S.C., 1837–39), VI, 503.

[19] J. Adams to Warren, April 16, 1783, quoted in Gottschalk, *Lafayette and the Close of the American Revolution*, 424; Benjamin Franklin to Samuel Huntington, March 4, 1780, Franklin to Washington, March 5, 1780, Franklin to James Lovell, March 16, 1780, Franklin to Robert Livingston, March 30, 1782, and April 8, 1782, in Albert Henry Smyth (ed.), *The Writings of Benjamin Franklin* (New York, 1907), VIII, 26–28, 35, 406, 422.

[20] Samuel Cooper to Franklin, January 4, 1779, in Smyth (ed.), *Writings of Franklin*, VII, 291. See also S. Adams to Lafayette, June, 1780, in Cushing (ed.), *Writings of Samuel Adams*, IV, 197.

defense of the American cause typed him as an American, at least symbolically. The notion of his American citizenship was reinforced by a widely publicized action, reported in the Boston *Independent Chronicle* in May, 1780: "The Marquis de la Fayette, when he took leave at the French Court, was dress'd in his American uniform. The particular attachment of the Marquis to America, led him to the choice of this dress on the occasion; the King made a delicate compliment to his new Allies in this indulgence; it being a new thing for a French Nobleman to appear at Court in a foreign uniform." [21] In 1784, as if to confirm the popular notion of Lafayette's "naturalization," several states and cities conferred citizenship on him.[22]

Lafayette's activities in France during the peace conference and in behalf of Franco-American commercial negotiations reinforced his image as servant of America.[23] A new side of this image developed in the 1780's, when he took on the role of public relations man and propagandist for his adopted country. In letters to various Americans, he pictured himself traveling throughout Europe counteracting "false assertions of News papers" and "the false ideas of Misinformed people" about the United States.[24]

[21] Boston *Independent Chronicle*, May 4, 1780, quoted in Allan Forbes and Paul F. Cadman, *France and New England* (Boston, 1925), I, 13. See also General Robert Howe to Washington, May 11, 1780, in Fitzpatrick (ed.), *Writings of Washington*, XVIII, 352n; Franklin to William Carmichael, March 31, 1780, in Smyth (ed.), *Writings of Franklin*, VIII, 51; J. Adams, Journal of Peace Negotiations, November 19, 1782, in Francis Wharton (ed.), *The Revolutionary Diplomatic Correspondence of the United States* (Washington, 1889), VI, 57; Lafayette to Washington, October 24, 1782, *ibid.*, V, 829.

[22] Gottschalk, *Lafayette Between the American and the French Revolution*, 145–47.

[23] Robert Morris to Franklin, November 27, 1782, Livingston to John Jay, November 28, 1782, in Wharton (ed.), *Revolutionary Diplomatic Correspondence*, V, 12–13, 30; Franklin, Journal of Negotiations for Peace, May, June, 1782, in Smyth (ed.), *Writings of Franklin*, VIII, 492–93, 550; Franklin to Livingston, December 5, 1782, *ibid.*, 630; extract of a letter from a gentleman in Paris, dated August 3, 1782, in *Pennsylvania Gazette* (Philadelphia), October 30, 1782.

[24] Lafayette to Jefferson, September 4, 1785, in Boyd (ed.), *Papers of*

From the American point of view, Lafayette was specially qualified as an advocate of America in Europe. Not only did his prominence and nobility insure that his arguments would be heard, but he was one of the few foreigners whom Americans trusted as sufficiently knowledgeable and sympathetic with regard to their affairs. This trust derived no less from the fact that Lafayette had lived in, and not simply visited, the United States, than from the vague notion that by virtue of his stay in America, he had begun to think as an American. "I have scarcely met with six foreigners in the course of my life who really understood American affairs," John Jay complained; the Marquis, it appears, was one of them. In a letter to Lafayette in June, 1786, Jay wrote, "I can easily conceive that, at the German courts you visited you have done us service, because I know how able, as well as how willing, you are to do it. I wish all who speak and write of us were equally well-informed and well-disposed." [25]

As self-appointed propagandist for the United States, Lafayette necessarily became a champion of union. A constant theme of his letters regarding the reputation of America in Europe was the tendency of Europeans to mistake "partial notions for a want of disposition to the federal Union." He argued that the image which the new republic presented abroad depended upon its ability to achieve unity at home.[26] When he visited America in 1784 he repeated his pleas for a firm union, warning his adopted countrymen that the dignity and independence of their country depended on it.[27]

Jefferson, VIII, 478. See also *ibid.*, 678–79n; Lafayette to J. Adams, February 19, 1780, in Wharton (ed.), *Revolutionary Diplomatic Correspondence*, III, 506.

[25] Jay to Lafayette, June 16, 1786, in Henry P. Johnston (ed.), *The Correspondence and Public Papers of John Jay* (New York, 1890–93), III, 201–202.

[26] Lafayette to the President of Congress, September 7, 1783, in Wharton (ed.), *Revolutionary Diplomatic Correspondence*, VI, 680–81; Lafayette to Washington, November 11, 1783, in Louis R. Gottschalk (ed.), *The Letters of Lafayette to Washington, 1777–1799* (New York, 1944), 271.

[27] See letters and speeches of Lafayette during his visit, quoted in Gotts-

Lafayette was successful as the champion of "a more perfect union" because he was a symbol of union. "More than any other man who had a claim to the gratitude of Americans, he belonged equally to all Americans." He was the one prominent figure of the Revolution who had no loyalty to a particular state or region. During the war he had fought in New England as well as in the middle and southern states. At the end of his visit in 1784 he had been in every state of the union except Georgia. He did not represent any of the states, yet he had the confidence and gratitude of all of them. As a symbol of the Revolution, he was also a symbol of the common cause, past and present, of the Confederation.[28] Washington, writing after the Marquis had departed, judged that his visit had indeed fostered unity among the American people.[29]

III

In the summer of 1790 American newspapers reported that the Marquis de Lafayette had sent the key of the Bastille to General Washington "as a proof of the triumph of French Freedom." [30] Lafayette wrote, "It is a tribute which I owe as a son to my adoptive father, as an aid de camp to my General, as a Missionary of Liberty to its Patriarch." Thomas Paine, who conveyed the memento to Washington, reinforced the symbolism of Lafayette's gesture by observing, "That the principles of America opened the Bastille is not to be doubted, and there-

chalk, *Lafayette Between the American and the French Revolution*, 31, 86, 120–21, 126–27, 137; Lafayette to Jefferson, October 11, 1784, in Boyd (ed.), *Papers of Jefferson*, VII, 438; *Pennsylvania Gazette* (Philadelphia), August 18, 1784; *Pennsylvania Journal* (Philadelphia), August 14, August 18, November 13, 1784, January 1, 1785.

[28] Gottschalk, *Lafayette Between the American and the French Revolution*, 91, 132–33, 143, 145.

[29] Washington to General Henry Knox, December 5, 1784, in Fitzpatrick (ed.), *Writings of Washington*, XXVIII, 5.

[30] *Pennsylvania Packet and Daily Advertiser* (Philadelphia), August 27, 1790. See also New York *Daily Advertiser*, June 14, September 17, 1790; New York *Journal*, August 13, 1790.

fore the Key comes to the right place." Washington in turn accepted the key in the spirit in which it had been given, as "the token of victory by Liberty over Despotism," signifying "triumph for the new World, and for humanity in general." [31]

The foregoing exchange dramatized the new image of Lafayette which developed in the 1790's, that of agent of the American mission, transporting liberty and republicanism from the New World to the Old. In part this new image was the outgrowth of the image of disinterested patriot. Lafayette's higher patriotism, transcending not only self-interest but nationalism as well, had already identified him with the cause of mankind as a whole, and his participation in the American Revolution had typed him as an emissary of liberty, ready to engage in the struggle for freedom wherever it might occur. His role in the French Revolution was easily seen as an outgrowth of these two causes, mankind and liberty.

The image of Lafayette as agent of the American mission also derived from the notion that he had learned the republican ideology in the "American school," a view which he himself propounded.[32] Indeed, his successful matriculation in the republican school gave credence to the traditional notion of Europe as "a potential pupil" of America.[33] In addition, Lafayette's relationship with General Washington—by 1789 one of the popular legends of the American Revolution[34]—also

[31] Lafayette to Washington, March 17, 1790, in Gottschalk (ed.), *Letters of Lafayette to Washington*, 348; Thomas Paine to Washington, May 1, 1790, in Moncure D. Conway, *The Life of Thomas Paine* (New York, 1892), I, 273; Washington to Lafayette, August 11, 1790, in Fitzpatrick (ed.), *Writings of Washington*, XXXI, 85–86.

[32] See, for example, Jefferson to Edward Carrington, January 16, 1787, in Boyd (ed.), *Papers of Jefferson*, XI, 48; address of Lafayette, Boston, October 15, 1784, in *Pennsylvania Journal* (Philadelphia), October 30, 1784.

[33] Cushing Strout, *The American Image of the Old World* (New York, 1963), 18.

[34] According to Gottschalk, by 1782 the affection of Washington and Lafayette had become "proverbial." *Lafayette and the Close of the American Revolution*, 363. During his visit in 1784, Lafayette's relationship with the

contributed to his image as agent of the American mission. Lafayette was portrayed as the disciple of Washington, who was celebrated not only as Father of His Country but as revolutionary leader, "the chieftain, the liberator . . . and the victor of the first great revolution of modern times." [35] As Washington's disciple, Lafayette was seen as one educated in revolutionary principles and destined to disseminate them wherever possible.

Lafayette's dual citizenship also helped to shape his image as agent of the American mission. As America's "adopted son," educated in the republican school, he could be counted on to represent her example fairly and persuasively. At the same time his French citizenship provided an entrée to the courts and salons of Europe. Even more important, it might serve as a kind of inoculation, immunizing him against Old World contagions that seemed to threaten the American character. Precisely because of his dual citizenship Lafayette was able, in a way that no native American was, to resolve the tension within the American sense of mission—between the nation's desire to serve as an example of freedom, encouraging revolutions for liberty and republicanism abroad, and her determination to remain aloof from the Old World and its endemic evils and ills.[36] Moreover, Lafayette was an ardent exponent of the notion of America as an example to the rest of the world. His farewell speech of 1784 articulated the American sense of mission in words few of his countrymen would have contested: "May this immense temple of freedom ever stand a lesson

American leader was celebrated in toasts and addresses. See, for example, Gottschalk, *Lafayette Between the American and the French Revolution*, 115; *Pennsylvania Gazette* (Philadelphia), September 8, 1784; *Pennsylvania Journal* (Philadelphia), October 30, November 3, 1784.

[35] Marcus Cunliffe, *George Washington, Man and Monument* (Boston, 1958), 18.

[36] On the tension within the American sense of mission see Strout, *American Image of Old World*, 18ff.

to oppressors, an example to the oppressed, a sanctuary for the rights of mankind." [37]

Most important in shaping Lafayette's new image as agent of the American mission was his role in the French Revolution. When news of the outbreak of the Revolution reached the United States, Americans congratulated themselves on the effect of the American example abroad. The Marquis de Lafayette and other French officers who had served in the American Revolution were credited with having transported "American principles" to their native country.[38] It came as no surprise to learn that Lafayette was leading the Revolution. His experience in the American contest, his republican education, his relationship with Washington—all of these qualifications marked him out as the obvious leader of the French Revolution.[39] Nor did Americans see anything incongruous in the fact that Lafayette, a member of the nobility, was leading the

[37] Ford (ed.), *Journals of the Continental Congress*, XXVII, 684 (December 13, 1784). According to Gottschalk, the farewell address was published in full in many American newspapers. *Lafayette Between the American and the French Revolution*, 137.

[38] *Pennsylvania Packet* (Philadelphia), October 16, December 1, 1789; Jefferson to Dr. Richard Price, January 8, 1789, in Adrienne Koch and William Peden (eds.), *The Life and Selected Writings of Thomas Jefferson* (New York, 1944), 453–54; Thomas Paine, *Rights of Man* (1791), in Moncure Daniel Conway (ed.), *The Writings of Thomas Paine* (New York, 1894–96), II, 336, 355–56. The role of French officers, who had served in America, in the French Revolution was seen as confirmation of the widely held notion that the American Revolution had inspired the French Revolution. See, for example, Jefferson to Washington, November 4, 1788, in Boyd (ed.), *Papers of Jefferson*, XIV, 330; Washington to Catherine Macaulay, January 9, 1790, in Fitzpatrick (ed.), *Writings of Washington*, XXX, 497–98; G. Morris to Washington, April 29, 1789, quoted in Louis Martin Sears, *George Washington and the French Revolution* (Detroit, 1960), 47–48. For the general reaction of Americans to the French Revolution see Charles Downer Hazen, *Contemporary American Opinion of the French Revolution* (Baltimore, 1897), 140–42, 145, 164, 291, 253–56, 275.

[39] *Pennsylvania Gazette* (Philadelphia), October 14, 1789; *Pennsylvania Packet* (Philadelphia), July 16, 1790; *Pennsylvania Journal* (Philadelphia), August 29, 1792.

Revolution with the support of the third estate and against his own class. In 1777 he had sacrificed the pleasures and privileges of courtly life. Now it was assumed he was again taking up the cause of liberty and mankind against aristocratic tyranny. As the *Pennsylvania Packet* explained, "The marquis de la Fayette was never disliked by the people of France. He was always deemed a nobleman of spirit and liberality; therefore, if he took any part in favour of the populace, it was likely that he would become a leading and a favorite character of the people." [40]

Thomas Jefferson, American minister to France, shared his countrymen's view of Lafayette as leader of the third estate. To Jefferson, Lafayette's election as a deputy of the nobility to the Estates-General seemed paradoxical. "Your principles," he wrote, "are decidedly with the tiers etat, and your instructions against them." If Lafayette tried to represent both the nobility and the third estate, he would lose the support of both classes. In the end, Jefferson predicted, Lafayette would "go over wholly to the tiers etat, because it will be impossible for you to live in a constant sacrifice of your own sentiments to the prejudices of the Noblesse." He urged such action on the Marquis, arguing that it would win for him the popularity of the third estate and would "be approved by the world which marks and honours you as the man of the people." [41]

But when "the people" turned into "the mob" and moderation gave way to violence, Americans were forced to revise their image of Lafayette. Originally they had identified him with the third estate, as military leader of the people against the aristocracy; now it appeared that he was becoming in-

[40] *Pennsylvania Packet* (Philadelphia), December 14, 1789.
[41] Jefferson to Lafayette, May 6, 1789, in Boyd (ed.), *Papers of Jefferson*, XV, 97–98. See also Jefferson to Washington, November 4, 1788, and May 10, 1789, and Jefferson to Jay, September 19, 1789, *ibid.*, XIV, 332, XV, 118–19, 459; Jefferson to Washington, December 4, 1788, quoted in Sears, *Washington and the French Revolution.*

creasingly unpopular with the people.[42] His efforts, some of them futile, to stem the growing tide of violence received extensive coverage in the American press.[43] For many Americans, Lafayette became a symbol of law and order—of "rational" or "constitutional" liberty as opposed to "licentiousness." [44] As agent of the American mission, he was expected to resist the temptation to extremism and to keep the French Revolution on the same moderate course which the American Revolution had followed.[45]

At the outset of the Revolution, Lafayette had appeared as a unifying force, linking royalists and republicans.[46] (To Americans, Lafayette's loyalty to the king was no contradiction of his republicanism. In the 1790's Louis XVI was still remembered as a "great, faithful and beloved friend and ally." Americans shared Lafayette's regard for a king whose support of their own revolution seemed to indicate a sympathy for the principle

[42] *Pennsylvania Packet* (Philadelphia), October 26, December 3, 1789, January 4, 5, August 27, November 15, 1790; *Pennsylvania Journal* (Philadelphia), October 5, 1791, September 12, 1792; William Short to Jay, October 9, 1789, and G. Morris to Jefferson, August 5, 1792, quoted in Sears, *Washington and the French Revolution*, 53–54, 140; Washington to Lafayette, July 28, 1791, in Fitzpatrick (ed.), *Writings of Washington*, XXXI, 324–25; John Quincy Adams Diary, July 7, 1794, in Charles F. Adams (ed.), *Memoirs of John Quincy Adams* (Philadelphia, 1874–77), I, 33–34; Gouverneur Morris Diary, October 4, 1789, in Anne Cary Morris (ed.), *The Diary and Letters of Gouverneur Morris* (London, 1889), I, 173.

[43] *Pennsylvania Packet* (Philadelphia), October 6, 15, November 27, December 17, 1789, January 1, February 19, June 23, August 24, 26, November 29, 1790; *Pennsylvania Gazette* (Philadelphia), October 7, 1789; *Pennsylvania Journal* (Philadelphia), October 5, 1791.

[44] William Short reported that Lafayette was considered "the *guardian angel* of the capital"; he wrote that "all agree, even those who are opposed to the revolution and consequently his enemies, that it is his influence alone which preserves the order and security which is enjoyed in the capital." Short to John Brown Cutting, June 9, 1790, and to Jay, May 23, 1790, in Boyd (ed.), *Papers of Jefferson*, XVI, 508, 438.

[45] See, for example, Washington to Lafayette, April 28, May 28, 1788, June 10, 1792, in Fitzpatrick (ed.), *Writings of Washington*, XXIX, 476, 508, XXXII, 54.

[46] See, for example, Jefferson to Jay, September 23, 1789, quoted in Sears, *Washington and the French Revolution*, 52.

of popular sovereignty.) Lafayette retained his image as a unifying force throughout the Revolution, though not the influence the image originally represented. In an atmosphere of factionalism and party spirit—which some Americans in the 1790's feared had spread to their own country—Lafayette appeared devoted to principle rather than party, as a champion of unity and reconciliation rather than an agent of divisiveness. This view gained in acceptance after his imprisonment and in the 1820's and 1830's, but it was articulated as early as November, 1791, in a report on the Paris mayoralty race, in which Lafayette ran against Jerome Petion de Villeneuve, a Jacobin. After reciting the qualifications of "the Hero of the two Worlds," the report added, "What seems further to designate the Marquis as the fittest man for this post at present, is the fear that party spirit, which now lies dormant, may be roused into action at the nomination of a man who is devoted to the republican *faction*." The implication was that Lafayette stood above party in his devotion to "the cause of liberty." By contrast, his opponent was "devoted to the republican *faction*" and was therefore likely to incite rather than allay the "party spirit," which was blamed for recent "convulsions of government." [47]

Indeed, Lafayette's denunciation of factionalism was thought to be the cause of his proscription by the National Assembly. As reported by American newspapers, the primary charge

[47] *Pennsylvania Journal* (Philadelphia), February 22, 1792. As early as November 15, 1790, the *Pennsylvania Packet* complained, "Party prevails so much in France, that it is become nearly impossible to distinguish on which side truth and justice lie." As Bernard Bailyn has pointed out, *faction* and *party* were terms of opprobrium in the eighteenth century, the former being "merely the superlative form" of the latter. Bernard Bailyn, *The Ideological Origins of the American Revolution* (Cambridge, Mass., 1967), 151. According to Charles Hazen, one reason for the growing hostility of Americans toward the French Revolution was its factionalism. *American Opinion of the French Revolution*, 275.

brought against "Washington's pupil" was his petition to the Assembly for the destruction of the Jacobin club.[48] But if Lafayette's seeming transcendence of party spirit brought about his downfall in France, it also accounted for his continuing popularity in the United States. In the American mind, Lafayette was not identified with any of the parties or factions in the National Assembly. He represented the universal cause of mankind rather than the particular interests of a single class or party. By the same token, he never became the possession of either the Republicans or Federalists in the United States. This was partly owing to the fact that he was imprisoned in 1792, before any substantial division of American opinion on the French Revolution had occurred.[49] More important was his identification with Washington, who also appeared to stand above parties, and with the American Revolution, on whose principles all Americans were agreed.

Nothing better illustrates Lafayette's nonpartisan appeal in the United States than the reaction to his flight from France in 1792. To be sure, the conduct of the Marquis posed something of a dilemma for Americans who sympathized with the French Revolution. Reports from France represented him as a deserter and traitor to his country. At the very least, his action indicated a loss of faith in the Revolution.[50] The ambivalence with which some Americans regarded his behavior is revealed in the following toast: "Our Friend and Brother, Lafayette.

[48] *Connecticut Courant* (Hartford), June 16, September 24, October 15, November 5, 1792; *Pennsylvania Journal* (Philadelphia), September 12, 19, October 10, 1792.

[49] Strout, *American Image of Old World*, 42–43.

[50] *Pennsylvania Journal* (Philadelphia), September 19, October 10, 17, 24, 31, 1792, January 23, 1793; *Connecticut Courant* (Hartford), October 29, 1792; Hazen, *American Opinion of the French Revolution*, 262. Cf. Philip Freneau, "Present View of France and Her Combined Enemies," in Fred Lewis Pattee (ed.), *The Poems of Philip Freneau, Poet of the American Revolution* (Princeton, 1902–1907), III, 85–86.

May a generous nation forgive his errors (if any) and receive him to her bosom." [51] Most Americans simply refused to sit in judgment of Lafayette, preferring to view him in the light of the reputation he had earned in the United States. Gouverneur Morris observed that "without examining his conduct in this country [France], which would doubtless be condemned, my fellow-citizens confine themselves to the grateful remembrance of the services he has rendered us." [52]

An article in the *American Museum* testifies to the power of the Lafayette image to dissolve doubts and evoke unconditional faith in the rightness of Lafayette's action. The author, "Americanus," admitted that Lafayette's "unfortunate situation . . . must be distressing to every American who had contemplated his real character, or witnessed his services to the cause of freedom." The implication was that there was a distinction, which any American could see, between Lafayette's "real" character, as evidenced by his "services to the cause of freedom," and the charges made by his enemies. Americans, after all, had a standard by which to measure Lafayette's conduct: "Americanus" claimed to "trace the strong features of his great model (our illustrious president) in every stage of his conduct, from the first speech in the assembly of the notables, to his last letter to the national assembly, cautioning them to guard against the cabals of a powerful faction." In the course of the Revolution Lafayette had advocated "the true principles of liberty"; on all occasions he had endeavored to check "lawless violence." The article concluded with an outspoken declaration of faith in Lafayette: "That such a man can be a traitor, cannot, and will not be believed. On the contrary, there is every reason to presume that a course of conduct so

---

[51] Quoted in Hazen, *American Opinion of the French Revolution*, 263.
[52] G. Morris to Washington, July 25, 1794, in Morris (ed.), *Diary and Letters of Morris*, II, 64. See also J. Q. Adams Diary, February 17, 1795, in Adams (ed.), *Memoirs of J. Q. Adams*, I, 78.

uniformly pursued, will terminate as gloriously as it began." [53]

In the view of most Americans, Lafayette was "the unfortunate victim of anarchy and despotism." [54] The fact that he had been forced to flee France for his life, only to be imprisoned by the Hapsburgs, seemed to cancel out any prior suspicion of ambition or self-interest. The most that might be said of him was that he had acted too hastily. An American correspondent for the *Pennsylvania Journal* argued that Lafayette should have stayed with the Revolution "a little longer." Had he done so, "he would have been the Washington of Europe." But seen in these terms, Lafayette's flight was no crime, merely an error of judgment. However precipitously Lafayette had acted, the correspondent hastened to add that he was "certain he acted from principle." He declared, "I know him to be an honest man, and a man of honor." [55]

Lafayette emerged from the era of the French Revolution virtually unscathed. His image, which was scarcely tainted by his flight from France, was probably enhanced by imprisonment. By the time of his liberation, his role in the Revolution had become something of a legend: Lafayette, the French Washington, inspired by the example of the American Revolution, had brought "rational liberty" to France, only to find himself the victim of factionalism and mob rule and eventually the prisoner of despotism. The picture was not an encouraging one. The legend, tragically glorious though it was, implied that Lafayette had failed as agent of the American mission. It was left to his American biographers, writing on the eve of his

[53] "The Illustrious Fayette," *The American Museum; or, Universal Magazine* (Philadelphia, 1792), October, 1792, p. 196. See also "M. La Fayette," and "Address from Americans to Fayette," *ibid.*, November, 1792, pp. 289–90, and December, 1792, pp. 348–49.

[54] *Connecticut Courant* (Hartford), July 7, 1794.

[55] Extract of a letter from Cadiz, in *Pennsylvania Journal* (Philadelphia), February 6, 1793. See also Jefferson to James Monroe, May 5, 1793, in Paul Leicester Ford (ed.), *The Works of Thomas Jefferson* (New York, 1904–1905), VII, 311.

last visit to the United States, to reveal the positive aspect of the legend.

IV

In the biographies of Lafayette published in the United States in 1824 and 1825, the separate images of Lafayette as model patriot, servant of America, and agent of the American mission merged. Lafayette was seen as the embodiment of republican virtue, "a *distinguished, consistent* and *undeviating* PATRIOT AND PHILANTHROPIST—the lover of liberty and the friend of mankind." [56] An examination of his career revealed two principal virtues: benevolence and consistency.

In celebrating Lafayette's "disinterested benevolence," biographers referred to an unselfish, even self-denying concern for the general welfare of mankind. They pointed to Lafayette's "benevolent affections" and his unremitting "pursuit of the only worthy object of human ambition, that of benefiting mankind." [57] As one writer observed, "The happiness of his fellow creatures seems to have been the leading object of all his actions, and we always find him engaged in acts of private beneficence of public utility." [58]

The proof of Lafayette's benevolence was to be found in an examination of his life. American biographers began with a pointed refutation of the charge that Lafayette had joined the American Revolution as "a desperate adventurer, without fortune, or friends, or honors," or that he was "influenced by motives of ambition." Instead they saw a "peculiar disinterestedness in the services and sacrifices of the Marquis La Fayette in defence of American independence." Lafayette had

[56] *American Military Biography* ([Cincinnati], 1825), 393.
[57] [Knapp], *Memoirs of Lafayette*, 119; *American Military Biography*, 397–98.
[58] *American Military Biography*, 330. See also *Lafayette, or Disinterested Benevolence* (Boston, 1825), especially 33–35; *An Authentic Biography of General La Fayette* (Philadelphia, 1824), 125; [Knapp], *Memoirs of Lafayette*, 63.

embraced the American cause "from a noble and enthusiastic love of liberty" and from "devotion to the cause of humanity." That he had done so "for strangers and in a foreign land," and "at a time too, when that cause was regarded as nearly hopeless," was further proof of his disinterestedness. Consequently, Americans revered Lafayette "not merely as a warrior, however successful, nor even chiefly as a hero shedding his blood most gallantly in a glorious cause," but "as a *philanthropist* the most pure, disinterested, zealous and active." His support of the American Revolution was termed "a singular instance of an heroic enterprize for the good of mankind." [59]

The particular significance of Lafayette's espousal of the American Revolution derived from its activism. Lafayette's "benevolent heart and ardent mind would not permit him to remain merely a well-wisher to the cause of independence and liberty in America, but prompted him to offer his services and his fortune to this glorious cause." [60] In a similar situation another man might have been induced by "the extraneous circumstances of birth and wealth" to refrain from "active self-exertion." But Lafayette possessed an "independence of spirit which spurned the advantages of birth when they came in competition with the excellencies of native worth." Seen in this light, Lafayette's generous support of the American Revolution indicated a kind of virtuous and democratic self-reliance: "that spirit which relies upon itself, that glories in its own exertion; that spirit . . . caused him to descend from the eminence of birth and wealth, to rank himself with his

[59] [Knapp], *Memoirs of Lafayette*, 14, 16; *American Military Biography*, 272; *Authentic Biography of La Fayette*, 123–25, 127. See also John Foster, *A Sketch of the Tour of General Lafayette* (Portland, Maine, 1824), 22; Robert Waln, *Life of the Marquis de Lafayette* (Philadelphia, 1825), 205–208; *A Complete History of the Marquis de Lafayette* (New York, 1826), 135–36; [George Ticknor], *Outlines of the Principal Events in the Life of General Lafayette* (Boston, 1825), 5, hereinafter cited as [Ticknor], *Outlines.*
[60] *American Military Biography*, 270–72.

fellow beings, to ease their load of oppression . . . and to teach mankind a lesson of philanthropy and humanity, to teach both kings and slaves that they were men." [61] Active exertion was the sign of the true republican: "A man's principles do not operate with full force, when they depend on speculative ideas; it is only by devoting our talents, our services, our blood or fortunes, to the defense of principles, that causes them to be revered, or their truth and importance justly appreciated." [62]

American speakers at Lafayette receptions in 1824 and 1825 echoed the theme of his biographers. The legend of Lafayette's participation in the American Revolution was frequently invoked, with the emphasis on his disinterested benevolence. Thus Judge John DeRossett Toomer of Fayetteville, North Carolina, admonished his audience to remember "that Washington . . . fought for country and for home, Lafayette for Liberty alone." Washington and other American patriots fought in a cause that was their own; Lafayette came to America a disinterested volunteer, and staked his fortune and his life in the defense of the rights of others.[63] The contrast was clear: Lafayette's love of liberty derived from a higher motive than the one that impelled American revolutionary heroes—not from patriotism but from benevolence. As another speaker explained, the Americans fighting for independence "were striving to secure their own happiness and the prosperity of their children. *They* found a motive for exertion in their own interest . . . . *Their* love of liberty was necessarily the sentiment

[61] *Historical Sketches Illustrative of the Life of M. de Lafayette* (New York, 1824), 5–7. See also [Knapp], *Memoirs of Lafayette*, 14–16; *American Military Biography*, 270–72; *Authentic Biography of La Fayette*, 5–6; Waln, *Life of Lafayette*, 12–13; *Complete History of Lafayette*, 5–6, 18.

[62] *American Military Biography*, 275, and see also 277.

[63] Address of Judge John DeRossett Toomer, Fayetteville, N.C., March 3, 1825, quoted in Edgar Ewing Brandon, *A Pilgrimage of Liberty* (Athens, Ohio, 1944), 33. See also address of Colonel Henry G. Nixon, Camden, S.C., March 8, 1825, quoted *ibid.*, 45–47.

of patriotism; *your's* [*sic*] was an ardent desire for the general welfare of mankind." [64]

Lafayette's American admirers stressed that his efforts in behalf of the "cause of humanity" had not been confined to America or to the struggle for political liberty. Speeches during his tour emphasized that the whole of his life had had the single goal of putting into practice the principles of the American Revolution to obtain the all-inclusive objective of "the good of mankind." For this reason, Americans venerated Lafayette not simply as a military hero, or as a patriot, but as "the *friend* of *man*, the *able advocate* of his rights, the great Apostle of liberty," whose object "has been—to *better* the *condition* of *man*—to enlarge the sum of *human happiness*, & maintain the right of *self government*." In Lafayette, Americans saw "a life sanctified in the sublime cause of heroic virtue and disinterested benevolence." [65]

Americans also found proof of Lafayette's disinterestedness in his career in the French Revolution. He had resisted all temptation to power, refusing "to be Dictator, Lieutenant-General of the kingdom, and constable of France." The fact that he had proposed that no individual command more than one department of the National Guards at one time, "when fourteen thousand deputies of four millions of armed citizens were about to

[64] Address of the selectmen of Portsmouth, in behalf of their fellow citizens, n.d., in Cornell Lafayette Collection (Rare Book Room, Cornell University Library), Carton XVIII.

[65] Address of a Judge Williams, Utica, N.Y., quoted in Brandon, *Pilgrimage*, 420; address on behalf of a village situated between Culpeper and Warington, [Va.], August, 1825, in Cornell Lafayette Collection, XVIII; address of Mayor Ambrose Spencer, Albany, in *Niles' Weekly Register* (Baltimore), October 2, 1824, pp. 69–70. See also addresses of Governor DeWitt Clinton, president of New York Literary and Philosophical Society, and of Governor of Pennsylvania, *ibid.*, October 2, 9, 1824, pp. 70–71, 86; address of the Hon. H. Baird, Washington, Pa., May 25, 1825, quoted in Brandon, *Pilgrimage*, 360–62; address of citizens of Rome, N.Y., by Wheeler Barnes, June, 1825, in Cornell Lafayette Collection, XVII.

entreat him to become their chief," was "a signal proof of the
disinterestedness of his principles." Even during the Champ de
Mars ceremony, when he had had "immense" power at his
disposal, he had remained uncorrupted.[66] "A virtuous love of
rational liberty" had enabled him "to resist the temptations of
power, and the workings of ambition . . . it was then that the
love of principle prevailed over the love of power, and virtue
triumphed over ambition." [67] Later, when his life was in danger, "he might have taken power to himself, and so have been
safe," George Ticknor observed. Instead, when the King accepted the Constitution of 1791, Lafayette had resigned his
command as chief of the National Guards "with a disinterestedness of which, perhaps, Washington alone could have been his
example." Sacrificing his own personal interests, he had acted
from a concern for the welfare of France.[68]

In addition to benevolence, the other virtue emphasized by
Lafayette's biographers in the 1820's was consistency, meaning
his constant and uniform attachment to republican principles.
During his long and varied career, he had succumbed neither
to ambition nor to fear, but had remained disinterested and
courageous throughout, always loyal to the republican principles he had learned in America. Lafayette, one biographer
declared, "possessed the same political principles, the same attachment to freedom, the same sacred regard to the rights of
the people, and steady adherence to the cardinal bases of civil
liberty, resting on free institutions, under all circumstances,

[66] *Complete History of Lafayette*, 234, 237–40; Foster, *Sketch of the Tour of Lafayette*, 26. See also *Biographical Notice of General Lafayette* (Philadelphia, 1824), 9.

[67] Burlington (Vt.) *Northern Sentinel*, July 15, 1825, quoted in "Pages from the Past," *Vermont Quarterly*, XIX (1951), 231. See also *Complete History of Lafayette*, 237–40; Foster, *Sketch of the Tour of Lafayette*, 26; *American Military Biography*, 340; [Ticknor], *Outlines*, 28; [Knapp], *Memoirs of Lafayette*, 67–68, 70.

[68] [Ticknor], *Outlines*, 29–30. See also *Biography of the Illustrious Citizen, General Lafayette* (Wilmington, Del., 1824), 8; Waln, *Life of Lafayette*, 397; *Complete History of Lafayette*, 259.

on both sides of the Atlantic; . . . and he has exhibited the same confidence in his principles and professions, the same integrity of purpose, in glory and in suffering, in popularity and power, and in proscription and disgrace." [69]

In the French Revolution, Lafayette had never varied from his original objective of a limited constitutional monarchy.[70] Even when his position became dangerous, he had remained "faithful to liberty, good order, and a government of laws." [71] Of course it was his adherence to principle that ultimately led to his downfall. Rather than violate the constitution to which he had sworn allegiance, he had "determined to fall with the constitution." [72] As one writer explained, "La Fayette was sincerely and ardently devoted to the constitution; to popular and free institutions, and to regulated liberty; he could admit of no compromise of principle, or violation of constituted authority, and his personal integrity as well as political principles required him to adhere in the most scrupulous manner to the oath he had taken, of fidelity to the constitution, the nation, and the king." To be sure, Lafayette had failed to preserve the constitution or to protect the monarchy. This writer went so far

[69] *American Military Biography*, 395–96, and see 330, 397–98. See also J. S. Benham, *An Oration on the Character and Services of General Lafayette* (Cincinnati, 1825), 12; [Knapp], *Memoirs of Lafayette*, 13. The image of Lafayette as consistent republican was first suggested in an English work which was widely read in America. See Lady Morgan [Sydney Owenson], *France [in 1816]* (New York, 1817), II, 126, 127, 130. Several of Lafayette's American biographers simply "lifted" or quoted large sections of Lady Morgan's work; others indicated their agreement with her view by paraphrase and imitation. See, for example: Waln, *Life of Lafayette, passim*; *Complete History of Lafayette, passim*; and *Authentic Biography of La Fayette*, 39, 168, 175, 177, 182.

[70] Waln, *Life of Lafayette*, 294–95, 267–72, 284–86; *Complete History of Lafayette*, 193, 175–78, 186–87; *Memoirs of General La Fayette* (New York, 1825), 215–18, 331–32; *Authentic Biography of La Fayette*, 60; *Biographical Notice of General Lafayette*, 10; [Knapp], *Memoirs of Lafayette*, 64–65, 69; *Historical Sketches of Lafayette*, 109–12; [Ticknor], *Outlines*, 27.

[71] *Northern Sentinel*, July 15, 1825, quoted in "Pages from the Past," 231.

[72] Waln, *Life of Lafayette*, 412. See also *Historical Sketches of Lafayette*, 120.

as to suggest that had Lafayette compromised his principles, by yielding to "popular opinion" while "endeavouring to maintain what control and direction he could over it," he might have saved himself from proscription and "possibly his country from the dreadful evils which afterward befell it." [73] But, as another biographer observed, Lafayette's "love of justice and his correct principles" prevented him from acting on the belief " 'that the end would justify the means.' " [74] Lafayette could not have taken the steps that might have saved the country and king "without compromising his personal integrity and political principles." According to one writer, Lafayette "did what was more important to his own reputation;—he maintained his integrity and fidelity under the most trying circumstances, to the last." [75] Moreover, to have stemmed the tide of violence and factionalism would have required more power than Lafayette could in conscience have assumed, and more power than Americans would have wished to see him exercise. As one biographer argued, "That La Fayette was not more efficient, or more despotic, when he commanded the national guards, and the populace went to Versailles and insulted the royal family; or when the jacobin faction, in June 1792, were ready to denounce him and to prostrate the constitution, did not argue want of energy, but the influence of principle and a salutary love of order." [76]

It is surely significant that none of Lafayette's biographers criticized his refusal to wield political power rather than compromise his personal reputation or principles. Lafayette's desire to maintain his personal reputation was not interpreted as "ambition" or self-interestedness because the way he chose to maintain his reputation was itself proof of disinterestedness. To an age preoccupied with the abuse of power by self-interested

---

[73] *American Military Biography*, 354–55.
[74] [Knapp], *Memoirs of Lafayette*, 85.
[75] *American Military Biography*, 354–55.
[76] [Knapp], *Memoirs of Lafayette*, 126–28.

men, and blind to the positive uses of power, the refusal to yield to the "temptation" of power was a clear sign of disinterestedness and republicanism.

Thus, in the view of his American biographers, Lafayette's apparent "failure" as agent of the American mission during the French Revolution was in fact a triumph of republican virtue. Had he not "failed," he would have participated in the crimes and excesses of the Revolution and in so doing would have tarnished his image. That would have constituted the real failure of republican principles. The fact that it did not happen signified Lafayette's ultimate triumph—a triumph of virtue over temptation, of liberty over power, of republicanism over tyranny.

Lafayette's biographers found further proof of his consistency in the career he followed upon returning to France after release from prison. His refusal of offices proffered by Bonaparte and his opposition to the election of Bonaparte as consul for life were cited as proof of disinterestedness and an "unvarying character." [77] In refusing to support the Bourbons when they returned to power in 1814, "he was animated by the same principles and sentiment which governed him in the part he acted in 1789 and 1792." [78] In 1818, when he came out of retirement to serve in the Chamber of Deputies, Lafayette "exhibited to his country, a bright, untarnished, model of the true, pure incorruptible constitutionalists of 1789." In all his votes he showed himself "constant to his ancient principles." [79]

[77] Frederick Butler, *Memoirs of the Marquis de La Fayette* (Wethersfield, Conn., 1825), 183–85. See also [Knapp], *Memoirs of Lafayette*, 100–102; Waln, *Life of Lafayette*, 459–61; *Complete History of Lafayette*, 300–301, 459–61; *Biographical Notice of Lafayette*, 13; *American Military Biography*, 368–69; *Authentic Biography of La Fayette*, 114; [Ticknor], *Outlines*, 51; *Biography of the Illustrious Citizen, General Lafayette*, 18.

[78] [Knapp], *Memoirs of Lafayette*, 105; Waln, *Life of Lafayette*, 462–63; *Complete History of Lafayette*, 302–303; *Authentic Biography of La Fayette*, 115. See also *American Military Biography*, 377–78.

[79] [Ticknor], *Outlines*, 58–59; Waln, *Life of Lafayette*, 483–84; *Complete History of Lafayette*, 316–17.

To his American biographers, Lafayette in 1824 was ideologically the same man he had been in 1777 or 1789, faithful to the same "principles of true and rational liberty and the rights of man, with which he commenced his public career of glory in 1777." [80] "He is the same patriot now," one writer observed, "and almost as sanguine in his hopes, as when fighting the battles of America, or directing the French Revolution." [81] Throughout his long and various career, Lafayette had acted "like one who deemed the voluntary allegiance which he had paid in his youth to the principles of freedom, as perpetually obligatory, and paramount to all considerations of personal interest and security." In remaining true to republican principles, he had "done honour to the political school in which he was formed, by proving that the true disciple can never be an apostate nor a prevaricator." [82] Coming to America in 1824, Lafayette would not merely call forth memories of the American Revolution. He would tour the United States as the embodiment of republican virtue—and at a time when Americans were greatly concerned about their own seeming lack of it.

[80] Butler, *Memoirs of La Fayette*, 22.
[81] *American Military Biography*, 398.
[82] Waln, *Life of Lafayette*, 483–84; *Complete History of Lafayette*, 316–17.

3 Last of the Founding Fathers

The name of La Fayette is identified
with our existence as a nation, with the
glory of our republic.

MAYOR ROBERT B. CURREY, Nashville[1]

Lafayette's legendary service in the American Revolution, his close relationship with George Washington, his persistent interest in the United States—all earned him the title among his adopted countrymen of one of the *"fathers of our republic."* [2] Indeed, as Mayor Currey's statement suggests, he was identified not only with the birth but with the continued existence of the republic. During the 1820's, as the ranks of the Founding Fathers were diminished by death, Americans turned increasingly to Lafayette as one of the last surviving patriarchs of the United States.

The 1820's and 1830's were decades of introspection and self-examination. Beginning with the party struggles of the 1790's, through the War of 1812 and into the period of turbulence and change known, ironically, as the Era of Good Feelings, Americans worried about a backsliding from republican principles.[3] It is not surprising that the presence of one of

[1] Nashville *Whig*, May 7, 1825, quoted in Brandon, *Pilgrimage*, 233.

[2] Address of a Mr. Finley, New York City Hall, *Niles' Weekly Register* (Baltimore), August 28, 1824, p. 428.

[3] See Perry Miller, *The Life of the Mind in America from the Revolution to the Civil War* (New York, 1965); William R. Taylor, *Cavalier and Yankee: The Old South and American National Character* (New York, 1961); Edwin

the founders of the republic should intensify discussion of the fate of the republican experiment. Lafayette's visit in 1824–25 offered an opportunity for subjecting the American system to critical examination. His reception became a forum in which Americans assessed the fruits of independence and republican institutions and articulated hopes and fears for the future of their country. Even after his return to France and until his death in 1834, Lafayette continued to serve as a focus of such discussion and concern for the republican experiment.

I

Writing in the *North American Review* in 1825, George Ticknor noted the "singular distinction" enjoyed by Lafayette during his visit to the United States:

> It is a strange thing in the providence of God, one that never happened before, and will, probably, never happen again, that an individual from a remote quarter of the world, having assisted to lay the foundation of a great nation, should be permitted thus to visit the posterity of those he served, and witness on a scale so vast, the work of his own sacrifices; the result of grand principles in government for which he contended before their practical effect had been tried; the growth and maturity of institutions, which he assisted to establish, when their operation could be calculated only by the widest and most clearsighted circumspection.[4]

The notion that Lafayette had returned after a lapse of forty years "to see for himself, the fruit borne on the tree of liberty" was a popular and provocative one.[5] As a result, Lafayette was

C. Rozwenc (ed.), *Ideology and Power in the Age of Jackson* (Garden City, N.Y., 1964), ix–xiv; Fred Somkin, *Unquiet Eagle: Memory and Desire in the Idea of American Freedom, 1815–1860* (Ithaca, N.Y., 1967); Marvin Meyers, *The Jacksonian Persuasion: Politics and Belief* (Stanford, Calif., 1957); Lyman H. Butterfield, "The Jubilee of Independence, July 4, 1826," *Virginia Magazine of History and Biography*, LXI (1953), 119–40.

[4] [Ticknor], *Outlines*, 63–64.

[5] Mayor of Baltimore to the city council, *Niles' Weekly Register* (Balti-

seen by his American hosts as a judge of the success of the republican experiment since its founding. At the same time, as a symbol of the American Revolution and an example of consistent attachment to republican principles, he also appeared as the embodiment of the standard by which any judgment of the United States would be made. Furthermore, the visit itself was seen as a test of the republicanism of the American people. How they responded to Lafayette was interpreted as an indication of *their* consistency and loyalty to republican principles. The symbolic significance attached to Lafayette and his visit inevitably intensified the process of introspection and justification which culminated in the celebration of the fiftieth anniversary of independence a year later.[6]

Much of the self-examination which Lafayette's presence elicited turned out to be little more than self-congratulation. His reception provided a podium for expressing the exuberant nationalism of the American people, for offering proof, not only to the Nation's Guest, but to the rest of the world (and perhaps to themselves), of the success of the republican experiment and of the progress of the American nation. Lafayette could see for himself that a system of government once considered "visionary" and "impossible" had endured and prospered. The nation whose independence he had helped to secure was now a "great and flourishing republic"—a result of "the order & harmony of a well balanced system" as well as of the

---

more), July 24, 1824, p. 340. See also the address of a Mr. Morris, president of the Frenchtown city council, *ibid.*, October 16, 1824, p. 102, and July 17, 1824, pp. 324–25. The notion was publicized by Henry Clay in a speech to the House of Representatives which was widely quoted by contemporary writers. Speaking on the occasion of Lafayette's reception by the House, December 10, 1824, Clay declared, "The vain wish has been sometimes indulged, that Providence would allow the Patriot, after death, to return to his country, and to contemplate the intermediate changes which had taken place . . . . General, your present visit to the United States is the realization of the consoling object of that wish." *Register of Debates in Congress* (Washington, 1825–37), I, 4.

[6] Butterfield, "Jubilee of Independence."

virtue and enlightenment of the people it served.[7] The American government, "the only example on earth of *a pure unmixed Republican form of government*," disproved the long-accepted notion "that, *'Elective governments* must end in *anarchy*—or in despotism.' " [8] Indeed, the republic had not simply endured. It was expanding. Lafayette's tour of the western states revealed the transformation of the wilderness by the principles for which he had fought in the American Revolution. "Such are the effects and influence of liberty," declared the intendant of Cahawba, Alabama, "and such is its Promethian [*sic*] power, in quickening with a teeming population the vast howling wilderness, and causing it to bud and blossom with the beauty and abundance of civilization and improvement." [9]

Such optimistic pronouncements, the core of many addresses honoring the Nation's Guest, suggest the themes of American nationalism in the 1820's. But Lafayette's reception was something more than an expression of nationalism. In sharp contrast to the exuberance described above, an undercurrent of doubt, anxiety, and apprehension runs through many of the responses to his visit. His tour found Americans in an ambivalent frame of mind: on the one hand proud and boastful—perhaps boasting a little too loudly and exuberantly—and on the other hand anxious and apprehensive. At the root of their anxiety was a question of identity. In the early nineteenth century, Americans were preoccupied with what they called "national feeling" or "national character." Broadly interpreted, the terms signified

[7] Address on behalf of a village situated between Culpeper and Warington, [Va.], August, 1825, in Cornell Lafayette Collection, XVIII; address of James Barron, [Philadelphia] Naval Station, n.d., *ibid.*; address by the University of Maryland provost, Baltimore, *Niles' Weekly Register* (Baltimore), October 23, 1824, p. 119.

[8] Address of the New York Historical Society, n.d., in Cornell Lafayette Collection, XVII; address on behalf of a village situated between Culpeper and Warington, [Va.], August, 1825, *ibid.*, XVIII.

[9] Address of a Dr. Heustis, intendant, on behalf of citizens of Cahawba, Ala., April 5, 1825, quoted in Brandon, *Pilgrimage*, 153.

a sense of nationhood, a sense of cohesiveness as a people. More particularly, and in the American context, they signified a republican consensus—agreement on the principles of the Revolution. The anxiety exhibited during Lafayette's visit derived from fears that this republican consensus was disintegrating under the impact of economic, political, and social changes. The panic of 1819, by widening the gulf between rich and poor, and the crisis of the Missouri question, which generated disturbing geographic and political divisions, had challenged American faith in the viability of the union. The westward movement raised the question of how best to extend republican principles and institutions to the wilderness. The election of 1824 raised the specter of factionalism in a country where "party spirit" was feared and detested. Moreover, certain incidents occurred in connection with Lafayette's visit that seemed to prove the disintegration of the republican consensus.

Some commentators on the reception charged the American people with behavior ill-befitting true republicans. They pointed to the "sycophancy" and "excess," the " 'servile adulation unbecoming freemen,' " exhibited at some of the receptions, particularly in the eastern part of the United States. *Niles' Weekly Register* reported that at one reception men "failed so far in self-respect as to contend with *horses* for the privilege of drawing the revolutionary chief in his carriage!" In several places horses were unhitched and Lafayette's carriage was drawn down the streets by men.[10]

James Elliot viewed such behavior with alarm. "You have seen the sycophants of our Country (the apt seeds of Aristocracy!)," he wrote to Lafayette, begging him to warn Americans to continue in the path of republicanism.[11] Indeed, such

[10] *Niles' Weekly Register* (Baltimore), August 28, 1824, p. 426; Timothy Pickering to Lafayette, Salem, July 23, 1828, in Cornell Lafayette Collection, XI; Brandon, *Pilgrimage*, 319–20.

[11] James Elliot to Lafayette, Sadsburyville, Pa., July 27, 1825, in Cornell Lafayette Collection, XVIII.

behavior not only exposed the unrepublican sentiments of some American citizens; it also constituted a grave insult to the man honored as a consistent republican and founder of the republic. "Insulted he must be," Hezekiah Niles declared, "when he sees the sovereigns of this great and glorious country, aiming at the most magnificent destinies, converted into asses or other beasts of burthen." Lafayette wanted and deserved "to be treated like a *man*, not as a titled knave or brainless dandy," the editor continued. "Let him be hugged to the heart of all that can approach him, so far as not to endanger his health, and incur the risk of 'killing him with kindness'—let the trumpet to the cannon speak, the cannon to the heavens, and the ardent prayers of free millions ascend to the throne of the Omnipotent, that blessings may be heaped upon him; but, in all this, let us remember that we are *men* like unto himself, and *republicans*." [12]

But to most Americans Lafayette was no mere man. The Cahawba *Press and Alabama State Gazette* lamented that "our respect approaches almost to idolatry and adoration." [13] But this was inevitable, given the extent to which Lafayette had become a legendary and symbolic figure. What Hezekiah Niles called "our secret respect to titles, which we pretend to despise," was also responsible for the excessive adulation of Lafayette.[14] During the revolutionary era, the "noble connections"

---

[12] *Niles' Weekly Register* (Baltimore), August 28, 1824, p. 426.

[13] Cahawba *Press and Alabama State Gazette*, April 16, 1825, quoted in Brandon, *Pilgrimage*, 156. Some Americans condemned the blasphemous nature of the reception from religious rather than political considerations. In a long letter to Lafayette, Georgium Siders enumerated "the direful evils" produced by his reception and wondered "how you can in any measure bear the extravagant and overwhelming gust of applauding thousands who daily bow at your shrine—and directly ascribe to you that which belongs to no human being but to God alone—I mean worship." Noting "how hateful must this appear in the eyes of the Great Eternal," Siders predicted the wrathful judgment of God on the nation. Georgium Siders to Lafayette, Philadelphia, September 29, 1824, in Cornell Lafayette Collection, XVII.

[14] *Niles' Weekly Register* (Baltimore), August 20, 1825, p. 386.

of the Marquis had had a peculiar attraction for Americans. Even in the age of the common man, they could not conceal their fascination with royalty and nobility.

Throughout Lafayette's visit, Americans wrestled with the problem of achieving a satisfactory balance between idolatry and adulation on the one hand and rank ingratitude on the other. "We wish to pay to your virtues the tribute of our gratitude," the Charleston intendant declared to Lafayette, "not in the courtly strains of adulation, but in the language of republican simplicity." [15] How to achieve this was also the concern of James Fenimore Cooper, who admonished planners and participants to be guided by the awareness that the reception was supposed to be that of a republic of freemen for their benefactor:

> Let no meagre imitations, no cold affectation, no foppery of any kind come between the genuine feelings of the people, and him they love to honour; let our American character be reflected in language suited to it. Since the most splendid arch of triumph was one built for Nero, should there be any thing in common between him and Lafayette? ...
>
> Let us then forbear to pollute with profane appellations, or ill sorted emblems, this holy jubilee. Whoever addresses this friend of our country, let him remember that his tongue is but the public organ, and his words the will of a people whose dignity he must maintain, and that his discourse is directed to one who well knows the value of a free people's love, and will doubly feel the glowing welcome, when uttered in the genuine dictates of nature.[16]

Similarly, commentators who saw the reception as a test of the republican character of the American people claimed that

[15] Address of the intendant, Charleston, S.C., March 14, 1825, quoted in Brandon, *Pilgrimage*, 66.

[16] From Cooper's description of the Castle Garden Fete, published in the *Port Folio*, October, 1824, and quoted in [Robert Waln], *An Account of the Visit of General Lafayette to the United States* (Philadelphia, 1827), 381–84, 386–87.

even to address Lafayette as "Marquis" would be an inappropriate gesture. George Ticknor went so far as to imply that only someone of "Ultra Royalist" sympathies, or who did not like Lafayette, would address him by his former title.[17] *Niles' Weekly Register* agreed that the use of the title would "be a sign of disrespect, . . . almost an offense, except in some old 'revolutioner,' who could not forget his former habits."[18] Lafayette had renounced his title during the French Revolution, thereby signifying his loyalty to republican principles. For Americans to revive the title could only suggest that they were less consistent republicans than their benefactor, honoring him on patently unrepublican grounds, for his title or wealth, rather than on the basis of merit and principles. "We would not desire the world to suppose that we offer homage to the nobleman resplendent with hereditary titles," one speaker protested; "blood has no claim to preeminence; . . . in you, we venerate that nobility no earthly sovereign can confer—the nobility of virtue."[19] Lafayette "is not beloved by us for his title," *Niles' Weekly Register* insisted.[20]

If the adulation displayed at Lafayette's receptions suggested a waning of republican faith, the plight of veterans of the Revolution also seemed to imply a weakening of the republican consensus. The attention and gratitude lavished on Lafayette contrasted sharply with public apathy toward native Americans who had fought for the republican principles on which the nation rested. Significantly, some congressmen opposed a government grant of land and stock to Lafayette on the grounds

17 [Ticknor], *Outlines*, 26–27.

18 *Niles' Weekly Register* (Baltimore), April 10, 1824, p. 87, June 26, 1824, p. 268, July 23, 1825, p. 321, August 20, 1825, p. 386. See also *American Sketches; by a Native of the United States* (London, 1827), 64; *Lafayette, or Disinterested Benevolence*, 8–9; John Brennan to Lafayette, Kingston, N.Y., August 1, 1825, in Cornell Lafayette Collection, XII.

19 Address of the intendant, Charleston, S.C., March 14, 1825, quoted in Brandon, *Pilgrimage*, 66.

20 *Niles' Weekly Register* (Baltimore), August 20, 1825, p. 386.

that it represented unequal treatment of the soldiers of the Revolution. James William Gazlay of Ohio pointed to "the multitude of claims which, for these ten years past, had been continually present [to the House] . . . for revolutionary services." "What I would not give to the poorest American soldier, I would not give to a king upon his throne, should he ask it of me," he declared.[21] Similarly, Governor Frederick Bates of Missouri worried about the effect on veterans' morale of an extravagant show of attention to Lafayette. Absenting himself during the general's visit to his state, Bates argued that there had been "enough of pageantry"; now "something is due to principle." He expressed the fear "that amidst this ostentation and waste, the wounds of our revolution, etc., which yet survive, many of them in poverty or but lately relieved might cause those Veterans to make comparisons very little to the credit of the nation." [22] As Bates's statement suggests, there were some Americans, not necessarily veterans of the Revolution, who were making such "comparisons" and finding the United States wanting.

II

Given the anxiety over the apparent disintegration of the republican consensus, Lafayette's connection with the American Revolution assumed a special significance during his tour. As one of the last of the fathers of the republic and "the only surviving *general* that fought for the liberties of the United States," he was a flesh-and-blood emissary from the revolutionary period and a link with departed patriots, particularly

21 *Register of Debates in Congress*, I, 34–35.
22 Thomas Maitland Marshall, *The Life and Papers of Frederick Bates* (St. Louis, 1926), I, 38–39, II, 323–24; Brandon, *Pilgrimage*, 214, 457–58n. See also Daniel Putnam to Lafayette, Brooklyn, Conn., July 28, 1826, in Cornell Lafayette Collection, XI; *American Sketches*, 77–78; Samuel Perkins, *Historical Sketches of the United States from the Peace of 1815 to 1830* (New York, 1830), 298.

Washington.[23] Thus, as the guest of a generation which had not known the Revolution at first hand, Lafayette served as a medium through which Americans could establish contact with that earlier time. For this reason, his presence was seen by many as an opportunity for engendering "national feeling" or a consensus on the republican principles born of the Revolution.

The cultivation of "national feeling" was a natural concern in a young nation bereft of the long historical tradition and physical monuments which inspired a sense of cohesiveness and identity in other peoples. After 1815, as divisive tensions surfaced abruptly amidst the turbulence of change and growth following the War of 1812, the cultivation of a national spirit became particularly crucial. Political unity appeared to depend on ideological unity—agreement on the republican principles on which the nation was founded. In their concern to foster this republican consensus, Americans looked to its source. The American Revolution became the touchstone of republican faith, and celebrations of it were seen as a way of cultivating the republican consensus.[24] According to Hezekiah Niles,

[23] *Niles' Weekly Register* (Baltimore), July 20, 1822, p. 322. See also Brennan to Lafayette, Washington City, June 26, 1823, in Cornell Lafayette Collection, XII; Jefferson to Lafayette, October 28, 1822, in Ford (ed.), *Works of Jefferson*, XII, 253–55. Apparently the notion that Lafayette was the last surviving general of the revolutionary army was well publicized. William Lee wrote to the general, "You will see by the public prints that you are now the only surviving general of the American Revolution." Lee to Lafayette, Washington, November 24, 1823, in Cornell Lafayette Collection, XIV. Lafayette was hailed as the "bosom friend," "copatriot," and "companion" of Washington, who in turn allegedly served as his "model" and "Prototype." Arches and banners at the receptions also emphasized Lafayette's connection with Washington. Address of B. W. Leigh, Yorktown, *Niles' Weekly Register* (Baltimore), October 30, 1824, p. 139; Foster, *Sketch of the Tour of Lafayette*, 94; Butler, *Memoirs of La Fayette*, 249; "La Fayette's Visits to the United States," *Niles' Weekly Register* (Baltimore), November 6, 1824, p. 146; letter of Committee of New-London, Conn., August 20, 1824, in Cornell Lafayette Collection, XVIII. According to Marshall W. Fishwick, Lafayette's tour "evoked a flood of Washington worship." *American Heroes: Myth and Reality* (Washington, 1954), 42. See also William A. Bryan, *George Washington in American Literature, 1775–1865* (New York, 1952), 158.

[24] The preoccupation with the American Revolution which marked the

"civic festivals" such as Washington's birthday and the Fourth of July "have a very powerful and beneficial tendency to cause the people to refer to first principles, and to compare the characters of the present actors on the stage with those who have made their exit; and between the two, a *standard* is established of inestimable value to the republic." [25]

The "civic festival" that marked Lafayette's visit to the United States was seen as serving a similar purpose. Writing in the *North American Review* in 1825, George Ticknor observed that Lafayette's visit "offers to us, as it were, with the very costume and air appropriate to the time, one of the great actors, from this solemn passage in our national destinies." [26] This redramatization of the Revolution which Lafayette's visit accomplished was credited with causing a remarkable upsurge of republican fervor throughout the United States—what Governor Israel Pickens of Alabama, in words echoing Niles's statement, called "a most signal recurrence to *'first principles.'* " Edward Livingston noted "the renovating impulse" Lafayette's tour "has given to the principles of our government," and John Browne Cutting wrote to the Nation's Guest thanking him "for contributing by the *ubiquity* of your presence and the diffusion of your opinions, to develop throughout this happy land the latent fire of republican sentiment." A toast offered at a public dinner in Lexington, Georgia, suggested the general effect of the visit: "*The revolution*—Its history has been revived in our memories, and its patriotism rekindled in our bosoms, by the visit of 'the nation's guest.' " [27]

---

early nineteenth century was not merely a by-product of burgeoning nationalism, but an outgrowth of the concern for the perpetuation of the republican experiment. Cf. Daniel J. Boorstin, *The Americans: The National Experience* (New York, 1965), 376–77.

[25] *Niles' Weekly Register* (Baltimore), March 6, 1824, p. 4.

[26] [Ticknor], *Outlines*, 62–63.

[27] Address of Governor Israel Pickens of Alabama, Montgomery, April 3, 1825, quoted in Brandon, *Pilgrimage*, 147; Edward Livingston to Lafayette, Red Hook, N.Y., September 2, 1825, and Cutting to Lafayette, Gadsby's

If Lafayette's presence caused a "reversion" to the American Revolution and "first principles," it also provided a "standard" —to use Niles's term—or model of republicanism for Americans to emulate. Lafayette was celebrated during his visit as the embodiment of the disinterested patriotism which had impelled the heroes of the Revolution and which was crucial to the maintenance of a republican society. As Judge James Hall observed at a reception for Lafayette, the American Revolution was unique among revolutions in being "impelled by the purest motives" and "effected by the most virtuous means." According to the judge, "a noble magnanimity of purpose and action, adorned our conflict for independence; no heartless cruelty marked the footsteps of our warrior patriots, no selfish ambition mingled in the council of our patriot sages." [28] And of all the "warrior patriots" who peopled the mythology of the American Revolution, none was more virtuous, none more principled than Lafayette. Lafayette's visit, George Ticknor pointed out, "brings . . . our revolution nearer to us, with all the highminded patriotism and selfdenying virtues of our forefathers." The effect on the youth of America, Ticknor noted, was particularly gratifying. They had not participated in the Revolution—had not known firsthand the oppression of tyranny, or the suffering and sacrifice which the winning of liberty had entailed and which made it dear to their fathers. There was some concern that they might therefore fail to

---

Hotel, Washington, September 5, 1825, in Cornell Lafayette Collection, XII; *Niles' Weekly Register* (Baltimore), May 21, 1825, p. 177. J. F. Conover, spokesman for the Cheraw, South Carolina, delegation, declared, "The mere *name* of Lafayette, is alone sufficient with every American to produce the most noble, hallowed and pleasing recollections: it associates all that is virtuous, amiable, patriotic, gigantic; it is therefore impossible to be in the presence of the man himself, and not be animated with a *new* patriotism, a *new* incentive to virtue, philanthropy, heroism, and every other kindred feeling." Quoted in Brandon, *Pilgrimage*, 39.

[28] Address of Judge James Hall, Shawneetown, Ill., May 15, 1825, quoted in Brandon, *Pilgrimage*, 226.

develop the republican zeal of their fathers and forefathers. But Lafayette's visit seemed to provide a solution, by offering Americans an opportunity "to transmit yet one generation further onward, a sensible impression of the times of our fathers . . . and thus leave in . . . young hearts an impression, which will grow old there with the deepest and purest feelings." [29]

The preceding quotation suggests the special significance which Americans attached to Lafayette's visit, a significance which may be understood by recalling the impact of "the Great Mr. Locke" on Americans of the 1820's.[30] His sensational psychology was interpreted to mean that ideas came from or through sense impressions and more particularly "that visual images were the primary, if not the exclusive, form in which men gained knowledge of external reality." [31] Viewed from the perspective of the sensational psychology, Lafayette's reception seemed to offer a peculiarly favorable occasion for instilling the republicanism associated with the founding of the nation. The visit of Lafayette, sole surviving general of the Revolution, made a "sensible," that is, a sense impression of that event on Americans in a way that the speeches, parades, and celebrations of other "civic festivals" did not. For Lafayette's presence provided a concrete visual image which, by virtue of its identification with the Revolution, could not fail to initiate a train of ideas—or "first principles"—associated with the Revolution.

Nor was the beneficent influence of Lafayette's visit confined to the youth of America. Its effect extended to the adult population also. As a model of disinterested patriotism and benevolence, he encouraged the growth or revival of republi-

[29] [Ticknor], *Outlines*, 62–63. See also address of Governor Edward Coles, Kaskaskia, Ill., April 30, 1825, quoted in Brandon, *Pilgrimage*, 220–22.

[30] See Merle Curti, "The Great Mr. Locke: America's Philosopher, 1783–1861," *Huntington Library Bulletin*, XI (1937), 117–18.

[31] Leo Marx, *The Machine in the Garden: Technology and the Pastoral Ideal in America* (New York, 1964), 82.

can virtue among his hosts. For this reason, the tour was seen as an "incalculable advantage" to the United States, occurring at a time when patriotic fervor seemed to be declining or obscured by political and social tensions. One writer claimed that it "aroused in all their earliest warmth . . . those latent feelings of love and pride of country, which by laying long concealed might have been in danger of being lost to some." The Albany *Argus* contended that the visit "kindles up feelings among ourselves that might otherwise rust and become extinct." [32]

The emphasis placed on the disinterested benevolence of Lafayette and his revolutionary compatriots, along with the tendency of commentators to identify it with patriotism, suggests its broad importance in the 1820's. It was not confined to religion or reform, but had a secular and political function as well. In an increasingly atomistic, acquisitive society, the notion of disinterested benevolence served as a counter to selfishness and extreme individualism. It emphasized the transcendence of self-interest by a concern for the general welfare, of factionalism by a concentration on principle. As such, it was a significant ingredient in the "national feeling" which some Americans were trying to nurture at the time of Lafayette's tour.

The precise connection between the cultivation of national feeling, or a republican consensus, on the one hand and recollection of the American Revolution on the other was never spelled out, but a speech by Governor Edward Coles of Illinois, during Lafayette's visit to that state, suggests that some Americans identified one with the other. "The love of liberty," Coles asserted, "which is the most prominent trait in the American character, is not more strongly implanted in every bosom than is an enthusiastic devotion and veneration for the patriotic

---

[32] *United States Gazette*, October 16, 1824, quoted in *The La Fayette Almanac, for the Year 1825* (Philadelphia, [1825]), 17; Albany *Argus*, quoted in Brandon, *Pilgrimage*, 430–31.

heroes and sages of the Revolution. We glory in their deeds, we consecrate their memories, we venerate their names, we are devoted to their principles and resolved never to abandon the rights and liberties acquired by their virtue, wisdom and valor." [33] According to this view, the veneration and devotion which Americans showed to Lafayette, the symbol of republican principles, would be a good measure of their veneration and devotion to those principles. Veneration for Lafayette was a sign of reverence for republican principles because both attitudes were believed to come from the same source, love of liberty, and because both testified to the persistence of that love. A speaker at the Fauquier County reception explained that the "veneration and love" which the citizens of that county offered the Nation's Guest "spring from the same elevated source that gave rise to his own heroic actions, and . . . [therefore] the consciousness of their love to him is also the proof of their love of that freedom, which he so nobly assisted them to achieve." [34]

The result of this kind of thinking was that Lafayette's reception, like other "civic festivals," became an occasion for Americans to express their loyalty to republican principles. Every celebration of his visit included a ritual affirming the republican faith of the American people as exemplified in their love for Lafayette. At Salem, Massachusetts, for example, Judge Joseph Story rehearsed the events of the Revolution with which Lafayette's name was "indissolubly united," and added, "We cannot forget these things if we would—We would not forget them if we could. They will perish only when America ceases to be a nation." According to one observer, "When the Judge came to that part which says, '*We could not forget them*

---

[33] Address of Governor Coles, Kaskaskia, Ill., April 30, 1825, quoted in Brandon, *Pilgrimage*, 220–22.

[34] Address on behalf of citizens of Fauquier County, Fauquier Courthouse, n.d., in Cornell Lafayette Collection, XVIII.

if we would; we would not forget them if we could;' the spontaneous assent of the assembled people to the sentiment, was given by 'no, never;' repeated by thousands of voices, and accompanied by deafening shouts of applause." [35]

If Lafayette's visit was an occasion for all Americans to affirm their republicanism, it was a particularly opportune time for certain sections or groups whose loyalty was doubtful or suspect to demonstrate their adherence to the principles of the Revolution. For example, westerners used the reception for Lafayette to reply to fears that rapid expansion threatened the republican experiment. One of the fundamental concerns of the 1820's was how to ensure the westward migration of republican principles as well as pioneers, thereby bringing the West within the republican consensus. But the necessity of cultivating national feeling in the western part of the United States was complicated by an even greater lack of physical monuments, of a historical heritage, than in the East. Most of the western states were wilderness at the time of the Revolution. The West was "a country barren of revolutionary incidents," as the governor of Ohio admitted, and therefore unable to produce the "recollections and associations" of the American Revolution that Bunker Hill and Yorktown evoked. [36] But Lafayette was assured that the real testimonies to liberty were to be found in the hearts of the people, "imprinted upon monuments more durable than brass." Replying to the fear that republican principles might degenerate on the frontier, removed from the original setting of the Revolution, westerners declared that "the principles of bold and uncompromising Freedom which animated our fathers in the east, have descended . . . unimpaired to their children in the west." [37]

[35] [Knapp], *Memoirs of Lafayette,* 179–81.

[36] Address of Governor Jeremiah Morrow, Cincinnati, Ohio, May 19, 1825, quoted in C. B. Galbreath, "Lafayette's Visit to Ohio Valley States," *Ohio Archaeological and Historical Quarterly,* XXIX (1920), 221–23.

[37] Address of Judge James Hall, Shawneetown, Ill., May 15, 1825, quoted

Indeed, some commentators claimed that the receptions for Lafayette not only proved the loyalty of the West, but revealed it to be *more* republican than the East. Citing the adulation which had marked the reception in eastern cities, the editor of the *Allegheny Democrat* declared scornfully that such activity would not be repeated in the West. As Lafayette approached that section he would "find the people more plain, more independent and more republican." In Pittsburgh, there were "neither fools enough to drag his carriage or blackguards enough to form a wondering and admiring mob at his heels." The Nation's Guest would receive "a decent and appropriate welcome," but the people of Pittsburgh had "too much self respect" to indulge in idolatry and extravagance.[38] Speakers at Lafayette receptions echoed such sentiments, contrasting "the unimposing forms of republican simplicity" exhibited in the West with "Eastern pomp" and extravagance, which were seen as a perversion of republican principles.[39] In their eagerness to dispel doubts about their national feeling and loyalty, westerners often betrayed the sectional bias that underlay feelings of self-consciousness and inferiority. Interestingly enough, at a time when the United States was almost completely agricultural, spokesmen for the small towns and rural parts of America often evinced the same scorn as westerners for the pomp and ceremony of urban receptions for Lafayette, which they contrasted with their "rustic salutations of welcome."[40]

in "Centennial of the Visit of General Lafayette to Shawneetown," *Illinois State Historical Society Journal*, XVIII (1925), 363–65; address of Robert H. Adams, Esq., Natchez, Miss., April 18, 1825, quoted in Brandon, *Pilgrimage*, 207. See also address of Governor of Louisiana, New Orleans, April 9, 1825, quoted in Brandon, *Pilgrimage*, 167, and addresses quoted in Galbreath, "Lafayette's Visit to Ohio Valley States," 168–69, 171–75, 221–23, 227, 245–46.

[38] Editorials, *Allegheny Democrat*, April 19, May 17, 1825, quoted in Brandon, *Pilgrimage*, 474–75n.

[39] Address of a Mr. Forward, Buffalo, June 4, 1825, quoted in Brandon, *Pilgrimage*, 398–99. See also address of General William Henry Harrison, Cincinnati, and *Kentucky Gazette*, May 12, 1825, quoted *ibid.*, 322–23, 282.

[40] Address of J. Collamer, Royalton, Vt., quoted in "Pages from the Past,"

The Masons were another group of Americans who looked upon Lafayette's visit as an opportunity to demonstrate their loyalty to republican principles. Already unpopular in many European countries and somewhat suspect in the United States, they received Lafayette with enthusiasm, confident of the beneficent effect of his visit. Masons pointed to the membership of Lafayette and other Founding Fathers, whose republicanism was beyond doubt, as proof of the loyalty of the entire order.[41] They also took advantage of the occasion of Lafayette's visit to celebrate the Revolution and to profess their devotion to republican principles. William G. Hunt of the Grand Lodge of Tennessee, in Nashville, cited such ceremonies as proof that "the Genius of our order, although justly averse to narrow and peculiar sentiments and feelings, not only approves, but strongly inculcates, the duties of patriotism." [42]

III

Nowhere was the notion of Lafayette's visit as a test of the national character stronger than in contemporary evaluations of his reception. Whatever their criticism of certain aspects of the reception, most commentators maintained that the national response to Lafayette demonstrated the revival, if not the persistence, of the republican consensus that had existed at the time of the American Revolution. Certain excesses notwith-

228–29. See also address of T. Hutchinson, Woodstock, Vt., quoted *ibid.*, 230; remarks of chairman of Charlottesville meeting, September, 1824, and Committee of Bath, Maine, to Lafayette, n.d., in Cornell Lafayette Collection, XVII; Auburn *Republican*, June 15, 1825, and Cheraw *Intelligencer*, March 11, 1825, quoted in Brandon, *Pilgrimage*, 410, 42.

[41] See Masonic addresses quoted in Brandon, *Pilgrimage*, 128, 140, 324, 356; address of the master of "La Fayette" Lodge, Maine, n.d., and letter from member of Maine Lodge, n.d., in Cornell Lafayette Collection, XVII; address of H. M. Shaw, Masonic Lodge, Louisville, May 11, 1825, quoted in Edgar Erskine Hume, "Lafayette in Kentucky," *Kentucky Historical Society Register*, XXXIII, 283–84.

[42] Oration of Brother William G. Hunt, Grand Junior Warden, Grand Lodge of Tennessee, May 4, 1825, quoted in Brandon, *Pilgrimage*, 239–42.

standing—and even those might be attributed more to exuberance than lack of patriotism—the American people had acquitted themselves in a manner entirely appropriate to their guest. Honoring the visit of the model of republican virtue, they had fashioned their gestures of gratitude and homage after his example.

Such thinking explains the considerable significance attached to the congressional resolution granting Lafayette $200,000 in stock and a township of unsold public land for his revolutionary services. The bill was seen as a test "of the character of the nation." Proponents argued that it must be "worthy of the American people," refuting the well-known adage that "Republics are ungrateful," and proving that gratitude was among the primary republican virtues.[43] "The question before us," declared Henry R. Storrs, a congressman from New York, "is, whether we will support the principles of our own government in our conduct towards one who has been considered on both continents as the great Apostle of Liberty." Storrs added, "General Lafayette now stands among posterity, and our act this day is to be the judgment of posterity on his merits and his fame. Are we then here to record our value for civil liberty and all the blessings it bestows, or is it that we may send one of the greatest benefactors her cause has ever known, back to his country as a witness of the ingratitude of Republics? . . . It is to be known to-day what we think to be due at least to our character as a nation."

Supporters of the resolution also urged its passage as a gesture worthy of Lafayette. His legendary act of benevolence and generosity toward the infant republic set an example which the American people were obliged to follow. Against the charge that the grant could only sharpen the already existing sense of neglect among Lafayette's former compatriots, native

[43] *Register of Debates in Congress,* I, 32, 46, 49. For text of the resolution see *ibid.,* I, appendix, 7.

revolutionary heroes, supporters pointed to the peculiar disinterestedness of Lafayette, entitling him to compensation not necessarily due other veterans of the Revolution. Since Lafayette was not a citizen at the time of the Revolution, one senator explained, he was not "one of those whose lives and fortunes were *necessarily* exposed during the vicissitudes of a contest for the right of self-government." Yet he had spent his personal fortune and asked no recompense for his services.[44] How else could Americans repay such benevolence except by an action equally disinterested and generous?

Considering the significance which various congressmen attached to the grant, the popular reaction following its passage is not surprising. Indeed, if the observations of a Scotsman traveling in the United States are correct, Americans seized upon the grant as an opportunity "to hold forth to the world . . . the magnificent liberality of their government." The newspapers, Peter Neilson acidly observed, "were crammed, day after day, with high-flown encomiums on the unheard of generosity and munificence of the government, when, if the plain and simple truth had been spoken, they were only paying back a part of their old debt . . . . Upon this La Fayette subject, many of their editors could dwell on nothing else for sometime, extolling the gratitude of Republics, and defying the whole world to show such an example of disinterestedness and munificence." [45]

The receptions themselves were also cited as proof of the "distinterested gratitude, and boundless generosity, exhibited by the republicans of America, towards their former benefactor." [46] But commentators were more likely to emphasize the way in which the receptions illuminated other aspects of

[44] *Ibid.*, I, 54–55, 29, and cf. 48, 50.

[45] Peter Neilson, *Recollections of a Six Years' Residence in the United States of America* (Edinburgh, 1830), 203–206. Cf. the observations of James Fenimore Cooper in *Notions of the Americans,* II, 282–84.

[46] Neilson, *Recollections,* 203–206.

the national character, revealing the existence of a truly republican consensus. The receptions showed that Americans emulated other of Lafayette's republican virtues besides benevolence. The spontaneity and voluntary nature of the homage rendered the Nation's Guest particularly impressed American observers. Lafayette's visit was indeed a "triumphal tour," but it was the triumph of a man of virtue, not a "hereditary monarch" or a "conquering tyrant." [47] A Caesar or a Tamerlane, an Alexander or a Napoleon, received "the constrained homage bestowed on a conqueror, at the head of a victorious army." [48] In contrast, Lafayette was the recipient of "the *voluntary homage* of the heart!" [49] He came to America as a "private individual," with no "power" or "influence" to command such homage except "his unexampled patriotism and distinguished services" and with "nothing but his blessings to give in return." And yet, although he arrived as a private individual, he was received in the United States "as a public or national character, as the guest of the country, and honoured as the distinguished and disinterested benefactor of America." As such he was offered "the homage and gratitude of an entire nation; unbribed and unbought, flowing spontaneously, the freewill offering of the heart." [50]

Commentators also emphasized the universality and unanimi-

[47] Excerpt from the *New England Galaxy*, September 3, [1824], quoted in *Memoirs of the Military Career of the Marquis de La Fayette* (Boston, 1824), appendix, 49–50.

[48] *American Military Biography*, 386–87. See also Charles J[ared] Ingersoll, *A Communication on the Improvement of Government* (Philadelphia, 1824), 19–20.

[49] Address of Colonel Josiah Dunham, principal of the Lexington Female Academy, May 15 or 16, 1825, quoted in Hume, "Lafayette in Kentucky," XXXIV, 59–61. See also *Port Folio*, XVIII, quoted in [Waln], *Account of the Visit of Lafayette*, 362–63; [Knapp], *Memoirs of Lafayette*, 179–81; address of Colonel Henry C. Nixon, Camden, S.C., March 8, 1825, quoted in Brandon, *Pilgrimage*, 45–47; Josiah Quincy, *Figures of the Past from the Leaves of Old Journals* (Boston, 1883), 55–56; address on behalf of citizens of Albemarle, N.C., n.d., in Cornell Lafayette Collection, XVIII.

[50] *American Military Biography*, 384–87; Ingersoll, *Communication*, 21–22.

ty of the homage paid Lafayette, a fitting tribute to the man who had long served as a symbol of union to many Americans. Taken together, the various demonstrations which greeted Lafayette throughout the United States constituted "the spontaneous burst of a NATION'S GRATITUDE." [51] Here was one more proof of the existence of a national consensus—the collective or corporate response to Lafayette, standing above individual manifestations of gratitude and respect and encompassing all of them, what one writer called "a universal impulse which vibrates as the pulse of the nation." The reception by the House of Representatives—"the *essence* of the people themselves, in their great sovereign capacity as a whole"—acting "as the organs of the public will" and "in the name of the nation," was a tangible expression of this collective response, and, as one observer noted, an event belonging "peculiarly to the 'nation's guest.' " [52]

The spontaneity and universality of Lafayette's reception evoked extravagant descriptions from contemporary observers. References to the "sublimity" of the reception were commonplace, and characteristic of the romantic vocabulary emerging during this period.[53] Applied to Lafayette's tour, the notion of sublimity had a number of meanings. The reception was said to be a "display of the moral sublime" in the sense that it represented a rare effusion of the "purest emotions of joy, love, and veneration," all the more striking and unusual because it was the spontaneous outburst of a whole nation in response to the

---

[51] Foster, *Sketch of the Tour of Lafayette*, 178. See also *ibid.*, 212; excerpt from the *New England Galaxy*, September 3, [1824], quoted in *Memoirs of the Military Career of La Fayette*, appendix, 49–50; Joseph Lyman, Sheriff of Hampshire County, to Lafayette, Chesterfield, June 15, 1825, in Cornell Lafayette Collection, XVII; address of intendant, Columbia, S.C., March 10, 1825, and Savannah *Georgian*, March 25, 1825, quoted in Brandon, *Pilgrimage*, 57, 120–21.

[52] *American Military Biography*, 384–85; *Niles' Weekly Register* (Baltimore), December 18, 1824, p. 241.

[53] See, for example, Miller, *Life of the Mind in America*, *passim*.

virtues and services of a single individual.[54] Describing Lafayette's brief stopover in Fayetteville, North Carolina, the *Carolina Observer* commented that it was "a season in which the purest incense of the heart was offered at the shrine of virtue and patriotism. It was a period in which none but the nobler feelings of the heart were exhibited." [55] The uplifting effect of such scenes also testified to the "sublimity" of Lafayette's visit. Virtually every commentator noted the "affecting" nature of the presence of the Nation's Guest. Frederick Butler described the Worcester reception as "a scene of feeling, in which all the people seemed to be wrought up to the extreme of exquisite emotion. Never did we witness any thing that wore so much the aspect of the moral sublime. Gratitude, veneration, sympathy, and affection, all combining in vigorous exercise, created a state of mind, such as very rarely exists, and which can be better conceived than described." [56]

The rare chemistry of the reception and its "sublime" results had an analogue in Lafayette's visit to Mount Vernon. The pilgrimage of the revolutionary hero to the tomb of Washington had a special poignancy for American commentators, who used it as a symbol of the pure patriotism and exalted emotions which all Americans should feel—and which they allegedly did feel—in contemplating the heroes and events of the Revolution. An account published in *Niles' Weekly Register* termed the pilgrimage "the greatest, the most affecting scene of the grand drama" and described it in sentimental, extravagant language:

'gazing intently on the receptacle of departed greatness, [Lafayette] fervently pressed his lips to the door of the vault, while

---

[54] Address of Charles Shaler, Pittsburgh, May 30, 1825, and Cincinnati *Advertiser*, May 25, 1825, quoted in Brandon, *Pilgrimage*, 380–82, 320–21. See also Oneida *Observer*, June 14, 1825, and address of W. B. Rochester, Rochester, June 7, 1825, quoted in Brandon, *Pilgrimage*, 419, 405–406.

[55] *Carolina Observer*, March 10, 1825, quoted in Brandon, *Pilgrimage*, 35–36.

[56] Butler, *Memoirs of La Fayette*, 309. See also [Knapp], *Memoirs of Lafayette*, 155, 251–52; *Niles' Weekly Register* (Baltimore), October 9, 1824, p. 86.

tears filled the furrows in the veteran's cheeks. The key was now applied to the lock—the door flew open, and discovered the coffins, strewed with flowers and evergreens. The general descended the steps, and kissed the leaden cells which contained the ashes of the great chief and his venerable consort, and then retired in an excess of feeling which language is too poor to describe. . . .

'Not a soul intruded upon the privacy of the visit to the tomb; nothing occurred to disturb its reverential solemnity. . . . Not a murmur was heard, save the strains of solemn music, and the deep and measured sound of artillery, which awoke the echoes around the hallowed heights of Mount Vernon.

' 'Tis done! The greatest, the most affecting scene of the grand drama has closed, and the pilgrim, who now repairs to the tomb of the father of his country, will find its laurels moistened by the tears of La Fayette.' [57]

If Lafayette's visit to Mount Vernon represented "an excess of feeling which language is too poor to describe," the same was true of his American reception. According to many commentators, the scenes marking the visit of the Nation's Guest and the emotions they elicited were ultimately indescribable. They produced "an effect of almost awful grandeur, which

[57] From a letter to the editors of the *National Intelligencer,* reprinted in *Niles' Weekly Register* (Baltimore), November 6, 1824, p. 158. See also *ibid.,* October 30, 1824, p. 138; [Robert Stevenson Coffin], "Lafayette at the Tomb of Washington," in *Oriental Harp: Poems of the Boston Bard* (Providence, 1826), 95–96; [Knapp], *Memoirs of Lafayette,* 243–44. Some of the accounts of Lafayette's visit to the tomb of Washington heightened its symbolic and mythic qualities by including a report that an eagle, "the emblem of our country," hovered over "the hallowed spot." According to John Foster, "It displayed those feelings which would seem to indicate that it was a special messenger, sent to welcome our illustrious guest on his visit to the sacred repose of the first of men—his friend and the friend of mankind. After the General had fulfilled his pious devotions, this bird, representing the gratitude of the nation, and emblematically the spirit of Washington, took its final departure." Foster, *Sketch of the Tour of Lafayette,* 193–97; [Waln], *Account of the Visit of Lafayette,* 405; Alexandria *Herald,* October 20, 1824, quoted in Brandon (comp.), *Lafayette, Guest of the Nation,* III, 49–50.

baffles description." [58] Writing about the Virginia reception, Samuel Knapp declared that "the moral effects of this spectacle were sublime. There was an effect in it, which no words can describe." [59] For Knapp, as for many other observers, the experience of Lafayette's visit was ultimately mystical in nature.

A more rational account of the reception's significance was offered by Horace Holley, president of Transylvania University in Kentucky. The American reception was no "mere pageant," according to Holley; nor was the homage of the American people "exclusively devoted to the man, after the manner of homage paid to a king or an emperor." Americans identified Lafayette, "as we do WASHINGTON, with the cause, the sentiments, the institutions, the blessings" of the American Revolution. Lafayette's reception was therefore nothing less than "THE JUBILEE OF LIBERTY." As such it was invested with a "moral and political grandeur" which constituted its real significance.

For Holley, the "political grandeur" of Lafayette's reception lay in its dramatization of "the efficiency of just and liberal principles in relation to the best civil and social purposes." The American response to Lafayette provided a convincing demonstration of the persistence of republican principles. Moreover, Lafayette's presence was "making impressions upon the ardent and ingenuous minds of the young men . . . which they will never forget." Holley did not doubt that "should duty call," these young men would "shed the last drop of their blood in

[58] *Niles' Weekly Register* (Baltimore), October 8, 1824, p. 86. See also *Carolina Observer*, March 10, 1825, and Cincinnati *Advertiser*, May 25, 1825, quoted in Brandon, *Pilgrimage*, 35–36, 320–21; Butler, *Memoirs of La Fayette*, 309.

[59] [Knapp], *Memoirs of Lafayette*, 251–52. The Raleigh *Register* explained, "At a distance, we can contemplate any event in which our feelings are interested with calmness and complacency, but when it comes upon us, there is a nameless feeling which almost paralyses the endeavor to expatiate upon it." Quoted in Brandon, *Pilgrimage*, 24.

defending the Cause, for which WASHINGTON and FAYETTE hazarded all they held dear, wealth and freedom, life and fame." Thus Lafayette's visit not only demonstrated the extent to which a government based on republican principles had succeeded; it also guaranteed the perpetuation of the republican experiment.

The "moral grandeur" of Lafayette's reception lay in its having stimulated the American people to a new awareness of self and society. The symbol of republican principles and one of the founders of the republican experiment, Lafayette made the American people "reflect seriously and deeply upon our laws and institutions, upon our civil and social character, upon our relations to one another, and upon the tendencies of our whole political and moral system." In Holley's view, such thinking signified an intellectual and moral liberation—from the complacency and apathy that threatened to undermine the republican consensus—as significant as the political liberation achieved during the American Revolution. Coming to America in 1824, Lafayette had cooperated with Americans "a *second time* in the establishment of our Freedom and Independence." The first time "was for our *bodies* and *outward* condition," the second "for our *souls* and our *sentiments*." Once again, and "in a still nobler sense than before," Lafayette served as "our Champion, and . . . one of the founders of our Liberty." [60]

IV

Lafayette departed the United States in September, 1825. The next year, on the Fourth of July, Thomas Jefferson and John Adams died. The occurrence of the fiftieth anniversary of independence was, in itself, a startling indication of the length of time separating the present generation from the Revolution and the principles it represented. But the departure of

[60] Address of President Horace Holley, Transylvania University, May 16, 1825, in Cornell Lafayette Collection, XVII.

the two patriarchs intensified a growing sense of estrangement from the Revolution; their passing created "an immense void" in American society, to use the words of Daniel Webster. "One great link connecting [Americans] with former times, was broken," Webster explained, and they "lost something more, as it were, of the presence of the Revolution itself, and of the act of independence." [61] Only a handful of men remained who had "acted with them, in the days of . . . tribulation." For the majority of Americans the revolutionary period was but "a matter of history." [62]

With the loss of two men "intimately, and for so long a time, blended with the history of the country, and . . . united . . . with the events of the Revolution," [63] Americans turned increasingly to Lafayette as a link with the revolutionary period. In 1828 *Niles' Weekly Register* named him one of the three surviving "founders of the republic," along with Charles Carroll of Carrollton and James Madison.[64] Though living in France, Lafayette continued to fill the roles he had played at the time of his visit in 1824–25—touchstone of republicanism, model patriot, benefactor of America. The voluminous correspondence between him and his American friends in the years following his visit attests to his continuing influence and authority. As William Giles declared, "Surely the example, and

[61] Daniel Webster, "A Discourse in Commemoration of the Lives and Services of John Adams and Thomas Jefferson, Delivered in Faneuil Hall, Boston, on the 2d of August, 1826," in *The Writings and Speeches of Daniel Webster* (Boston, 1903), I, 290, 293. See also William Wirt, "Eulogy on Thomas Jefferson and John Adams, Delivered in Washington, D.C., on October 19, 1826, in the Hall of the House of Representatives of the United States," in Andrew A. Lipscomb and Albert Ellery Bergh (eds.), *The Writings of Thomas Jefferson* (Washington, 1904), XIII, liv; Edward Everett, "Address Delivered at Charlestown, [Mass.], August 1, 1826, in Commemoration of John Adams and Thomas Jefferson," in *Orations and Speeches, on Various Occasions* (Boston, 1836), 122–24.

[62] Richard Peters to Lafayette, Belmont, [Mass.?], December, 1826, in Cornell Lafayette Collection, XI.

[63] Webster, "Discourse in Commemoration of Adams and Jefferson," 290.

[64] *Niles' Weekly Register* (Baltimore), August 30, 1828, p. 6.

opinion of no human being could be entitled to greater regard in this Country; than those of one, who is here, universally admitted to be the most uniform and experienced friend of the 'plain rights of man': and in all other countries universally admitted, at least, by all liberals, to be, the undeviating apostle of human liberty." [65]

The fact that Lafayette continued to evince a concern for the welfare of his adopted country helped to keep his image alive in the American mind. His annual appearances at Fourth of July celebrations in Paris were faithfully reported by American newspapers, and he received an unending flow of American visitors at La Grange, many of whom returned home to testify to the General's interest in and familiarity with American developments. An editor of a New York newspaper described an evening with Lafayette and his family in which the conversation covered "a variety of topics, chiefly relating to our country." He reported that "the whole family talk, and seem to think of nothing else than the United States, where their feelings, their hopes, and wishes all centre. The general considers himself emphatically, a citizen of the American republic, and familiarly speaks of it precisely in the same way, as if he had been there born and educated." Lafayette received "a great number of American newspapers, reviews and other publications," the New Yorker continued, "and regularly corresponds with many of his friends, in every part of the union. These various sources of information . . . added to the astonishing accuracy of his observations and recollections of circumstances connected with his tour, render him better acquainted with the condition of the country, than almost any one of its actual residents." [66]

[65] William B. Giles to Lafayette, Richmond, Va., May 15, 1828, in Cornell Lafayette Collection, XVII.

[66] Extract of a letter ascribed to a Mr. Carter, editor of one of the New York journals, Paris, January, 1826, quoted in [Waln], *Account of the Visit of Lafayette*, 485–86.

The fact that Lafayette's image had not been tarnished by involvement in partisan politics also contributed to his influence and authority in the late 1820's and early 1830's. This was a valuable asset in a period of increasing factionalism and sectionalism and one which few Americans could claim. Following his tour as the Nation's Guest, Lafayette was more than ever "the nations [*sic*] property" and consequently, one correspondent explained, "every citizen of this republic claim[s] a privilege of addressing you." [67]

A number of Americans wrote to Lafayette expressing concern about the republican experiment. As a symbol of consistent republicanism, Lafayette was still the best judge of the success or failure of the American effort, still the best model of the virtues necessary to perpetuate a republican government and society. To the dismay and disappointment of his American friends, the reawakening of republicanism and patriotism which his visit had stimulated did not outlast his return to France. "There are *now* no such exigencies as we passed thro' in our arduous struggle for national existence," Richard Peters wrote to Lafayette in 1826; "but there are constantly occurring enough to exercise & call forth the Talents & patriotism of our best & wisest citizens. Yet such do not always appear in our public bodies." Similarly, James Brown lamented the "great decline in publick spirit and Patriotism" and declared that "office hunting, and servility, corruption and Calumny, the elevation of the ignorant and vulgar, while exclusion of the patriotick seem to have become the prevailing vices of the Country." [68]

A letter by William Ellis offers a striking contrast to the proud boasts of Americans during Lafayette's visit. Ironically,

[67] Phinehas Rainey to Lafayette, Middletown, Conn., August 25, 1833, in Cornell Lafayette Collection, XIV. See also Robert Walsh to Lafayette, Philadelphia, November 27, 1831, *ibid.*, XV.

[68] Peters to Lafayette, Belmont, [Mass.?], December, 1826, *ibid.*, XI; James Brown to Lafayette, Philadelphia, March 8, 1834, *ibid.*, XII.

the prosperity that had then been a source of pride was now a reason for fear, threatening to undermine the patriotism and republican principles on which the United States was founded. Writing in 1831, Ellis reported that many of his countrymen feared "that an uninterrupted prosperity, renders the people of any Nation Effeminate,—That wealth and Luxury, may prove the destroyer of courage and patriotism." [69] Indeed, Ellis' explanation of the decline of patriotism was quite similar to the theory of Alexis de Tocqueville, who was visiting America in the same year that Ellis wrote his letter. Tocqueville argued that "equality of condition," the by-product of American prosperity, explained "why so many ambitious men and so little lofty ambition are to be found in the United States." In democratic nations, Tocqueville continued, "life is generally spent in eagerly coveting small objects that are within reach." Moreover, equality of condition tended "to keep men asunder" by nurturing an individualism which "disposes each member of the community to sever himself from the mass of his fellows and to draw apart with his family and his friends, so that after he has thus formed a little circle of his own, he willingly leaves society at large to itself." Equality of condition thus intensified "private interest" and even selfishness, to the exclusion of a concern for the public welfare.[70]

Against the petty ambition and selfishness of the majority of Americans, Lafayette stood out in sharp contrast. His disinterested espousal of the American cause of liberty and his benevolent concern for the welfare of mankind exemplified the kind of patriotism so sadly lacking in the United States. What would happen to the republican experiment when he no longer served as a living example of such virtues? The deaths of

69 William Ellis to Lafayette, Dedham, Mass., July 4, 1831, *ibid.*, XIII. See also John L. Watson to Lafayette, Germantown, Pa., September 1, 1830, and Giles to Lafayette, Richmond, Va., May 15, 1828, *ibid.*, XVII.

70 Alexis de Tocqueville, *Democracy in America*, ed. Phillips Bradley (New York, 1954), II, 100–102, 104–106, 109–13, 256–58.

Adams and Jefferson had intensified fears of a decline of patriotism. Ellis admitted that "fears are sometimes entertained that after the Revolutionary Patriots are gone, our people, in the midst of prosperity, luxury and good feeling, might forget that their Enjoyments were purchased at the price of blood, and neglect to cherish the Sacred Principles which originated, and which alone can preserve these 'Pearls of great price' to after generations." [71] The desperate way in which Americans clung to Lafayette suggests the nature and extent of their anxiety over the fate of the republican experiment. As the last surviving link with the Revolution and the virtues and principles it represented, Lafayette was identified, in the minds of Americans, with the republican experiment itself. What would happen to it when he, like Adams and Jefferson and other patriarchs, was gone?

V

As a symbol of the principles of the Revolution, Lafayette also received appeals from reformers who sought to fulfill the promises of the Revolution or who believed the republican experiment threatened by certain evils. Edward Delavan, for example, solicited Lafayette's support for the temperance crusade, arguing that intemperance threatened American liberty and effected a tyranny over men as oppressive as that of the British crown fifty years earlier. The result of intemperance, he explained, was "the slavery of vice." Moreover, intemperance endangered the republican experiment, for "all history shows, that a nation cannot long be free, after it has become vicious." Given these assumptions, the objective of the New York State Temperance Society (whose report he included in his letter to Lafayette) equaled, if it did not surpass, the American Revolution in significance. "When that day shall come, which shall see

[71] Ellis to Lafayette, Dedham, Mass., July 4, 1831, in Cornell Lafayette Collection, XIII.

America free from the guilt and pollutions of drunkeness [*sic*],
it will be a prouder and a more glorious day, than that which
beheld the British Lion yielding to the American Eagle on the
plains of Yorktown," Delavan declared. Then would the heroes
of the Revolution be vindicated: "with what delight will Washington and Fayette, and other kindred spirits look down from
the fields of the blessed, and see the Nation to which they gave
freedom, in the fulltide of successful experiment, giving to the
world an example of virtuous liberty, and of unrivalled
prosperity." [72]

As Delavan's letter suggests, antebellum reformers viewed
their crusades as part of the larger cause of liberty that had inspired the American Revolution. Perhaps too they identified
with Lafayette. Just as he had sacrificed worldly pleasures, impelled by a concern for humanity to take up the cause of freedom, American reformers were also missionaries of liberty
seeking to free the oppressed—slaves, women, alcoholics—from
the last remaining bonds of tyranny, thereby fulfilling the liber-
tarian promise of the Revolution. Certainly Lafayette's legendary philanthropy and demonstrated love for humanity made
him a natural target for reformers preaching "disinterested
benevolence" as a motive for reform. "To whom . . . could I
with so much propriety direct . . . a communication?" asked
an advocate of the movement to abolish capital punishment.
"From whom do the great mass of the people so readily take
counsel, as from the disinterested—the wise and the good?" [73]
For American reformers, as for many of their countrymen,
Lafayette functioned not only as an example of benevolence
but as a figure of authority and, they hoped, of influence on
behalf of their causes.

[72] Edward C. Delavan to Lafayette, Albany, August 16, 1832, *ibid.*, XII.
[73] S. M. Stilwell to Lafayette, New York, July 28, 1832, *ibid.*, XV. See also
Thomas Thompson, Jr., to Lafayette, Boston, October 25, 1830, *ibid.*; Jacob
Griswold to Lafayette, New York, July 4, 1825, and Thomas Herttell to
Lafayette, New York, July 13, 1825, *ibid.*, XIII; Israel Canfield to Lafayette,
Morris Town, N.J., July 14, 1825, *ibid.*, XVII.

The most numerous appeals to Lafayette came from the ranks of the antislavery movement. His reputation as a friend of African emancipation was well known in the United States.[74] The biographies published on the occasion of his visit in 1824–25 had pointed to his support of emancipation during the French Revolution and portrayed him as a gradual emancipationist, and the tour itself had underscored that reputation.[75] A ceremony at the African Free School in New York reaffirmed his honorary membership (dating from August, 1788) in the New York Manumission Society, and the American Colonization Society made him a vice president in recognition of "a long and most illustrious life, consecrated to the maintenance of human rights & to the happiness of the world."[76] Lafayette's public pronouncements in favor of emancipation during the tour were few and indirect in nature.[77] Nevertheless, at least

[74] See, for example, Samuel F. B. Morse to Lafayette, New York, August 6, 1833, *ibid.*, XI; George Ticknor to Jared Sparks, Washington, January 3, 1825, in Herbert Baxter Adams (ed.), *The Life and Writings of Jared Sparks* (New York, 1893), I, 347.

[75] Biographers credited Lafayette with being "the first Frenchman, who raised his voice against the slave trade"; and they pointed to his membership in the *Amis des Noirs*, "a society whose object was, the gradual emancipation of the blacks held in slavery, particularly in the French colonies," and his "experiment for the gradual emancipation of the blacks." He was said to support "citizenship for Negroes" and "the civil rights of men of colour." [Ticknor], *Outlines*, 18; *American Military Biography*, 330; *Biographical Notice of Lafayette*, 7, 9; Waln, *Life of Lafayette*, 264; *Complete History of Lafayette*, 173–74. See also *Authentic Biography of La Fayette*, 49; *Lafayette, or Disinterested Benevolence*, 29, 30; [Knapp], *Memoirs of Lafayette*, 63; *Biography of the Illustrious Citizen, General Lafayette*, 7. For a short history of Lafayette's efforts on behalf of the slaves, see John T. Gillard, "Lafayette, Friend of the Negro," *Journal of Negro History*, XIX (1934), 355–71.

[76] *Niles' Weekly Register* (Baltimore), September 18, 1824, p. 42; R. R. Gurley to Lafayette, Washington, September 5, 1825, in Cornell Lafayette Collection, XIII.

[77] See, for example, Lafayette's remarks at Gallipolis, Ohio, May 22, 1825, quoted in Brandon, *Pilgrimage*, 351–52. Apparently Lafayette talked with some Americans about a plan for gradual abolition. John Marshall analyzed it at length in a letter to Lafayette and concluded by pronouncing it unworkable. Ralph R. Gurley, president of the American Colonization Society, wrote to Lafayette requesting "to know more *of the plan*, which was *only* mentioned, in a recent conversation." John Marshall to Lafayette, Oak Hill,

one American maintained that his visit had a direct effect in inspiring hopes of freedom in American slaves. "The general facts of the American revolution are known to the coloured population," John Paxton observed. "It is impossible to hide from . . . them the fact, that they are held in slavery in direct opposition to the fundamental principles of our free institutions." The mere name of Lafayette, Paxton pointed out, was "so connected with freedom, that almost every slave in the land, when he hears the one will think of the other." Given Lafayette's function as a symbol of revolutionary principles of freedom and equality, and the calculated revival of those ideals during his tour, the effect on the slave population was inevitable. "The visit of General De Lafayette, with the excitement it produced from Dan to Beersheba, with the dinners and toasts, and speeches and balls, and processions, and talk about our struggle for liberty, and our gratitude to him for espousing our cause, &c., gave a lesson to our slaves about the worth of liberty and the way to get it, which they will not forget during the present generation." [78] Perhaps fearing the effect of such celebrations on slaves and free Negroes, several southern newspapers published orders prohibiting slaves and "persons of color" from attending processions or ceremonies connected with Lafayette's visit.[79] But the prohibitions were not always heeded. Near Charleston, one observer reported, "The astonished Blacks flocked in numbers to get a glimpse of the *giniral* [*sic*]—whose fame had reached even their Ethiop ears." [80]

A poem published in the *Columbian Centinel* in October, 1824, "Address to General Lafayette, from 'The Slaves' in the

---

August 26, 1825, in Cornell Lafayette Collection, XIV; Gurley to Lafayette, Washington, September 5, 1825, *ibid.*, XIII.

[78] John D. Paxton, *Letters on Slavery; Addressed to the Cumberland Congregation, Virginia* (Lexington, Ky., 1833), 31, 34–37.

[79] For notices in southern newspapers, see Brandon, *Pilgrimage*, 92, 259.

[80] *American Sketches*, 80. See also New Orleans *Courier*, April 19, 1825, quoted in Brandon, *Pilgrimage*, 181–82.

Land of Freedom," also suggested the revolutionary potential inherent in the tour of "the Liberty man." Even more significant was the author's use of Lafayette's visit to expose the hypocrisy of white Americans who had once "fought for Freedom and for Life," yet now kept "one sixth of the nation" enslaved. To the revolutionary hero and judge of the republican experiment, returned to see the progress of the nation he helped to found, "the slaves" directed "some questions":

> As the Whites gained the Freedom for which
>   they contended
> Could you have suppos'd, when the war
>   had thus ended,
> That they would bind over the African race,
> To thraldom unceasing, and endless disgrace,—
> Inflicting more evils, as thousands to one,
> Than the Rulers of Britain on them had e'er done,—
> Ah, hold us as cattle for barter and sale,
> And leave us as hopeless our state to bewail?
>
> Did you, Sir, imagine such Pleaders for *right*,
> Would quickly prove Tyrants and substitute *might*,—
> And kill the poor Negroes who seek, tho' in vain,
> To shake off their fetters, their Freedom to gain?

Having betrayed the purposes and principles of the Revolution, Lafayette's hosts revealed their hyprocrisy in their reception for him. Praising liberty, they maintained a system of slavery. "While they report that '*ten millions*' of men, / Unite in proclaiming your praises again, / *One million and a half* of this very number, / Are treated as *Slaves*." Indeed, their masters' rehearsal of the Revolution and its principles, hypocritical though it was, could not but serve as a lesson to the oppressed slaves:

> What, Sir, can you fancy our feelings to be,
> When White men proclaim—'It is good to be free,—
> That violence and slaughter in Liberty's cause,
> Are sanctioned by Heaven with loudest applause,—

That men who thus hazard their lives and their name,
Shall shine as *Immortals* in Temples of fame?'

How plainly they tell us the course to pursue,
In all the applauses they lavish on you!
The plaudits and speeches pronounced by their breath,
Inculcate the doctrine of '*Freedom or Death.*'
We have their example in word and in deed,
To rouse us to action tho' thousands may bleed—
Tho' innocent victims by myriads may fall,
To settle the question by powder and ball!

But the slaves hoped to avoid resorting to violence, "altho' we are *told* that such measures are lawful." Knowing Lafayette's benevolence and love of liberty, they appealed to him to persuade his American friends to lift the shackles, thereby preventing inevitable "insurrection, destruction and fire!"

Approving in age what you did in your youth,
In fighting for Freedom, for Glory, and Truth,
You can't be contented to see us enslav'd,
By freemen who laud you for valor that saved?

We therefore solicit assistance from you,
As one to whom deference is own'd to be due;
If millions to you have surrendered the heart,
Direct them, O General; to act the good part,
To take off our fetters with wisdom and grace,
To treat us as brothers—tho' sable our race.[81]

Thus at least one observer was struck by the hypocritical posture of Americans who boasted so loudly and enthusiastically of the "Grand effects of Liberty." For him, and perhaps for others, Lafayette's tour provided a visible demonstration of that hypocrisy. Possibly too, in recalling the Revolution and its principles of liberty and equality, the visit revived the sense of a contradiction between the Declaration of Independence and the fact of slavery that had marked the postrevolutionary

81 "Address to General Lafayette, from 'The Slaves' in the Land of Freedom," *Columbian Centinel* (Boston), October 20, 1824.

period.[82] In thus heightening sensitivity to the iniquity of slavery, Lafayette's visit may have contributed to the escalation of antislavery protest in the late 1820's.

Although Lafayette's visit occurred during the "neglected period" of the antislavery movement, at least two reformers sought his influence in behalf of emancipation. "Capac," calling upon Lafayette to complete the work of liberation begun during the American Revolution, wrote that the man who had conferred freedom on America as a youth, had in "old age" the power to confer a "greater" favor on that country. America "has a million and a half of sons and daughters who have never tasted the freedom you gave the rest of her children," he wrote. "Why should you be partial? You and only you can break the chains and let the captives free." Should Lafayette support or organize an abolition project, "Capac" argued, "all America must combine to promote it. If you were to reengage in cause of freedom, Government could no longer withhold funds or measures to aid in the good work, while a slave continued to breathe our air." The importance of Lafayette's intervention was underscored by "Capac's" declaration that "no other man can so well unite the energies of the American people." [83] Martha Miller made a similar appeal to "the friend of freedom" to use his influence on behalf of abolition. "Not that you should again enter the field of blood," she wrote, "but to influence a nation who has made such loud professions of gratitude, it is only for him to say let them go free, and we would be ashamed to deny him on request, who has so frequently been exposed to peril for us." [84]

[82] For a discussion of the sense of contradiction see Bailyn, *Ideological Origins of the American Revolution*, 232–46.

[83] "Capac" to Lafayette, Ohio, January 1, 1826, in Cornell Lafayette Collection, XII.

[84] Martha M. Miller to her cousin, May 7, 1825, *ibid.*, XVIII. There were also appeals to Lafayette for aid to individual slaves. See for example Gurley to Lafayette, Washington, August 5, 1825, *ibid.*, XIII.

In the late 1820's and early 1830's, as the antislavery crusade gained momentum, reformers increased their appeals to Lafayette to intervene on their side. As during his tour, the notion of Lafayette's "reengaging in cause of freedom" appealed to those who saw the antislavery movement as a struggle for liberty comparable to the American Revolution, which had won Lafayette's support in an earlier day. In addition, Lafayette's nonpartisan image, and the fact that he served as a symbol of union, also contributed to his appeal in a question which excited sectional tensions. Writing to Lafayette from St. Augustine, Florida, M. E. Levy noted the "delicate" nature of the slavery question and expressed the hope that Lafayette might "be made in the hands of providence [*sic*] an instrument to awaken our southern people from their dangerous slumber and save them from this canker-worm of slavery that is undermining their happiness." [85]

Lafayette never took a public stand on the issue of slavery in the United States. The closest he came to intervening in the politics of the slavery question was in writing letters to James Monroe and James Madison expressing the hope that the Virginia constitutional convention might adopt " 'measures tending first to meliorate, then gradually to abolish the slave mode of labor.' " [86] Still, it was known that Lafayette had been made a perpetual vice president of the Colonization Society in 1825, and he espoused the colonization scheme in letters to his American friends.[87] Indeed, the Colonization Society was not un-

[85] M. E. Levy to Lafayette, St. Augustine, Fla., April 28, 1829, *ibid.*, XIV. See also Marshall to Lafayette, Richmond, Va., May 2, 1827, *ibid.*, XI; George Washington Parke Custis to Lafayette, Arlington House, May 25, 1826, and November 20, 1827, *ibid.*, X.

[86] Lafayette to Monroe, June 17, 1829, quoted in James Schouler, *History of the United States of America, Under the Constitution* (New York, 1904), III, 470. Lafayette's letter to Madison, September 28, 1829, was similar to the letter to Monroe.

[87] See, for example, Lafayette to Henry Clay, Paris, March 8, 1829, in Calvin Colton (ed.), *The Life, Correspondence, and Speeches of Henry*

aware of the powerful recommendation which Lafayette's support afforded. In 1829 the board of managers passed a resolution thanking him for "his enlightened approbation of their benevolent scheme" and expressing the hope "that General Lafayette will continue to afford them the weight of his influence and the honour of his name." [88] And when "immediate emancipation" began to attract converts, Lafayette was asked to offer a word of "paternal advice" to free Negroes in behalf of the colonization plan. [89]

In contrast, the Negro leader James Forten wrote to Lafayette hoping to persuade him to change his mind on colonization. Forten transmitted the sentiments of the Convention of the Free People of Color held in Philadelphia in June, 1833: "The convention deeply sensible of the interest which you excelent [*sic*] Sir, have throughout the course of your long life, ever shown in behalf of their oppressed race, are urged by a sense of duty which they owe to you as the great advocate of the liberty and happiness of *all* the human family; to lay before you these views of the Colonization Society, from which Sir, you may judge, wether [*sic*] *Liberty* and *Happiness* can ever dawn on the Man of color, from the operations of this Society." [90]

Forten's letter suggests that for some Americans Lafayette's general reputation "as the great advocate of the liberty and happiness of *all* the human family" outweighed his specific espousal of the colonization plan. [91] Thus Elizur Wright cited La-

---

Clay (New York, 1864), IV, 224; Lafayette to Jefferson, Paris, February 25, 1826, in Gilbert Chinard (ed.), *The Letters of Lafayette and Jefferson* (Baltimore, 1929), 437–38, and see also 359; Albert J. Beveridge, *The Life of John Marshall* (Boston, 1916), IV, 476n; *Niles' Weekly Register* (Baltimore), December 2, 1826, p. 219.

[88] Copy of a resolution passed at a meeting of the board of managers of the American Colonization Society, in Washington City, April 20, 1829, in Cornell Lafayette Collection, XIII.

[89] Morse to Lafayette, New York, August 6, 1833, *ibid.*, XI.

[90] James Forten to Lafayette, Philadelphia, July 31, 1833, *ibid.*, XIII.

[91] Whether by choice or not, Lafayette was inescapably linked with a more radical antislavery scheme than gradual emancipation or colonization

fayette's "peculiar & generous affection for this land of your adoption, as well as your long tried and uncompromising regard for the cause of human rights" in requesting his support for immediate emancipation. For abolitionists like Wright, Lafayette was a symbol of liberty, a representative of the Revolution and its objectives, which they were trying to fulfill in order to perpetuate the republican experiment. "We see no hope for our Country but in effecting by peaceable and constitutional means, such a change in public sentiment in regard to slavery as will abrogate the laws by which it exists, & extend *to all men*, upon *this soil* consecrated to liberty, the benefit of just & equitable laws," Wright explained.[92] But, as the letters from various wings of the antislavery movement attest, the meaning and promise of the Revolution were themselves in question. Did the principles of the Revolution, embodied in the Declaration of Independence, "extend *to all men*," or only to white men? The ambiguity of the Revolution was transferred to its chief symbol, Lafayette, to whom both colonizationists and immediatists appealed for support and advice.

VI

Besides functioning as a symbol of the Revolution and lib-

—the Nashoba community of the Wright sisters, who had accompanied Lafayette on his visit of 1824–25 and remained in America to prosecute their antislavery experiment. For the relationship between Frances Wright and Lafayette, see Frances Wright, *Views of Society and Manners in America*, ed. Paul R. Baker (Cambridge, Mass., 1963), xiv–xv; William Randall Waterman, *Frances Wright* (New York, 1924), 62–65. For American comments (optimistic and pessimistic) on the Nashoba experiment, see the following letters to Lafayette: Cadwallader David Colden, New York, August 19, 1826, June 29, 1827, October 19, 1827, June 9, 1828, August 8, 1829, January 25, 1830, in Cornell Lafayette Collection, X; Richard Peters, Belmont, [Mass. ?], December, 1826, *ibid.*, XI; "Capac," Ohio, January 1, 1826, and C. P. Bennett, Wilmington, September 10, 1829, *ibid.*, XII; Charles Wilkes, New York, September 30, 1826, June 27, 1827, February 27, 1828, *ibid.*, XV.

[92] Elizur Wright to Lafayette, New York, November 20, 1833, in Cornell Lafayette Collection, XV. See also "Capac" to Lafayette, Ohio, January 1, 1826, *ibid.*, XII.

erty, Lafayette also served as a symbol of union, a role that became increasingly important as factionalism and sectionalism threatened to sunder the republic. The tour of 1824–25, which included all the states of the union, had enhanced his reputation as a figure belonging equally to all states and sections. At the beginning of the visit, Thomas Jefferson predicted that the Nation's Guest would have a "salutary" effect on Americans "by rallying us together and strengthening the habit of considering our country as one and indivisible." [93] As Jefferson anticipated, Lafayette toured the nation as a spokesman of union, which he termed "so essential, not only to the fate of each member of the confederacy, but also the general fate of mankind, that the least breach of it would be hailed with barbarian joy, by an universal warwhoop of European aristocracy and despotism." [94] Moreover, many Americans credited the general with diminishing the factionalism called forth by the election of 1824. James Fenimore Cooper wrote that Lafayette's arrival "paralyzed all the electoral ardour."

> The newspapers, which, the evening before, were furiously combating for their favorite candidate, now closed their long columns on all party disputes, and only gave admission to the unanimous expression of the public joy and national gratitude. At the public dinners, instead of caustic toasts, intended to throw ridicule and odium on some potent adversary, none were heard but healths to the guest of the nation, around whom were amicably grouped the most violent of both parties. Finally, for nearly

---

[93] Jefferson to Richard Rush, Monticello, October 13, 1824, in Lipscomb and Bergh (eds.), *Writings of Jefferson*, XVI, 78–79. Congressman Charles Mercer wrote to Lafayette in July, 1825, thanking him "for all the labour you have . . . encountered, to make your fourth visit to the United States, as useful in cementing our Union, as your first appearance, was in founding our Freedom and Independence; of which that Union, is the surest safeguard." Mercer to Lafayette, Aldie, Va., July 20, 1825, in Cornell Lafayette Collection, XVIII.

[94] *Niles' Weekly Register* (Baltimore), August 13, 1825, p. 370; also published in the *Missouri Advocate and St. Louis Public Advertiser*, May 6, 1825, quoted in Brandon, *Pilgrimage*, 216.

two months all the discord and excitement produced by this election, which, it was said, would engender the most disastrous consequences, were forgotten, and nothing was thought of but Lafayette and the heroes of the revolution.[95]

Other Americans testified to the harmonizing effect of Lafayette's tour. Jefferson wrote to Richard Rush that the "eclat" of the "visit has almost merged the Presidential question, on which nothing scarcely is said in our papers." [96] The *New England Galaxy* remarked on the national feeling exhibited at receptions for the general: "The multitudes we see are not assembled to talk over their private griefs—to indulge in querulous complaint—to mingle their murmurs of discontent—to pour forth tales of real or imaginary wrongs—to give utterance to political recriminations. The effervescence of faction seems for the moment to be settled, the collision of discordant interests to subside—and hushed is the clamor of controversy." One saw "an assembled nation, offering the spontaneous homage of a nation's gratitude to a nation's benefactor." [97]

Lafayette himself believed that his tour allayed factionalism and controversy. "I have the satisfaction of thinking that my presence has effected many reconciliations between the political parties," he wrote; "men, who have not spoken to one another for more than twenty years, have made arrangements together and have invited one another to entertainments in our honor, and revive together common memories of the Revolution." In another letter he observed that the "trip has contributed to tighten the union between the states and to soften political parties, by bringing them all together in common hospitality toward a ghost from another world." [98]

[95] [Cooper], *Notions of the Americans*, II, 23–24.
[96] Jefferson to Rush, Monticello, October 13, 1824, in Ford (ed.), *Works of Jefferson*, XII, 380–81.
[97] Excerpt from the *New England Galaxy*, September 3, [1824], in *Memoirs of the Military Career of La Fayette*, appendix, 49–50.
[98] Quoted in Henry Dwight Sedgwick, *La Fayette* (Indianapolis, 1928), 396–97, 399–400.

Lafayette's letters suggest the reasons he was able to generate a spirit of harmony and union even in the heat of the presidential campaign. As "a ghost from another world" he revived "common memories of the Revolution," focusing attention on a period in their history about which Americans were, or thought they were, in complete agreement and which the national mythology pictured as an era of nonpartisan feeling. As Edward Everett explained in an oration delivered in Lafayette's presence in August, 1824, "Divisions may spring up, ill blood may burn, parties be formed, and interests may seem to clash; but the great bonds of the nation are linked to what is past." [99] As a symbol of that past, Lafayette served to strengthen the "bonds of the nation."

Even after his return to France, Lafayette continued to function as a powerful symbol of union for Americans. When the election of 1828 threatened to produce the same kind of bitter, and unrepublican, factionalism that had characterized the campaign of 1824, some of Lafayette's correspondents wistfully recalled his patriotic services. Daniel Bryan wrote in 1826, "God grant that you could be here to harmonize, by your presence, our public councils and smooth the rough tide of party faction—on the eve of our next presidential election." [100] The nullification controversy also prompted letters to Lafayette. To be sure, some of his correspondents viewed the dispute

[99] Edward Everett, "The Circumstances Favorable to the Progress of Literature in America," in *Orations and Speeches on Various Occasions* (Boston, 1879), I, 38–39.

[100] Daniel Bryan to Lafayette, Alexandria, D.C., June 11, 1826, in Cornell Lafayette Collection, XII. Most of Lafayette's American friends, though they admitted that the "acrimony" and "abuse" of the presidential campaign might "bring discredit on the general cause of Republican Liberty," viewed the contest with equanimity. Many of them shared the attitude of Philip Howe, who predicted that the contest would cause "much irritation, and party excitement," but was confident that it involved "no question of Principle, and whether Adams or Jackson should succeed, the Peoples [*sic*] rights will not be endangered, or their happiness be compromitted." Howe to Lafayette, July 23, 1827, *ibid.*, XIII. See also James Barbour (U.S. minister in London) to Lafayette, London, November 11, 1828, *ibid.*, X.

as a minor aberration—a necessary evil in a republican society—
and expressed confidence that "public sentiment" would triumph over faction. Albert Gallatin assured Lafayette that "the
real community of interests, patriotism, and a growing National
spirit and feeling, will . . . ultimately prevail; and the United
States continue to offer the most glorious model of Republican
institutions which the world has as yet exhibited." [101]

Nevertheless, even Gallatin's assurance suggests that many
of Lafayette's American friends viewed the nullification controversy as a crisis of the republican experiment. The dispute
raised anew the old question of how to perpetuate—and whether
it was possible to perpetuate—the republican principles of the
American Revolution, once their original exponents had gone
to their graves. "I hope the storm is past," Morgan Neville wrote
to Lafayette; "but I fear, when all our Revolutionary *Nestors*
are gone, our golden age of *Rational* Liberty will end. Already
have intrigue & management become powerful Engines in our
government." [102]

In 1833, of course, at least one revolutionary Nestor remained, and Lafayette's connection with the revolutionary
period took on a special meaning during the nullification controversy. For Lafayette was a link with the Founding Fathers
and with the principles of the Revolution on which the republic was based. At the same time, he was the one truly nonpartisan figure whose judgment all Americans could honor. Each
side in the controversy appealed to him for support, representing its case as a defense of "first principles" against political
innovation.[103]

[101] Albert Gallatin to Lafayette, New York, May 30, 1833, *ibid.*, XI. See
also Colden to Lafayette, Jersey City, March 29, 1833, *ibid.*, X; Morse to
Lafayette, New York, January 26, 1833, and John P. King to Lafayette,
Columbia, S.C., July 11, 1828, August 8, 1830, *ibid.*, XI; J. K. Tefft to Lafayette,
Savannah, January 14, 1833, *ibid.*, XV.
[102] Morgan Neville to Lafayette, Cincinnati, April 29, 1833, *ibid..* XI. See
also Joseph S. Lewis to Lafayette, Philadelphia, April 20, 1833, *ibid.*, XIV;
E. L. Winthrop to Lafayette, New York, December 23, 1832, *ibid.*, XV.
[103] See, for example, the following letters to Lafayette: John C. Calhoun,

Ultimately the opponents of nullification secured Lafayette's intervention on their side. At least two letters by him, deploring the nullification controversy, were published in American newspapers. The New York *Journal of Commerce* reprinted a letter by the "veteran apostle of liberty," which it addressed "*to all disunionists* throughout *the United States!*" urging them to "listen to the voice of *Lafayette!* a man who has no private interests to subserve, and no sectional feelings to bias his judgment." In the letter Lafayette pointed to the "ill-natured handle . . . made of the violent collisions, threats of a separation, and reciprocal abuse, to injure the character and question the stability of republican institutions." While professing his faith in "the patriotism and good sense of the several parties in the United States," Lafayette did not dismiss the possibility that dissension might end ultimately in "a final dissolution of the union." But he hoped that the event would be postponed: "*deprecated as it has been by the last wishes of the departed founders of the revolution,* WASHINGTON *at their head,* IT OUGHT AT LEAST, IN CHARITY, NOT TO TAKE PLACE BEFORE THE PERIOD (not now remote) WHEN EVERY ONE OF THOSE WHO HAVE FOUGHT AND BLED IN THE CAUSE SHALL HAVE JOINED THEIR CONTEMPORARIES." [104]

Pendleton, S.C., October 23, 1830, *ibid.,* X; Nicholas Fish, New York, August 12, 1830, *ibid.,* XI; John Stocking, Jr., on behalf of members of the Hickory Club, Mobile, December 27, 1832, *ibid.,* XIII; Richard T. Manning, Sumter District, S.C., January 22, 1832, *ibid.,* XIV.

[104] The letter had been written to Samuel F. B. Morse, who had just returned from a visit with Lafayette at La Grange. Letter reprinted from the New York *Journal of Commerce* in *Niles' Weekly Register* (Baltimore), December 1, 1832, pp. 217–18. The *Journal of Commerce* admitted copying the letter from the New York *Observer.* J. K. Tefft of Savannah reported to Lafayette that his letter "has been generally published in the *Union* newspapers here." Tefft to Lafayette, Savannah, January 14, 1833, in Cornell Lafayette Collection, XV. In a letter of October 2, 1832, Morse wrote, "The leaders at the South happen to be my personal friends and I shall take the opportunity to send them an extract from your letter the moment I land." Apparently Morse gave a copy of the letter to the New York newspapers on arriving in the United States. By January, 1833, he was able to report to Lafayette that the letter "has produced a very happy effect throughout the

No doubt Lafayette's declaration was more a tactical strata-
gem than a sincere expression of uncertainty about the future
of the union. Yet it demonstrates that the American Revolution
was still charged with emotion and ideological significance
some fifty years after the fact. The notion that succeeding generations of Americans had incurred a debt to the patriots of
the Revolution for their suffering and sacrifices was still potent
in 1832. To renege on the debt or repudiate it outright would
be to render those sacrifices futile and unmeaning.

In a second letter, dated October 8 and published in *Niles'*
Weekly Register, the notion that disunionism sabotaged the
endeavors of Washington and his revolutionary compatriots
was made more explicit. According to Lafayette, such "partial
quarrels" over "the maintenance of the union" concerned "the
unanimous and fond object of every one of us, who have fought
and bled in the revolution." Again he asserted his faith in "the
general good sense of the American people" but pointed out
that the nullification dispute was "adroitly handled by the ad-
versaries of republican institutions" and therefore "very in-
jurious to the popular cause" and to the image of the United
States in Europe.[105] As a symbol of union, Lafayette offered
the same arguments in 1832 that he had made in the 1780's and
in 1824–25: dissension among the American people obstructed
the fulfillment of the promise of the American Revolution at
home and abroad. It prevented the consolidation of a republican system of government; it also hurt the image of the United
States abroad, thereby undermining the American mission to

---

country. I made an extract of that part which relates to our unhappy dis-
sensions, and prefacing it by some remarks, had it inserted in the paper edited
by my brothers, from which it has been copied into almost all if not *all* the
papers in the union. From many expressions in the public documents which
have lately appeared I have no doubt that the latter remark of your letter
has been deeply felt." Morse to Lafayette, Havre, October 2, 1832, and New
York, January 26, 1833, in Cornell Lafayette Collection, XI.

[105] Richmond *Enquirer*, reprinted in *Niles' Weekly Register* (Baltimore),
January 19, 1833, p. 330.

spread liberty and republican institutions throughout the world.

Lafayette's usefulness as a symbol of union was not confined to his own correspondence. In 1833 Peabody and Company of New York published an eighteen-page pamphlet entitled *Letter on the President's Message; Supposed to Be Written by General Lafayette, to His Adopted Countrymen, on the Receipt of the President's Message, on the Opening of the Second Session of the Twenty-second Congress, December 4, 1832.* Written by "a gentleman of Boston" according to the publisher, the pamphlet purported to be an open letter from Lafayette to his "Friends and Fellow-Countrymen in America," from La Grange, dated January 14, 1833, and discussing the issues raised by President Andrew Jackson in his annual message to Congress.[106] The letter termed protection "the true interest and policy of the nation," praised Jackson's Nullification Proclamation as "such as a patriot could wish," and warned of the effect of continued controversy on the image of the United States in Europe and on the cause of liberty throughout the world. In expressing these views, "Lafayette" claimed to be acting on the basis of distinterested benevolence and nonpartisanship. "The love I have for you, and the interest I feel in your prosperity and happiness, has induced me to address you," he explained at the beginning of the letter. "Situated as I am, distant and aloof from your petty strife, and distracting jealousies, and having no interest except your general welfare, my observations, I hope, will have some influence. I belong to no party; I am neither masonic nor anti-masonic; national nor antinational; northerner or southerner; but one alone, with a single eye to the good of all." The purpose of the letter was an "im-

---

[106] *Letter on the President's Message; Supposed to Be Written by General Lafayette, to His Adopted Countrymen* (New York, 1833). The copy of the pamphlet in the Harvard University Library bears the signature of Theodore Sedgwick, Jr., and the notation "by a Gent: of Boston as Peabody says."

partial review" of the President's message, by which "Lafayette" hoped to "allay party animosities and sectional strife." [107] Whoever had written the letter clearly recognized the popular appeal of Lafayette as American patriarch, disinterested patriot, and symbol of union.

By his intervention in the nullification controversy (whether fabricated or not) Lafayette was credited with saving the union from the "calamity" of secession. By January, 1833, J. K. Tefft of Savannah was confident no "separation" would occur, partly because of the "good sense[,] virtue & patriotism *of the People*," but also because of "the deserved influence of those, who in their youth were the active supporters of our beloved country, and in the vale of years, speak with the voice of another and better age, the counsels of wisdom & or warning!" [108]

But what would happen when there were no more revolutionary Nestors to "speak with the voice of another and better age," to call attention to the first principles on which the republic was founded? What would happen when no survivor of the Revolution remained to serve as a touchstone of republican faith? Many of the appeals to Lafayette written in the late 1820's and early 1830's contain an implicit recognition of his mortality, an urgency not always explained by the exigencies of the situation at hand. Preparing for the time when Lafayette's direct, active intervention and influence would no longer be available, one of his correspondents requested that he issue something like a farewell address to the American people, to serve as a guide after his death. William Ellis, who proposed the project in 1833, even implied that Lafayette might be more fitted than Washington, by virtue of his long acquaintance with the United States, to write such a document. Not

---

[107] *Ibid.*, 3, 7, 9.
[108] Tefft to Lafayette, Savannah, January 14, 1833, in Cornell Lafayette Collection, XV. See also Morse to Lafayette, New York, March 5, 1833, *ibid.*, XI.

only had Lafayette taken "a conspicuous part in our struggles for Independence"; as if "by a special destination of divine Providence" he had visited America "nearly half a Century afterwards, thereby from personal observation, testing the value of that *Liberty* and *happiness*, resulting from that Republick, which he had so long before, suffered so many privations to Establish." In Ellis' view, Lafayette "has better means of judging of the *tendancy* [*sic*] the *Utility* and the *duration* of *Republican Governments*, than any other man can at this time possess, on the habitable Globe." Therefore, Lafayette should write for the American people "*A Letter of advice and Caution for futurity*." Such a document, Ellis suggested, "united to the 'farewell Address' of our political Father Washington, might not only furnish the American People with a sheet Anchor, sufficient to sustain their Republic, during any sudden Storms of Tyrany [*sic*] without, or the Hurricanes of faction within, but it would constitute a durable Beacon, 'a cloud by day, and a Pillar of Fire by night'—to direct the devoted Patriot of future Ages, in his pursuit of that *Justice* and *Liberty*, which alone can secure the felicity of social man." [109]

In suggesting the analogy between Lafayette's letter and the presidential address, Ellis revealed the extent to which Lafayette, friend and adopted son of Washington, had become a Washington-like figure for many Americans. If he did not achieve equal status with the Father of His Country, he had nevertheless functioned since the beginning of the nineteenth century as a father-figure to his adopted country: a symbol of wisdom, authority, and benevolence, and above all, of the birth of the nation at the time of the Revolution.

---

[109] Ellis to Lafayette, July 1, 1831, *ibid.*, XIII. See also Giles to Lafayette, Richmond, May 15, 1828, *ibid.*, XVII. In 1825 Thomas Tolman, a revolutionary veteran, had suggested that Lafayette, "after the example of *Washington*, bless us with a *Farewell Address* to the nation." Tolman to Lafayette, Greensborough, Vt., August 1, 1825, *ibid.*, XVIII.

4 Agent of the American Mission

Heaven saw fit to ordain, that the
electric spark of liberty should be
conducted, through you, from the
New World to the Old . . . .
DANIEL WEBSTER[1]

In the role of agent of the American mission, Lafayette became the focus of the American desire to promote the cause of liberty and republicanism throughout the world. Indeed, it is no exaggeration to say that after his release from prison in 1797, Lafayette carried almost the entire burden of America's hopes for the liberalization of France and the rest of Europe. For Americans, he was an ideological certainty amidst the confusing complexities of European politics. Tested by imprisonment and martyrdom, he had proved his consistent devotion to principles learned in the United States. Thus Jefferson wrote to Lafayette that he functioned as "the index of the orthodox party of your government for us who have no means of knowing the details." [2] Moreover, because Lafayette was France's link with the principles of the American Revolution, his continuing influence could be interpreted as a sign that those prin-

[1] Webster, "The Bunker Hill Monument, An Address Delivered at the Laying of the Corner-stone of the Bunker Hill Monument at Charlestown, Massachusetts, on the 17th of June, 1825," in *Writings and Speeches of Daniel Webster*, I, 246.
[2] Jefferson to Lafayette, March 22, 1821, in Chinard (ed.), *Letters of Lafayette and Jefferson*, 402.

ciples were not totally lost to France, despite the failure of the French Revolution and the eventual restoration of the Bourbon monarchy.[3]

Lafayette himself encouraged Americans to look to him as the agent of the American mission. His annual appearances at Fourth of July celebrations in Paris, faithfully noted by American newspapers, reinforced the notion that he represented Europe's link with the American Revolution. In his toasts he never failed to reiterate the wish that American principles might triumph in Europe: "American liberty, founded on the rights of men and nations; may this doctrine open all eyes, fortify every arm, and may the cause of Europe triumph over the late convulsions of despotism and privilege."[4] To bolster confidence among "the friends of liberty" in the United States, he engaged in a voluminous correspondence. In a typical letter he declared, "Far am I to be discouraged with Respect to the first establishment of freedom in the European world. The liberal part of the Revolution shall not Be lost."[5] In 1822 *Niles' Weekly Register* published a letter from Lafayette assuring an American correspondent that " 'the friends of freedom need not . . . despond. They may carry with them the consoling hope, that its cause is not lost in Europe, and in France less than any

[3] George Bancroft Journal, May 30, 1821, in Mark Antony De Wolfe Howe (ed.), *The Life and Letters of George Bancroft* (New York, 1908), I, 406. Americans were greatly encouraged by Lafayette's election to the Chamber of Deputies in 1818. William Lee wrote that the American public had received the news "with great satisfaction." According to Lee, "They consider it as one of the best proofs yet given by France of the return to correct principles—It creates indeed a consoling hope for her future destinies." William Lee to Lafayette, April 9, 1819, in Cornell Lafayette Collection, XIV. See also the following letters to Lafayette: E. Livingston, February 10, 1823, *ibid.*, XI; J. Brown, October 15, 1818, *ibid.*, XII; William H. Crawford, November 7, 1817, *ibid.*, X.

[4] *Niles' Weekly Register* (Baltimore), September 22, 1821, p. 61, and August 30, 1823, p. 410. See also *ibid.*, September 28, 1816, p. 80, September 27, 1817, p. 79, September 16, 1820, p. 47.

[5] Lafayette to Clay, December 26, 1815, in James F. Hopkins (ed.), *The Papers of Henry Clay* (Lexington, Ky., 1959–63), II, 114.

where else. All that is great and useful in the revolution, will, I trust, be preserved.' " [6]

I

For many Americans, Lafayette's career in Europe seemed to embody the career of liberty itself; and their reaction to Lafayette was frequently identical with their reaction to the progress of liberal principles abroad. For example, the response to the French Revolution closely paralleled the response to Lafayette's role in it: optimism and enthusiasm at first, later disillusionment and despair. Much of the optimism and enthusiasm derived from the belief that Lafayette was the leader of the Revolution. By the same token, his fall from power was interpreted as a sign that the Revolution was taking a different course from the one originally charted.[7] Lafayette's flight from France, which Americans identified with a change in the leadership and direction of the Revolution, planted seeds of doubt that ultimately blossomed into widespread disenchantment with the entire Revolution.

The fate of America's Marquis, "the unfortunate victim of anarchy and despotism," seemed to symbolize the fate of American principles.[8] Americans believed that Lafayette had been trying to spread those principles, and his failure to do so caused great disappointment. Assessing the outcome of the French Revolution, Americans could not be other than pessimistic. What had begun as a revolution for liberty, based on the American example and led by America's adopted son, had degenerated into the tyranny of party spirit and mob rule. Lafayette, "the true friend of rational liberty," had been forced by the

[6] *Niles' Weekly Register* (Baltimore), June 29, 1822, p. 274.

[7] Short to Secretary of State, August 24, 1792, in U.S. Department of State, Diplomatic Despatches, The Hague and Spain, Library of Congress. See also Short to Secretary of State, August 31, 1792, *ibid.*

[8] *Connecticut Courant* (Hartford), July 7, 1794.

Jacobins to flee the country.[9] Publicly, Americans boasted that their unique virtues rendered them immune to the political diseases spawned by the French Revolution. Privately they worried that factionalism and "the tyranny of the majority"— a euphemism for mob rule—were taking root in American soil. Both reactions indicated a determination to stay out of European affairs, lest American principles be tainted or destroyed. Ironically, Lafayette's downfall so reinforced such isolationist tendencies that Americans were unwilling to involve themselves in European affairs even to effect Lafayette's release from prison.[10]

II

R. R. Palmer has characterized the American attitude toward Europe following the French Revolution as a "feeling of self-chosen and fortunate isolation, a belief that the vices of Europe were incorrigible, and that Americans should be as little involved as possible with an old world where true liberty could

[9] "To the printers of the Connecticut Courant," signed GUSTAVUS, New-London County, April 27, *ibid.*, May 8, 1797. See also "The AMERICAN," *ibid.*, February 4, 1793; *Pennsylvania Journal* (Philadelphia), October 31, 1792, December 19, 1792; "The Illustrious Fayette," 196.

[10] On the issue of Lafayette's imprisonment, Americans were caught between two conflicting impulses: sympathy for Lafayette and fear of foreign involvement. Their ambivalent state of mind is most clearly seen in George Washington. Privately he confessed his concern for Lafayette and his desire for his release. Publicly he maintained a silent, hands-off policy, fearing that any official interference on Lafayette's behalf might involve the United States in the European war. When he ultimately wrote to the King of Prussia seeking Lafayette's freedom, it was as a "private individual," and he made the request not on the ground that the Marquis was an American citizen (as Lafayette himself had suggested) but because of his own "personal and affectionate anxiety" for the welfare of his adopted son. American diplomatic officials also assumed an ambivalent posture for similar reasons. Statements of sympathy for Lafayette which appeared in American newspapers were largely rhetorical.

In the House of Representatives, a resolution authorizing the President to take any "expedient" measures for Lafayette's liberation failed, despite appeals to remember his services in the American Revolution. Opponents

not exist." [11] Yet the voluminous correspondence between Lafayette and the "friends of liberty" in America suggests otherwise. To be sure, Americans tended to view events in Europe
with more skepticism and detachment than they had exhibited
in the early 1790's. The chastening experience of the French
Revolution had made them wary of revolution as a means of
reform. They were no longer confident that American principles could be transplanted intact to the rest of the world,
or that once transplanted they would operate according to
the same orderly and moderate process as had occurred in
America. The later phases of the French Revolution indicated
that the soil of the Old World was very different from that of
the New and that the tree of liberty would have a more difficult
time taking root in Europe than it had in the United States:
therefore the planting and cultivation of republican principles
in the Old World would necessarily be a slow and gradual
process. But such thinking did not lead to complete pessimism
and isolation. The American sense of mission survived the trau-
ma of the French Revolution. It emerged, somewhat modified,

---

of the resolution declared their gratitude to Lafayette but worried about the
political consequences of attempting to gain his release. Like Washington, the
congressmen were victims of a conflict of sympathies: between the obligations
which gratitude to Lafayette implied and considerations of national interest.
Washington to Thomas Pinckney, February 20, 1796, and to the Duc de La
Rochefoucauld-Liancourt, August 8, 1796, in Fitzpatrick (ed.), *Writings of
Washington*, XXXIV, 473–74, XXXV, 168; Sears, *Washington and the French
Revolution*, 143, 199; G. Morris to Short, November, 1792, in Morris (ed.),
Diary and Letters of Morris, II, 3; extract of a letter from Short to G. Morris,
September 7, 1792, and extract of an answering letter from G. Morris to
Short, September 12, 1792, both enclosed in a letter from G. Morris to Jeffer-
son, September 27, 1792, in U.S. Department of State, Diplomatic Despatches,
France, Library of Congress; *Connecticut Courant* (Hartford), July 11, 1796,
May 1, 1797; Hazen, *American Opinion of the French Revolution*, 263; House
of Representatives, March 3, 1797, *Annals of the Congress of the United
States* (Washington, 1834–56), VI, 2362–67.

[11] R. R. Palmer, *The Age of the Democratic Revolution: A Political History of Europe and America, 1760–1800* (Princeton, 1959–64), II, 571, and
see also 548. Cf. Strout, *American Image of Old World*, 47.

in the early nineteenth century in the form of a cautious realism based on a theory of social and political relativism, which anticipated the ultimate, though not immediate, triumph of republicanism and liberty in Europe.

The basic elements of this new sense of the American mission are clearly revealed in a letter which Thomas Jefferson wrote to Lafayette in 1815. Initially Jefferson had been an ardent supporter of the French Revolution, but ultimately had become disillusioned by its excesses (and by the political embarrassment it caused him at home). Now, in 1815, he cautioned Lafayette that "a full measure of liberty is not now perhaps to be expected by your nation, nor am I confident they are prepared to preserve it." In Jefferson's estimation, it would take "more than a generation" before the people of France "will be capable of estimating the value of freedom, and the necessity of a sacred adherence to the principles on which it rests for preservation." That would come only with "the progress of knowledge in the general mass of the people, and their habituation to an independent security of person and property."

Jefferson implied that the different tolerance for liberty in France as opposed to America derived from the different nature of their revolutions. "Instead of that liberty which takes root and growth in the progress of reason, if recovered by mere force or accident, it becomes, with an unprepared people, a tyranny still, of the many, the few, or the one." In America, Jefferson seemed to be saying, liberty had been a natural growth of which the Revolution was an offshoot. But in France the purpose of the Revolution had been to transplant an alien species in largely unharrowed soil. The result had been a blighted growth.

At the very beginning of the French Revolution, Jefferson reminded Lafayette, he had been dubious about the amount of liberty which France might be able to bear. He had urged Lafayette and others "to enter then into a compact with the king, securing freedom of religion, freedom of the press, trial by jury, *habeas corpus*, and a national legislature, all of which it was known he would then yield, to go home, and let these work on the amelioration of the condition of the people, until they should have rendered them capable of more, when occasions would not fail to arise for communicating to them more." Lafayette, Jefferson recalled, had "thought otherwise, and that the dose [of liberty] might still be larger." Events had proved him right: the people of France "were equal to the constitution of 1791."

Had the Revolution stopped there, with a "limited monarchy," Jefferson was confident it would not have degenerated into the "tyranny" of Robespierre and Bonaparte. But, he observed, "unfortunately, some of the most honest and enlightened of our patriotic friends, (but closet politicians merely, unpractised in the knowledge of man,) thought more could still be obtained and borne. They did not weigh the hazards of a transition from one form of government to another, the value of what they had already rescued from those hazards, and might hold in security if they pleased, nor the imprudence of giving up the certainty of such a degree of liberty, under a limited monarchy, for the uncertainty of a little more under the form of a republic." This was the "fatal error" of the "republicans." "You differed from them," Jefferson reminded Lafayette. "You were for stopping there, and for securing the Constitution which the National Assembly had obtained." Once again, Lafayette had been right. To the republicans' separation from Lafayette and the "constitutionalists," Jefferson attributed "all the subsequent sufferings and crimes of the French nation." The lesson to be learned was clear. With the Bourbon Restoration, French liberals should "be contented with a certain portion of power, secured by formal compact with the nation, rather than, grasping at more, hazard all upon uncertainty, and risk meeting the fate of their predecessor, or a renewal of their own exile." [12]

The distinction Jefferson made between "republicans" and "constitutionalists" was a revealing one. Jefferson was himself a republican. Like most Americans he considered Lafayette to be one too. Yet in narrating the history of the French Revolution, he had linked Lafayette with the constitutionalists and in opposition to the republicans. In contrasting the two factions, Jefferson seemed to be saying one of two things: that American republicanism was not the same as French republicanism, or that France was simply unprepared for republicanism and would have to learn to live, at least temporarily, in the halfway house of constitutionalism. Either way, the distinction indicated an awareness of certain crucial differences between French and American politics.

Narrowly defined, constitutionalism meant limited monarchy. Broadly interpreted, it seemed to signify that balance of liberty and authority which Jefferson had suggested was the *sine qua non* of a truly republican form of government. "How does the new constitution work?" Jefferson inquired of Lafayette in 1819; "is your government and people getting in the habit of viewing it as sacred, [word effaced] as [a] real fetter on their actions which they cannot break, & [that] it is sacrilege to attempt it? For until they acquire this veneration for it, it will be treated but as an ordinary law, & broken whenever convenient." [13] This from the man who, some forty years earlier, had penned the manifesto of the American mission, counseling the right and duty of revolution against monarchy; and—an even more striking contradiction—who had declared as a "self-evident" principle, "that the *earth belongs in usufruct to the*

[12] Jefferson to Lafayette, February 14, 1815, in Ford (ed.), *Works of Jefferson*, XI, 454–58.

[13] Jefferson to Lafayette, March 8, 1819, in Chinard (ed.), *Letters of Lafayette and Jefferson*, 397. See also E. Livingston to Lafayette, October 24, 1820, in Cornell Lafayette Collection, XI.

living" and that "no society can make a perpetual constitution," a view which he had reaffirmed only a few years before
in a letter to Lafayette.[14] Yet the French experience had shown
that the right of revolution, in the hands of "an unprepared
people," brought not liberty but "a tyranny still." Seeing this,
and drawing on a theory of political and social relativism, Jefferson advocated a constitutional monarchy for France.[15]

The realistic approach was not an easy one for some Americans to take. Edward Livingston, writing to Lafayette in 1820,
could not reconcile himself to the intermediary stage of development which limited monarchy represented. He predicted
that France "will never be tranquil but under a Despotism or a
Government *Entirely* representative." At the same time, he
did not doubt that Lafayette would disagree with him on that
point, and Livingston admitted that he was therefore probably
wrong. But he excused himself on the ground that "it is Difficult to get rid of errors in which one has been educated, hard
& grown old, even if they be Errors—Therefore you will excuse
an American Democrat of the Old School for judging ill of
the affairs of France under the New Doctrines." [16] In the 1820's
Americans were beginning to disagree over the meaning of the
American mission. "Old school" adherents continued to hope
for the total and complete victory of American principles in
Europe. "New school" supporters moved increasingly toward
a more realistic policy. Neither school entirely escaped further
discouragement and disillusionment.

14 Jefferson to Madison, September 6, 1789, in Lipscomb and Bergh (eds.),
Writings of Jefferson, VII, 454–61. See also Jefferson to John W. Eppes, June
24, 1813, and to Samuel Kercheval, July 12, 1816, *ibid.*, VIII, 270, XV, 40.
Jefferson had written to Kercheval, with regard to the American scene,
"Some men look at the constitutions with sanctimonious reverence, and deem
them like the ark of the covenant, too sacred to be touched." Yet he inquired
of Lafayette whether Frenchmen had come to look upon *their* constitution
as "sacred," and revolution as "sacrilege."

15 Koch, *Philosophy of Thomas Jefferson*, 129–32.

16 E. Livingston to Lafayette, April 18, 1820, in Cornell Lafayette Collection, XI.

The realistic view of the prospects of liberty in Europe in turn shaped a new conception of America's role in promoting liberty abroad. Writing to Lafayette in 1817 about "the fate of civil liberty in Europe," William Crawford predicted that it would be decided when representative government was established in France and Germany. In the struggle for that objective, Crawford wrote, "we shall aid and uplift you as much as possible, by precept and example." The United States could do no more. In the face of the Holy Alliance, "it is our interest, it is the interest of all free governments, that we should obtrude ourselves upon their attention as slightly, as a due regard to the interests of the nation will permit. Any exhibition of our principles—any signal eclat, might draw upon us the formidable combination which now controls the affairs of Europe." Such was the "modest retirement" which "prudence" imposed upon the United States. Such indeed was the logical outgrowth of the realistic spirit that was beginning to infuse the American sense of mission. Just as Jefferson had appealed to France's national interest in counseling Lafayette to compromise his republican principles and accept a limited monarchy, so Crawford justified American passivity and aloofness on the basis of an assessment of the power structure of Europe and its implications for America. At some more propitious time the United States might "be ready to countenance the exertions of those who are struggling for the rights of man more openly, & distinctly, than it would be proper at this time to attempt." But until such time, Crawford explained, the United States "must be content to assist the friends of liberty in the old world" as an "example, modest & unobtrusive." [17]

The Monroe Doctrine translated into official policy the notion of America as the propagator of republican principles by

[17] Crawford to Lafayette, November 7, 1817, *ibid.*, X. See also John Quincy Adams, *An Address Delivered . . . on the Fourth of July, 1821* (Cambridge, Mass., 1821), 31–32.

passive example rather than active interference. President Monroe voiced the "friendly sentiments" of the American people "in favor of the liberty and happiness of their fellow-men," but there was no indication that the United States contemplated active intervention to further those ends. Indeed, the message was an explicit declaration of noninterference, confirming the "modest retirement" which William Crawford had defended six years earlier.[18] Lafayette encouraged Americans in thinking that the message would prove "a lesson of political civilization for the Nations of Europe" and an inspiration to "the friends of liberty" outside the United States.[19] He wrote to Monroe that he was "delighted with your message, and so will be every liberal mind in Europe and South America." [20] To an American agent he remarked that the doctrine was "the best little bit of paper that God had ever permitted any man to give to the World." [21]

If theories of social and political relativism reshaped the American sense of mission, they also raised questions about Lafayette's role in the French Revolution. Americans of the first decades of the nineteenth century were forced to judge Lafayette's competence as agent of the American mission in the light of such questions. The ambivalent response they made to those questions suggests the ambivalence with which they confronted the mission itself.

Most Americans agreed that Lafayette had attempted in the French Revolution to apply to his native country the principles he had learned in America. But the disastrous results of that

18 James Monroe, Seventh Annual Message, Washington, December 2, 1823, in Stanislaus Murray Hamilton (ed.), *The Writings of James Monroe* (New York, 1898–1903), VI, 339–41.

19 Lafayette to the President of the United States, January 11, [1824], in Cornell Lafayette Collection, XVI.

20 Hamilton (ed.), *Writings of Monroe*, VII, 14n.

21 Quoted in Dexter Perkins, *Hands Off: A History of the Monroe Doctrine* (Boston, 1943), 55–56. See also Monroe to Madison, March 27, 1824, in Hamilton (ed.), *Writings of Monroe*, VII, 14.

Revolution raised a question about the wisdom of introducing such principles into a country unprepared for them, thereby precipitating an upheaval that terminated not in republican government but despotism. Should Lafayette be condemned for his foolish and visionary attempt to apply American principles in France, without regard for the temporal or geographical context in which he was operating? (In other words, should he have compromised his principles to suit France's peculiar heritage and problems?) Or should he be praised for his fidelity to principles in the face of momentous obstacles and real personal danger? Was Lafayette a visionary and irresponsible idealist or a consistent republican?

The answers of Lafayette's biographers suggest the way most Americans reconciled new political and social theories with the legend of "the Washington of France." Writing in the 1820's, American biographers judged Lafayette's role in the French Revolution on the basis of his intentions, not on the results of that Revolution. In an age of individualism they chose to view him as an autonomous individual (true to himself and his principles) rather than as a political leader (interacting with other men and responsible for the effects of his and their actions). Thus Lafayette's actions in the Revolution were said to have been impelled by "the most pure and patriotic motives"; he was uniformly portrayed as the enemy of "anarchy" and the friend of "rational freedom." [22]

Given his fidelity to liberal republican principles, the most that could be said in criticism of his role was that he erred in judgment. For example some biographers blamed the excesses of the Revolution on the Constitution which Lafayette had helped to frame, arguing that it "tended directly to destroy the whole power of the monarch." But the defects of the Constitution were termed the result of an "error in judgment" and it was emphasized that Lafayette and those who formed it "were

[22] Waln, *Life of Lafayette*, 267–72; *Complete History of Lafayette*, 175–78.

men of the best intentions." Robert Waln suggested that "a more temperate and mature judgment would, probably, have led him to oppose that fatal degradation of the executive power, which finally proved the ruin of authority, of government, and of order, in France." But even Waln excused Lafayette's action as "the error of a young and ingenuous mind, which, in its ardent zeal for the liberty and happiness of his fellow-creatures, did not permit him to distinguish what was practicable, from what was merely speculative and visionary." In erring, Lafayette had given further proof of his absolute fidelity to principles. "Though, in his judgment, he may have erred, it must be admitted he was always consistent in his principles." [23]

In contrast to Waln, most of Lafayette's biographers avoided even the mildest criticism of his actions. In their view, France, not Lafayette, was responsible for the failure of the Revolution. The Constitution had not succeeded because of "the unfitness of the French people . . . for the blessings of a more popular government." [24] Lafayette's failure to establish a free, representative government was "no impeachment of his patriotism or his capacity." Indeed, one biographer asserted, "it is by no means probable that any body of men, not even Washington and the American Continental Congress, could have been more successful." [25] Thus was Lafayette absolved of any errors during the French Revolution. Yet the terms in which his acquittal was drawn reveal the influence of theories of social and political relativism and the new sense of mission they produced. In the 1820's Lafayette's efforts to spread American principles abroad were seen as an essentially futile attempt to promote the cause of liberty among a people unprepared for

23 [Knapp], *Memoirs of Lafayette*, 64–65; Waln, *Life of Lafayette*, 267–72, 421–22; *Complete History of Lafayette*, 175–78, 275–76.

24 [Knapp], *Memoirs of Lafayette*, 65–66.

25 *American Military Biography*, 353. See also [Knapp], *Memoirs of Lafayette*, 121–28.

it. To be sure, Lafayette's biographers stressed his pure intentions, but they unconsciously conceded his imprudence when they admitted "the unfitness of the French people . . . for . . . popular government." Though most of his biographers avoided the word, they viewed Lafayette's actions in the French Revolution as those of a visionary who, because of his youth and naïveté, failed to see that France was not ready for liberty. The implied critique did not detract from Lafayette's image as agent of the American mission. If anything, his image was enhanced by the emphasis placed on his consistent attachment to liberal principles, beside which his errors of judgment during the French Revolution paled into insignificance.

III

Given Lafayette's role as agent of the American mission and the situation of Europe in the 1820's, it was almost inevitable that his visit to the United States would take on a symbolic meaning. To Americans, Lafayette was the champion of liberalism in the Old World—the "friend of mankind," the "Apostle of Liberty," the "hero of two worlds" who had imbibed republican principles while fighting in the American Revolution and returned to France to try to establish them in his own country. Even in 1824, his career still served as an index to the state of liberty in France. His failure to win reelection to the Chamber of Deputies in that year symbolized the decline of liberal principles in general.[26] On the eve of his visit liberalism appeared to Americans to be a lost cause in Europe: constitutional monarchy had degenerated into autocracy, and

[26] See, for example, *N.E.P.* [*New England Palladium?*], April 23, 1824, and April 30, 1824, in "Lafayette in the United States, 1824–1825" (MS in Benjamin Thomas Hill Collection, Library of Congress), I, 19. Americans were not incorrect in seeing Lafayette's defeat as symbolic of the decline of liberalism in general. The elections of 1824 returned only 19 liberals to the Chamber in contrast to 410 royalists. Nora E. Hudson, *Ultra-Royalism and the French Restoration* (Cambridge, 1936), 102n.

the Holy Alliance seemed ready to stamp out republicanism and revolution in Europe and perhaps to annihilate it everywhere in the western hemisphere. France, once the vanguard of republicanism in the Old World, had joined with the counter-revolutionary powers.[27]

In this context, Lafayette's reception was seen as an instrument for fulfilling the American mission—a means of fostering the extension of liberty abroad without abandoning the position of passivity and detachment from European politics. As we have seen, the reception for Lafayette was an opportunity to advertise the success of the republican experiment, the model government for the rest of the world to follow. It provided a demonstration of the unexampled prosperity and unity of the United States. Even President Monroe, who worried about the effect of Lafayette's reception on American relations with the Holy Alliance, rejoiced at the show of republican unity which the reception exhibited. "The holy Alliance, & all the govt. of Europe, must . . . look to us, as an united people, devoted to the principles of our revolution & of free republican government," he declared.[28]

Lafayette's reception was also an opportunity to fulfill the demands of the American mission in another way—by offering a reproach to European despotism. If the reproach was mainly rhetorical, it nevertheless satisfied a desire to vent hostility toward the Holy Alliance and to articulate disappointment with the progress of liberty abroad. The least subtle manifestation of

[27] Louis R. Gottschalk, *The United States and Lafayette* (Rock Island, Ill., 1958), 7–8. For the American attitude toward France in the 1820's see Howard Mumford Jones, *America and French Culture, 1750–1848* (Chapel Hill, 1927), 561–64; Elizabeth Brett White, *American Opinion of France from Lafayette to Poincaré* (New York, 1927), Chap. 3.

[28] Monroe to Jefferson, October 18, 1824, and to Madison, October 18, 1824, in Hamilton (ed.), *Writings of Monroe*, VII, 41–42, 40. See also Calhoun to Monroe, October 2, 1824, in James Monroe Papers (microfilm copy of Presidential Papers in Louisiana State University Library, Baton Rouge), Film 1722; Calhoun to Monroe, October 28, 1824, in J. F. Jameson (ed.), *Correspondence of John C. Calhoun* (Washington, 1900), 226–27.

the reproach was a direct attack on the Holy Alliance, usually in the form of a toast at one of the many public dinners celebrating Lafayette's visit. A toast offered in Frankfort, Kentucky, and appropriately greeted with jeers, was typical: "The 'Holy Alliance'! An insolent and wicked conspiracy against the independence of nations and the rights of man." In Savannah, Georgia, citizens raised their glasses to "The Holy Alliance,—The bitterness of political death to those who are no friends to 'the world, or the world's Law.' " Speakers at Lafayette receptions condemned the "intrigues and machinations" of the "*sacrilegious coalition* against the sacred rights of mankind." [29] With the threat of intervention in the Americas presumably eliminated by Monroe's famous declaration, Americans could safely denounce infringements of liberty on the other side of the Atlantic without fear of reprisal.

The more indirect ways of demonstrating American hostility toward European despotism depended on the interpretations which the Old World might attach to Lafayette's reception. Americans maintained that the demonstrations in favor of Lafayette exposed the illegitimate relation between rulers and subjects under so-called legitimate governments. Virtually all the descriptions of Lafayette's reception included an invidious comparison, either implicit or explicit, with the monarchs of Europe. The homage paid to Lafayette, commentators pointed out, was motivated by gratitude, not fear; it was spontaneous and freely given, not "constrained." (Such remarks were particularly relevant following American denunciation of the forced and artificial ceremony attending the death and

---

[29] Hume, "Lafayette in Kentucky," 293; Savannah *Georgian*, March 21, 1825, Schenectady (N.Y.) *Cabinet*, June 15, 1825, and *Missouri Advocate and St. Louis Public Advertiser*, May 6, 1825, quoted in Brandon, *Pilgrimage*, 99, 429, 217. See also Pittsfield (Mass.) *Sun*, June 16, 1825, quoted *ibid.*, 436; *Northern Sentinel*, July 15, 1825, quoted in "Pages from the Past," 225; *Niles' Weekly Register* (Baltimore), July 17, 1824, p. 333; Hooper Cumming, *An Oration* (New York, 1824), 11.

funeral of Louis XVIII of France and the coronation of Charles X.[30]) Moreover, "the unbought and unbribed homage of a free and great people . . . to their benefactor" indicated the superiority of popular governments, where the loyalty of the people as well as the power of the ruler rested on "consent" rather than fear.[31] Lafayette's reception exposed the fundamental weakness of tyrannical governments. "Where," asked the Cincinnati *Advertiser*, "has been, or who is the king or emperor . . . that ever possessed the esteem and gratitude of ten millions of people?" [32]

There was still another way in which Lafayette's reception appeared to serve as an instrument of the American mission. The homage Americans paid to Lafayette was, as Sarah Seaton remarked, "our homage to Liberty in the person of Lafayette." [33] His reception was "the reward of a man who is the enemy of tyrants and oppression, and whose life and blood have been devoted to the cause of liberty and the rights of mankind." [34] His reception might not sit well with the sovereigns of Europe, but it could not fail to have a beneficial effect on their subjects.[35] The demonstrations in favor of "the uniform

[30] See, for example, White, *American Opinion of France*, 82–83, 85.

[31] *American Military Biography*, 267–69. See also scrapbook of newspaper clippings, 1824–25, relating to Lafayette's visit to America and his service in the Revolution (Rare Book Room, Library of Congress), 16.

[32] Cincinnati *Advertiser*, May 25, 1825, quoted in Brandon, *Pilgrimage*, 332. See also Louisville *Public Advertiser*, May 14, 1825, and address of John Bradford, Lexington, Ky., May 16, 1825, quoted *ibid.*, 270, 286.

[33] Sarah (Mrs. William) Seaton to her mother, January, 1825, in William Winston Seaton, *A Biographical Sketch* (Boston, 1871), 173. See also *Mississippi Gazette*, April 23, 1825, quoted in Brandon, *Pilgrimage*, 209; N. Crookshank to Lafayette, Harrison, Ohio, June 20, 1825, in Cornell Lafayette Collection, XII; address of citizens of Orange, N.J., n.d., and address of Samuel W. Dana, mayor of Middleton, Conn., September 4, 1824, *ibid.*, XVIII.

[34] *American Military Biography*, 267–69. See also address of John Bradford, Lexington, Ky., May 16, 1825, quoted in Brandon, *Pilgrimage*, 286.

[35] See, for example, Jefferson to Rush, October 13, 1824, in Ford (ed.), *Works of Jefferson*, XII, 380–81; Monroe to Madison, December 13, 1824, in Hamilton (ed.), *Writings of Monroe*, VII, 53; Cincinnati *Advertiser*, May 25, 1825, Louisville *Public Advertiser*, May 14, 1825, Savannah *Georgian*,

friend of liberal institutions" would serve as an inspiration to "the friends of liberty in Europe" and elsewhere.[36] Lafayette, one writer explained, "is the connecting link between the United States, and the friends of free principles in France; the *electric rod*, if we may be allowed the expression, uniting the two nations, and communicating to the hearts of Frenchmen the etherial [*sic*] spark of freedom, which animates the breasts and nerves the arms of their cis-atlantic brethren." The same writer predicted, "The accounts of his reception here; the numerous addresses of all classes of our citizens, and his replies, together with his toasts and sentiments, breathing uniformly the undaunted spirit of liberty, and hostility to the slavish doctrines of the Holy Alliance, will be widely circulated, and read on the continent of Europe, notwithstanding all the efforts which may be made by despots to suppress them." What would be the effect of all this? The writer anticipated "extensive and powerful reaction in favour of liberal principles." The news of Lafayette's reception would not "produce a revolution; but it will . . . exert a more propitious influence, than any even since the establishment of American independence." Other commentators were less cautious in predicting the effect of Lafayette's reception on the cause of liberty abroad. The possibility that it might spark another revolution was not unimaginable. The *Connecticut Courant* suggested that "freedom may again be encouraged in Europe to rear up her head against the oppressions of royalty and despotic power." [37]

March 21, 1825, quoted in Brandon, *Pilgrimage*, 340, 270, 99; Ingersoll, *Communication*, 23–24; "Lafayette in the United States," II, 4.

[36] Message of Governor Joseph Desha, November 1, 1824, in Joseph Desha, "Extracts from the Messages of Governor Desha," *Kentucky Historical Society Register*, XI (1913), 71. See also "Lafayette in the United States," II, 12; *N.E.P.*, August 31, 1824, October 8, 1824, *ibid.*, VI, 37, VII, 83; clipping from Richmond *Enquirer*, scrapbook, no p., Savannah *Georgian*, March 25, 1825, quoted in Brandon, *Pilgrimage*, 120–21.

[37] Newspaper clipping, scrapbook, 15; *N.E.P.*, August 31, 1824, in "Lafayette in the United States," VI, 37. See also Foster, *Sketch of the Tour of Lafayette*, 211.

The conviction that Lafayette's reception would encourage liberals in Europe and elsewhere was not without validity. According to Edgar Ewing Brandon, "the enthusiastic reception accorded Lafayette in the United States furnished the liberal press of both England and Continental Europe an excellent occasion to advocate republican doctrines, and full advantage was taken of it in countries where the censorship would permit." Liberal writers in France such as Charles Ogé Barbaroux exploited the visit.[38] Pierre Jean de Béranger, the most popular poet and songwriter of the Restoration, celebrated Lafayette's reception as a republican fete.[39] From Buenos Aires came a letter, published in *Niles' Weekly Register*, which suggested the effect of Lafayette's reception on liberals "in the most distant region of the 'new world.'" The writer observed, "That ten millions of souls, actuated by pure sentiments of gratitude and friendship, should, with one voice, pronounce this individual the 'Guest of the Nation,' and pay him the highest honors the citizens of a free nation can offer, is an event which must excite the astonishment of Europe and show the inestimable price of liberty."[40]

American confidence as to the effect of Lafayette's reception on the cause of liberty abroad was part of a more general optimism regarding the progress of liberal principles throughout the world. Notwithstanding the alleged threat to liberty posed by the Holy Alliance, Americans of the mid-1820's analyzed political developments in the western hemisphere from a more sanguine and realistic point of view than previously. The new appraisal was articulated by Daniel Webster at the laying of the cornerstone of the Bunker Hill Monument during Lafayette's visit. Looking back on the half-century since the Ameri-

---

[38] Brandon, *Pilgrimage*, 464n. See also Gottschalk, *United States and Lafayette*, 8; [Waln], *Account of the Visit of Lafayette*, 478–83.

[39] P.-J. de Béranger, "Lafayette en Amérique," *Oeuvres Complètes* (Paris, 1847), I, 119–20.

[40] *Niles' Weekly Register* (Baltimore), April 9, 1825, pp. 85–86.

can Revolution, Webster noted "the great changes" which had occurred throughout the world. The process of change had been twofold. While the various nations had made "separate and individual advances in improvement," they had also participated in "a common progress." Webster likened the nations to "vessels on a common tide, propelled by the gales at different rates, according to their several structure [*sic*] and management, but all moved forward by one mighty current, strong enough to bear onward whatever does not sink beneath it."

The simile reveals two important assumptions underlying the new appraisal of the struggle for liberty. First, it suggested a relativistic view of progress. Webster implied that the past history and present condition of nations caused them to advance "at different rates." Second, his simile embraced the idea of the inevitability of progress. The ships, or nations, are propelled "on a common tide" by "one mighty current," suggesting an elemental or natural force moving and supporting the vessels. The analogue of the "one mighty current" was the law of progress which made possible both the individual improvement and "common progress" of the various nations.

A third assumption underlying the new appraisal of the struggle for liberty was the notion that progress occurred gradually, through the growth of knowledge. Webster pointed to "a community of opinions and knowledge amongst men in different nations, existing in a degree heretofore unknown," as the "chief distinction" of the age and basis of progress in the area of "human liberty and human happiness." [41] Another speaker at a reception for Lafayette echoed Webster's words, observing that "some of the great and leading truths of political oeconomy [*sic*], have been gradually unfolded to suffering Europe." He asserted his "conviction, that the march of moral and intellectual improvement, though slow, is certain; and that sooner or later, those iron systems of oppression that over-

[41] Webster, "Bunker Hill Monument," 247–50.

shadow some of the fairest portions of the globe, will dissolve and vanish before the light of truth, as the darkness flees before the morning beam." [42] Thus the new appraisal of the struggle for liberty was based on the notion that the advance of liberty, promoted by the law of progress, occurred gradually and inevitably, though at different rates depending on the history and conditions of individual nations.

As proof of the progress of liberal principles, Americans pointed to the republics of South America. Their triumph over Spanish despotism was a theme sounded by many speakers at receptions for Lafayette. Webster reckoned the South American revolution one of "the great events" of the fifty-year period since Bunker Hill. He admitted that the new republics still had "much to learn"—presumably from the United States—but considering their peculiar history and problems he could not be other than optimistic. The former Spanish colonies had won their independence "under circumstances less favorable, doubtless, than attended our own revolution," Webster observed. Notwithstanding certain political, religious, and educational deficiencies, "they have risen to the condition of settled and established states more rapidly than could have been reasonably anticipated." They furnished "an exhilarating example of the difference between free governments and despotic misrule." [43]

The appraisals of France offered at the receptions for Lafayette also reflect the optimism with which Americans viewed

[42] Address on behalf of citizens of Waterford, [Pa.?], n.d., in Cornell Lafayette Collection, XVIII.

[43] Webster, "Bunker Hill Monument," 251–52. The receptions for Lafayette provided the occasion for numerous toasts celebrating the South American revolutions and their leaders, particularly Simon Bolívar (who was often likened to Washington and/or Lafayette), in tones reminiscent of the enthusiasm with which Americans had greeted the French Revolution in 1789. See Brandon, *Pilgrimage*, 18, 74, 75, 81, 99, 102, 126, 136, 154, 223, 235, 276, 364, 374, 385, 392, 429, 435, 480n; Galbreath, "Lafayette's Visit to Ohio Valley States," 176–77, 213–14; "Pages from the Past," 225; *Niles' Weekly Register* (Baltimore), May 1, 1824, p. 135, January 8, 1825, p. 290, April 2, 1825, p. 70.

the progress of liberal principles. This is not to say that Americans approved the policies of the Bourbons. As we have seen, the reception for Lafayette was looked upon by some Americans as a perfect opportunity to indicate disappointment with the reactionary policies of the French government. Even celebrations of the Franco-American alliance, though conciliatory in appearance, had a critical edge to them. Indeed, they were less celebrations of Franco-American amity than demonstrations of the ideological and political gulf that had grown up between the two countries.[44] In toasting France as "our revolutionary ally" and "friend in need" Americans toasted the France of 1778, not the France of 1825. In 1778 France had appeared to Americans as a patron of revolution; in 1825 she was seen as the enemy of revolution. Implicit in many of the toasts to France was the hope that she might assume her earlier posture: "America, & France in union with her, As by the aid and prowess of distinguished Frenchmen, American Liberty has been established—so may their remaining patriots save and make permanent the liberties of their own nation." [45]

Notwithstanding this kind of veiled criticism, the striking thing about most of the appraisals of France is their fundamental optimism, in contrast to the despair and resignation of earlier estimates. Thus for M. Ludwell Lee, France was "yet a Country of heroes & of Sages." His sanguine view of France led him to predict that "the small leaven of freedom" existing in that country "may ere long ferment the map" and bring about similar progress throughout Europe.[46]

Behind this optimistic view of France lay a new interpretation of the French Revolution, which Lafayette himself en-

[44] See White, *American Opinion of France,* 79–80.

[45] Raleigh *Register*, March 11, 1825, and *Georgia Journal*, April 5, 1825, quoted in Brandon, *Pilgrimage*, 28, 137. For other toasts see *ibid.*, 223, 235, 276, 429, 436, 480n; "Pages from the Past," 224–25.

[46] Address of M. Ludwell Lee, Leesburg, Va., August, [1825], in Cornell Lafayette Collection, XVIII.

dorsed.[47] In the past, Americans had treated that struggle with contempt. But some speakers at Lafayette receptions, instead of rehearsing the horrors of the Terror, emphasized the long-term benefits which the Revolution had bestowed. Speaking at Uniontown, Pennsylvania, Albert Gallatin, former American minister to France, enumerated the "mass of improvements" brought about by the Revolution and explicitly challenged the orthodox interpretation of the Revolution. "It has perhaps been a common error to believe that France had reaped no other fruits from her revolution than wretchedness and bloodshed, that no material benefits had ultimately accrued to the nation from that portentous event," he observed. "If, however, the magnitude of the obstacles to be overcome in every quarter shall be duly considered, and if we compare what France was at the epoch of our revolution with what it now is, there will be found less cause of astonishment that no more was affected, than of regret that it should have been purchased at so dear a price." In Gallatin's view, the French Revolution had effected "a radical change in the internal policy of France, far greater than ever had been effected, within the same time, in any age or in any country."

Probably Gallatin offered the new interpretation of the Revolution partly out of deference to Lafayette, in recognition of the role he had played in it. As Gallatin observed, "The part you took, on all the monstrous questions agitated at that time, is known to the world." He conceded that most of the improvements he had listed "were obtained in the course of the three first years of the French revolution, of that short period during

<hr/>

[47] In a reply to an address by the Frenchmen of New York, Lafayette argued "that the revolution of 1789 has greatly meliorated the condition of an immense majority of the people." He counseled his former countrymen not to "despair . . . of the cause of liberty," assuring them that "it is still dear to the hearts of Frenchmen, and we shall one day have the felicity of seeing it established in our beloved country." *Niles' Weekly Register* (Baltimore), August 28, 1824, p. 429; Butler, *Memoirs of La Fayette*, 237. See also *N.E.P.*, August 24, 1824, in "Lafayette in the United States," II, 21.

which alone you had an influence, and a most powerful influence over the affairs of France." Nevertheless, the mere recognition of the good results of the Revolution, for whatever reason, was a significant departure from the earlier American interpretation.

The primary impulse behind such revisionism was the idea of progress. Gallatin measured the ultimate benefits of the Revolution against "the magnitude of the obstacles to be overcome" and evaluated the success of the Revolution by contrasting France's situation at the time of the American Revolution with her situation in 1825. Like Webster, he suggested that nations improved at different rates, depending on their condition and structure. In comparison with the progress effected by the American Revolution, France's struggle was bound to appear a failure. But looking at the French Revolution from a relativistic point of view, one would have to admit that the changes it had wrought were not only quite radical in nature but an improvement over France's former situation. Indeed, France's progress was but one example of the influence of the law of progress governing the universe. The moral and intellectual improvement effected by that law evoked a flourish of rhetoric from Gallatin. "A new spirit pervades, animates the whole civilized world," he declared. "It has penetrated through every class of society, teaching every man, in the most obscure and latterly oppressed [social classes], to feel and assert his rights; making every day new converts, even amongst the privileged ranks, sitting on the very footsteps of the thrones." A "few infatuated men" might attempt to arrest the progress of mankind. Gallatin dismissed them as men "who only dream what they cannot hope." "The planets also, to the eye of man, appear at times to have a retrograde motion," he observed, "but they still pursue their unerring course, in obedience to the laws of Nature and to the first impulse of the Creator." So it was "in the moral world" also—"people, nobles, statesmen, monarchs, all are carried away by the irresistable [*sic*] stream of public opinion & of growing knowledge." [48]

Gallatin had implied that any comparison of the French Revolution with its American counterpart was in some sense illegitimate. But such comparisons were inevitable given the popular notion that the French Revolution had been, at least in its inception, what one American called "a Scion from our American republican stock." [49] The difference between the comparisons made in 1824–25 and those made during and soon after the French Revolution reveals the influence of the early nineteenth-century philosophy of progress. Judging the two revolutions relativistically, Americans conceded that both the "success" of the American Revolution and the "failure" of the French Revolution were to some extent foreordained by the structure and condition of the two countries in which they occurred. Daniel Webster delineated the familiar comparison for his Bunker Hill audience: "The great wheel of political revolution began to move in America. Here its rotation was guarded, regular, and safe. Transferred to the other continent, from unfortunate but natural causes, it received an irregular and violent impulse; it whirled along with a fearful celerity; till at length, like the chariot-wheels in the races of antiquity, it took fire from the rapidity of its own motion, and blazed onward, spreading conflagration and terror around."

On the one hand, the comparison reveals Webster to be more of a gradualist than Gallatin. The latter had applauded the French Revolution for producing "a radical change . . . far greater than ever had been effected, within the same time, in any age or in any country." In contrast, Webster suggested that the change wrought by the Revolution had proceeded *too* rapidly, degenerating into anarchy and violence. Believing in

[48] Address of Albert Gallatin, Uniontown, Pa., May 27, 1825, quoted in Brandon, *Pilgrimage*, 367–73.
[49] *Union Sentinel and Gazette*, June 14, 1825, quoted *ibid.*, 480n.

the law of progress, Webster assumed that beneficial change was gradual and orderly, and therefore "safe." At the same time, a belief in the relative nature of progress led Webster to attribute the excesses of the French Revolution to "unfortunate but natural causes." He implied that certain political, economic, social, and psychological factors inherent in the French situation—beyond the control of either men or Providence—had caused the wheel of political revolution to veer in a disastrous direction. The absence of such factors, and the presence of other factors, had produced an entirely different kind of revolution in America, one that was "guarded, regular, and safe":

> The possession of power did not turn the heads of the American people, for they had long been in the habit of exercising a great degree of self-control. . . . They were accustomed to representative bodies and the forms of free governments; they understood the doctrine of the division of power among different branches, and the necessity of checks on each. The character of our countrymen, moreover, was sober, moral, and religious; and there was little in the change to shock their feelings of justice and humanity, or even to disturb an honest prejudice. We had no domestic throne to overturn, no privileged orders to cast down, no violent changes of property to encounter.

Americans should not be surprised, Webster concluded, "that, under circumstances less auspicious, political revolutions elsewhere, even when well intended, have terminated differently. It is, indeed, a great achievement, it is the master-work of the world, to establish governments entirely popular on lasting foundations; nor is it easy, indeed, to introduce the popular principle at all into governments to which it has been altogether a stranger." Recognizing the relative nature of progress, Webster was inclined to be somewhat skeptical of the possibility of an immediate triumph of liberal principles. The results of the French Revolution, though not so disastrous as many had thought, reinforced this attitude. But such skepticism never degenerated into the stark pessimism of earlier decades, and it was balanced by a generally optimistic outlook based on a long-range view of developments over the past fifty years. "It cannot be doubted . . . that Europe has come out of the contest, in which she has been so long engaged, with greatly superior knowledge, and, in many respects, in a highly improved condition," Webster argued. Moreover, he declared, "whatever benefit has been acquired is likely to be retained, for it consists mainly in the acquisition of more enlightened ideas." Progress deriving from an increase in knowledge was self-perpetuating. According to Webster, "it is the glorious prerogative of the empire of knowledge, that what it gains it never loses. On the contrary, it increases by the multiple of its own power; all its ends become means; all its attainments, helps to new conquests. Its whole abundant harvest is but so much seed wheat, and nothing has limited, and can limit, the amount of ultimate product." [50]

Although Americans shared Webster's conviction that the cause of liberty was advancing, they could not agree on the part their country should play in furthering such progress. They anticipated a "good effect" from Lafayette's reception, viewing it as an instrument of the American mission, but there was no consensus on the question of the role of the United States in carrying out its providential task of spreading republican principles. As a result, Lafayette's visit became a forum in which the meaning of the American mission was debated, with the majority of speakers and writers supporting a conservative conception of the United States as a passive example or model for other nations to follow, and a minority espousing a more radical view, arguing for active intervention in and direct support of the cause of liberty throughout the world.

The conception of America as a passive model of republicanism was endorsed by Daniel Webster at Bunker Hill. Exulting in "the benefit which the example of our country has produced,

[50] Webster, "Bunker Hill Monument," 248–49.

and is likely to produce, on human freedom and human happiness," Webster described the role assigned "in the great drama of human affairs" to the United States: "We are placed at the head of the system of representative and popular government. Thus far our example shows that such governments are compatible, not only with respectability and power, but with repose, with peace, with security of personal rights, with good laws, and a just administration." Cast in such a role, Americans incurred a unique responsibility. If the representative system should fail in the United States, "popular governments must be pronounced impossible," Webster warned. Therefore, "the sacred obligations" which devolved on the American people were the "defence and preservation" of the republican system, and its "improvement" through the advancement of peace, union, and harmony. The "appropriate object" of American energies was "OUR COUNTRY, OUR WHOLE COUNTRY, AND NOTHING BUT OUR COUNTRY." Through such efforts the United States might "become a vast and splendid monument, not of oppression and terror, but of Wisdom, of Peace, and of Liberty, upon which the world may gaze with admiration for ever!"

As Webster defined it, the American mission consisted in defending, preserving, and improving the republican system established by the Founding Fathers. "We can win no laurels in a war for independence," he declared. "Earlier and worthier hands have gathered them all. Nor are there places for us by the side of Solon, and Alfred, and other founders of states. Our fathers have filled them." Even the active proselytizing of liberal principles was dismissed. "We are not propagandists," Webster declared. "Wherever other systems are preferred, either as being thought better in themselves, or as better suited to existing condition [*sic*], we leave the preference to be enjoyed." In Webster's view, the American mission implied no involvement or interference in conflicts or systems outside the national boundaries. It meant only serving as a model of repub-

lican government, destroying tyranny by passive example
rather than by active intervention.

The conservative view of the American mission derived
much of its force and conviction from the prevailing philosophy of progress. The law of inevitable progress seemed to
guarantee the eventual establishment of republican principles
throughout the rest of the world, without the active interference of the United States. This was one reason why the
primary "duty" of Americans, as Webster said, was "to preserve the consistency of this cheering example, and take care
that nothing may weaken its authority with the world." For
Americans to intervene directly in the struggle for liberty
beyond their boundaries would be to risk the decline or over-
throw of liberty at home, thereby destroying the only existing example of republicanism and with it, "the last hopes of
mankind." [51]

Webster was not alone in propounding the conservative view
of the American mission. Lafayette's visit called forth other
samples of that view in the form of toasts, speeches, and com-
mentaries. Thus one speaker pointed to the contrast between
Europe and the American example—a contrast between "an
alliance, hypocritically denominated HOLY, the ostensible object of which is, to forge chains for the very subjects it is bound
to protect," and "a *real* holy alliance of free states, extending
the blessings of liberty to every citizen, protecting him in the
possession of property, and all his natural and social rights."
In his opinion, the contrast alone "must possess a powerful
influence in strengthening the cause of liberty wherever it
exists." [52] Lafayette too endorsed the notion of America as
an example to the rest of the world. In the nation's capital he

[51] *Ibid.*, 253–54.

[52] Quoted in Foster, *Sketch of the Tour of Lafayette*, 211–12. For other
toasts see Brandon, *Pilgrimage*, 28, 29, 74, 127, 363, 386; "Lafayette in New
Brunswick in 1824," *New Jersey Historical Society Proceedings*, n.s., V
(1920), 115.

toasted "the city of Washington: The central star of the constellation which enlightens the whole world." [53]

In opposition to the conservative view other Americans argued for a radical conception of the American mission, calling for active and direct support of republican principles throughout the world. Instead of minimizing and circumscribing human effort and relying on the inevitable law of progress, they demanded volunteers to fight on behalf of liberalism wherever threatened. In the 1820's the focus of the radical conception of mission was the Greek revolution. The Greeks had won the sympathy of the American people almost as soon as news of their uprising against the Turks reached the United States. According to Edward M. Earle, "The autumn and winter of 1823–1824 were a period in which sentiment for Greek independence reached a high point, strenuous efforts were put forth to render active assistance to the revolutionary forces, and serious consideration was given to a possible recognition of Greek belligerency and independence by the government of the United States." [54]

Lafayette's arrival in the United States intensified American interest in the Greek struggle.[55] He was known to sympathize with the Greeks. " 'His cause,' " wrote James Gallatin, " 'is the emancipation of the Spanish Colonies and of Greece.' " [56] Consequently, receptions for the Nation's Guest

[53] *Niles' Weekly Register* (Baltimore), October 23, 1824, p. 123. See also *ibid.*, September 4, 1824, p. 14, November 6, 1824, p. 157; William Cutter, *The Life of General Lafayette* (New York, 1857), 370–71; White, *American Opinion of France*, 81–82; *N.E.P.*, September 10, 1824, in "Lafayette in the United States," V, 31.

[54] Edward M. Earle, "American Interest in the Greek Cause, 1821–1827," *American Historical Review*, XXXIII (1927), 47. See also Stephen A. Larrabee, *Hellas Observed: The American Experience of Greece, 1775–1865* (New York, 1957), 55, 65–74, 104, 304–305n.

[55] See, for example, *N.E.P.*, March 12, 1824, in "Lafayette in the United States," I, 14.

[56] Larrabee, *Hellas Observed*, 74. See also J. Q. Adams Diary, February 6, 1825, in Adams (ed.), *Memoirs of John Quincy Adams*, VI, 498; Foster,

often were the scene of pro-Greek toasts.[57] At the same time, some Americans looked upon the visit as an opportunity to continue discussion of American policy regarding the Greek struggle. Congress had officially disposed of the issue during the "Greek Debate" of 1824, but proponents of material, in addition to moral, support of the Greeks continued to appeal for a reconsideration.

Essentially, the debate during Lafayette's visit over American policy regarding the Greek revolution was a debate between the conservative and radical conceptions of the American mission. Webster was the spokesman for the conservative view. He stood for limited support of the Greek cause in the form of an aroused public opinion which would exert a moral influence in favor of Greece throughout the world and encourage that country in its struggle for independence: "Let her be assured, that she is not forgotten in the world; that her efforts are applauded, and that constant prayers ascend for her success," Webster advised.[58] Albert Gallatin articulated the radical opinion on American aid to Greece.[59] In his address to Lafayette at Uniontown, he reviewed the critical situation of the Greeks and called for American intervention in their behalf. "The cause is not yet won," he cried. "An almost miraculous resistance may yet perhaps be overwhelmed by the tremendous superiority of numbers. And will the civilized, the christian [*sic*] world . . . look with apathy on the dreadful

---

Sketch of the Tour of Lafayette, 114; address of William Thornton, Washington, September 6, 1825, in Cornell Lafayette Collection, XV; Lafayette's reply to an address by Albert Gallatin, Uniontown, Pa., May 27, 1825, quoted in Brandon, *Pilgrimage*, 373.

[57] See Brandon, *Pilgrimage*, 28, 81, 126, 137, 374, 386, 392, 480n; "Pages from the Past," 224–25.

[58] Webster, "Bunker Hill Monument," 251.

[59] While in Paris, Gallatin had received agents of the Greek government and had consulted with Lafayette on the Greek struggle. Influenced by the Frenchman, the American minister had even proposed sending the United States fleet to aid the Greeks. Larrabee, *Hellas Observed*, 65–74.

catastrophe that would ensue? a catastrophe which they, which even we alone could prevent with so much facility and almost without danger?" [60]

Gallatin's passionate appeal for aid to Greece did nothing to alter the official noninterventionist position of the United States government. Nor did Lafayette's visit, in spite of the popular enthusiasm it evoked in favor of the Greeks. Congress had already settled the issue within the framework of the conservative view of the American mission. Appeals for active support of Greece were more successful on the personal and individual level. Proponents of the radical conception of mission took advantage of the celebration of the American Revolution occasioned by Lafayette's tour to solicit aid for the Greek cause. Comparisons between the Greek struggle and the American Revolution, and recollections of Lafayette's participation in the latter, were the basis for toasts such as the following: "*The sons of classic Greece*—Whose ancestors shed an imperishable lustre on the military and literary world, now bravely contending against fearful odds for independence; may they find among their natives a Washington, and among their allies a Lafayette, to lead them on to victory, to glory, and a *free government*." [61] An explicit call for volunteers in the Greek struggle was made by Henry Ware before the Phi Beta Kappa Society of Harvard College at a meeting honoring Lafayette. [62]

Most of the appeals for volunteers pointed to Lafayette as an example of active, disinterested support of liberty. Indeed, Lafayette's legendary role in the American Revolution served

[60] *Genius of Liberty*, June 7, 1825, quoted in Brandon, *Pilgrimage*, 368–73. See also *N.E.P.*, March 12, 1824, in "Lafayette in the United States," I, 14; Larrabee, *Hellas Observed*, 74.

[61] Nashville *Whig*, May 7, 14, 1825, quoted in Brandon, *Pilgrimage*, 235. See also *ibid.*, 154, 429; Dorothy Mackay Quynn, "Lafayette's Visit in Frederick, 1824," *Maryland Historical Magazine*, XLIX (1954), 297.

[62] Larrabee, *Hellas Observed*, 113.

as a paradigm for proponents of the radical conception of mission. After rehearsing the story of Lafayette's participation in the American war for independence, the intendant of Milledgeville, Georgia, expressed "the hope that our country is destined to produce other Lafayettes, who profiting by your example and aided by the God of Battles, will give liberty and independence to nations now groaning under the yoke of tyranny and oppression." [63] The gratitude which Americans felt toward their benefactor was also cited as an incentive to aid the Greeks. Samuel Gridley Howe was surprised that more "young men of fortune do not come to Greece; that they do not enlist heart and soul in this most sacred of all causes, and gain for themselves the gratitude of a nation and a place in history; more particularly, too, when they have such a scene before their eyes as is presented by the treatment of Lafayette in our happy and flourishing country." [64]

Such appeals apparently influenced at least two Americans to offer their services to the Greeks. One of them, Estwick Evans of New Hampshire, actually spent the month of July, 1825, in Greece. No doubt the congressional debate of 1824 first aroused his interest in the struggle. According to Stephen A. Larrabee, "The death of Byron probably increased his interest in the Greeks, and the enthusiasm over the visit of Lafayette to the United States may have encouraged him to think of being something like his counterpart in Greece." [65]

Another volunteer, twenty-three-year-old Bedinger Morgan of Kentucky, revealed his motivations in a long, semiliterate

[63] Address of the intendant, Milledgeville, Ga., March 27, 1825, quoted in Brandon, *Pilgrimage*, 135.

[64] Samuel Gridley Howe to his father, March, 1825, in Laura E. Richards (ed.), *Letters and Journals of Samuel Gridley Howe* (Boston, 1906), I, 29–30. At the time of Howe's death, the General Court of Massachusetts passed a resolution citing him for "emulating . . . the noble career of his friend and the friend of mankind—the illustrious Lafayette." *Ibid.*, II, 598. See also Earle, "American Interest in the Greek Cause," 56.

[65] Larrabee, *Hellas Observed*, 135–36, and see also 137, 316–17n.

letter requesting Lafayette's aid and support for his benevolent enterprise, which he believed to be "congenial with your wishes and policy." Morgan explained that he had watched the struggle "for Grecian liberty" with considerable "interest and anxiety." It had partially succeeded. But the battle was not yet done. "The prayers of America has been put up for them," Morgan observed. "Our Congress has recognised them free and Independant." But "something else must be done[;] unless Individuals contribute there mite—Greece may yet be enslaved," he declared. "I therefore as an Individual of these United States —and a Sitizen of Kentucky—Volentarily step forward and tender to her my cirvaces my *fortune* and if necessary my *life* —with the full determination with her to live—or with her to perish—concurring in the sentiments contained in the American *Declaration* of *Independance* . . . . I feel it a duty to protect and assist so far as it is in my power the opressed." [66]

Why did Lafayette's example inspire so few imitators in the 1820's? The answer is that the conservative view of the American mission was dominant in the early nineteenth century. Indeed, as we have seen, it even affected assessments of Lafayette's role as agent of the American mission, raising disturbing questions about the validity and success of his attempt to carry republican principles to France. Thus while Lafayette's visit was the occasion for a renewal of the American sense of mission, the number of Americans who interpreted it from a radical point of view was small. Most, like Webster, interpreted it to mean serving as a passive example of republicanism for other nations to follow. Though Americans praised Lafayette for having transcended national loyalty in espousing a foreign cause, the disinterested benevolence which he symbolized was absent from their own sense of mission. In the 1820's the dominant American attitude toward foreign policy

[66] Bedinger Morgan to "Friend of Washington," Russellvill Logan Ct [*sic*], Ky., May 20, 1825, in Cornell Lafayette Collection, XVII.

was based on realism rather than idealism, self-interest rather than benevolence. Like the revival of republicanism, the renewal of the American sense of mission which Lafayette's visit fostered was primarily conservative in its effects.

IV

Just as an earlier generation had seen Lafayette as the "index" of true liberalism in the Old World, so Americans in the decade following the Triumphal Tour tended to read European politics largely in terms of his career. At the same time Lafayette resumed correspondence with his American friends—their number greatly enlarged as a result of his visit—on the progress of liberty abroad. Consequently, many Americans viewed the European scene almost exclusively through his eyes. They continued to see him as the agent of the American mission—a mediary between the Old World and the New, through whom they could encourage and oversee the cause of liberty without abandoning their passive role as an example of republican government.[67]

The American reaction to foreign events in the late 1820's and early 1830's exposed certain contradictions and tensions in their sense of mission. Despite their acceptance of the notion of relative progress, Americans still became disillusioned when other countries failed to adopt their example. The enthusiasm for the Greek cause manifested during Lafayette's visit had soured by 1826. Richard Peters wrote to Lafayette that he had "never believed them [the Greeks] fit for a republican Government," and he complained that "the Greeks deceive our Judgments by our associating their ancient Fame with their modern character. They are at least Semi barbarians; & it is to be regretted that so good a cause is in such incompetent

---

[67] See, for example, clipping from Richmond *Enquirer*, scrapbook, no p.

hands." [68] The South American revolutions evoked a similar response.[69]

In a way, such disillusionment was inevitable, given the American attitude toward revolution. Convinced that upheavals throughout the world were inspired by their own example of "guarded, regular, and safe" revolution, Americans expected that the outcome of such upheavals would be similar to that of the American Revolution. Despite their professed belief in relative progress, they measured every revolution by their own, pressing its example on foreign liberals and protesting any deviation from it. They failed to appreciate what Lafayette had once termed the "elasticity" within "the revolutionary spirit of freedom." [70] Nor were they able to maintain any "elasticity" in their own response to revolution. By the late 1820's their reaction to revolution had become as stereotyped as their image of it.

Nowhere is the stereotyped response to revolution more clearly revealed than in the reaction to the Revolution of 1830. The response to the events of the "Three Days" and their aftermath followed the typical pattern of initial rejoicing and ultimate disillusionment. There were celebrations in cities and towns across the nation, and private citizens wrote letters of congratulation to Lafayette expressing enthusiasm for "the late glorious revolution." [71] Fears of a repetition of the "con-

[68] Peters to Lafayette, December, 1826, in Cornell Lafayette Collection, XI. See also Marshall to Lafayette, May 2, 1827, and Josiah Quincy to Lafayette, May 6, 1828, *ibid.*

[69] See the following letters to Lafayette: Edward Everett, December 6, 1826, George Washington Parke Custis, November 20, 1827, Alexander H. Everett, October 26, 1828, *ibid.*, X; William Henry Harrison, May 5, 1829, *ibid.*, XI.

[70] Lafayette was chiding critics of the Greek Revolution who demanded that it follow the American pattern. Lafayette to Clay, January 22, 1826, in Colton (ed.), *Life, Correspondence, and Speeches of Clay*, IV, 136.

[71] Fish to Lafayette, September 22 and December 19, 1830, in Cornell Lafayette Collection, XI. See also the following letters to Lafayette: E. Everett, October 29, 1830, A. H. Everett, September 15, 1830, *ibid.*, X; E. Livingston,

vulsions" of the earlier revolution had proved "groundless," Josiah Quincy observed. The Revolution of 1830 was a success; it had been "effected without other bloodshed, than that, which flowed in the first and inevitable combat!" In Quincy's view, the "virtue" and "moderation" of Lafayette's compatriots demonstrated that "the lapse and lessons of forty years had materially changed the character of the French people." [72]

This notion of the progress that France had made in acquiring a "respect for legality and good order"—obviously lacking in the 1790's, yet vital to any system of "rational liberty"— inspired confidence that the French, under the guidance of Lafayette, would this time be able to follow the American example not only in revolting against oppression, but in establishing stable constitutional government. Writing to Lafayette, Albert Gallatin contrasted the motivation of the revolutionaries of 1789 and those of 1830, describing the latter in terms strikingly similar to those usually applied to patriots of the American Revolution. Frenchmen of 1830 "fought purely for liberty and not for revenge," according to Gallatin; "their fathers had been maddened by ages of inexpiable wrongs: your heroes & martyrs were enlightened freemen actuated by none but the most generous feelings of human nature." [73] The implication was that since the motivation of the Revolution of

December 26, 1830, W. C. Rives, July 31, August 1, and November 8, 1830, *ibid.*, XI; John S. Cogdell, November 19, 1830, *ibid.*, XII; James G. King, October 1, 1830, *ibid.*, XIII; Joseph S. Lewis, January 23, 1831, *ibid.*, XIV.

[72] Quincy to Lafayette, January 31, 1831, *ibid.*, XI. See also the following letters to Lafayette: E. Livingston, October 10, 1830, *ibid.*; J. Brown, October 9, 1830, *ibid.*, XII; Philip Howe, September 28, 1830, Daniel Foster, November 22, 1830, *ibid.*, XIII; and Monroe to a committee of Tammany Hall, 1831, in Hamilton (ed.), *Writings of Monroe*, VII, 220–21. For a more qualified judgment of the Revolution see Calhoun to Lafayette, October 23, 1830, in Cornell Lafayette Collection, X; J. Q. Adams Diary, December 23, 1830, in Adams (ed.), *Memoirs of John Quincy Adams*, VIII, 253.

[73] Gallatin to Lafayette, November 1, 1830, in Cornell Lafayette Collection, XI.

1830 was essentially the same as that of the American Revolution, the outcome of the former would prove as auspicious as that of the latter.

To be sure, France had stopped short of a republican form of government, establishing a constitutional monarchy instead, and most of Lafayette's friends gave this development their hearty approval. Their support was based on the notion of relative progress. "For myself," James Madison wrote to Lafayette, "Republican as I am, I easily conceive that the Constitutional Monarchy adopted, may be as necessary to the actual condition of France, internal & external, as Mr. Jefferson thought the system, which left Louis XVI on the Throne, was an eligible accommodation to the then State of things." [74] Most Americans agreed that it was necessary to stop at constitutional monarchy not only to prevent a repetition of the anarchy and terror of the 1790's, but also to allow a period of time for the growth of knowledge and of experience in self-government. The moral transformation of the French people had not proceeded far enough to support a republican form of government. Thus Gallatin wrote to Lafayette, "Notwithstanding what I have said of your political education, it is more applicable to Paris and towns than to your peasantry. They are as yet too ignorant, and Bonaparte has left too deep an impression to have risked a Republic. This might, I still fear, have degenerated into a Military Government. For France I prefer a Constitutional Monarchy." [75]

[74] Madison to Lafayette, December 12, 1830, *ibid.* Jefferson's views of the Revolution of 1789 were set forth in Thomas Jefferson Randolph (ed.), *Memoir, Correspondence, and Miscellanies, from the Papers of Thomas Jefferson* (Charlottesville, Va., 1829) and published the year before the Revolution of 1830. See I, 56, 75–76, 81–82; IV, 246–48, 384. For the general impact of the *Memoir*, see Merrill D. Peterson, *The Jefferson Image in the American Mind* (New York, 1962), 19–20, 29.

[75] Gallatin to Lafayette, November 1, 1830, in Cornell Lafayette Collection, XI. See also the following letters to Lafayette: Peters, December, 1826, E. Livingston, October 10, 1830, *ibid.*; Samuel H. Perkins, January 4, 1831, *ibid.*,

Republican though they were, Americans were "much more *sage* than is thought in the matter of monarchy," as Alexis de Tocqueville and Gustave de Beaumont discovered in 1831. The two visitors admitted that "the middle classes, the masses, and the newspapers representing popular passions . . . have a blind instinct which drives them to adopt the principles of liberty professed in Europe, and the men who foster them." But they reported that "the enlightened classes" agreed with them that "a republic would not in the least suit France." Tocqueville wrote, "Perhaps it is because, seeing at close range the path taken by popular passions acting in their own country in perfect freedom, they are better situated than we to judge how difficult it is to obtain good government, and above all a stable government, from such elements; since all believe that a people, to be republican, must be poised, religious, and very enlightened. Many admit that, besides these conditions, it is necessary that there be found a condition of material happiness such that there be hardly ever any interior unrest resulting from unsatisfied needs." [76]

Yet acceptance of constitutional monarchy did not mean giving up the American example. James Madison argued in favor of constitutional monarchy precisely because it left open the opportunity of evolving a republican government when "internal and external conditions" permitted. "It may . . . be more easy, if expedient, to descend to a more popular form, than to controule [*sic*] the tendency of a premature experiment to confusion and its usual result in arbitrary Government," he observed. When such a change became possible, Madison urged Lafayette to consider "a federal mixture." Pressing the American example on its chief agent, he wrote,

---

XIV. See also Monroe to John Quincy Adams, January 25, 1831, in Hamilton (ed.), *Writings of Monroe*, VII, 217.

[76] Quoted in George Wilson Pierson, *Tocqueville and Beaumont in America* (New York, 1938), 146, 370–71.

"A federal system will improve any Republic, and . . . it is essential to one in a Country like France." [77]

Indeed, Americans who expected the French to follow their example quickly became impatient. By 1831 the French government had begun to deviate from the original policies of the "Three Days," and Lafayette was criticizing the government and demanding the extension of "republican institutions" in pursuit of his idea of a popular throne surrounded by republican institutions. At least one of his correspondents, Eliza Custis, wanted Lafayette to demand alterations and innovations in the French system even more radical than he himself was proposing. She had approved the creation of a popular monarchy as a first step toward the establishment of a purely republican form of government. But in her view, "One error was committed by the Patriots at first." The peers and deputies should have dissolved themselves and called a convention "to form a Constitution on liberal principles—have a Senate & deputies like ours or nearly so & give no King power to dissolve them nor to issue one ordanance [*sic*] of his own will." Reciting an anecdote, she betrayed her unqualified faith in the validity of the American example for France:

A friend of mine by birth a frenchman writes me, that he sympathises in all my feeling for the french, & regrets that your revolution has stop'd—without securing the rights of the people, by full & just representation of the whole nation[.] He says his friends in france write him they wish the Americans would send some of their wise men to teach the french how to make good Laws—. . . . I should have answer'd them . . . "you have the constitution of the United States—you have the constitutions of twenty four sovereign & independant States—have them translated, publish'd in your Paris newspapers, & circulated through all france["]—if after studying those constitutions & forms of government, which have made this Country the wonder of the

---

[77] Madison to Lafayette, December 12, 1830, in Cornell Lafayette Collection, XI.

world—the french will not rally Round the banner of freedom
& remembering all they have suffer'd for centuries, determine *to
secure a full representation & free constitution to their posterity*
neither could they be aroused to their duty, if all the Patriots of
America went to instruct them—nor even if the Immortal Washington descended from heaven to tell them the blood of the
Martyrs of July 1830 should not be shed in vain.

And after all, the French did have Lafayette. America "speaks
to you," Mrs. Custis wrote, "& says—while you have a house
of Peers—& your King can by those *vile ordenances* dissolve
your deputies at his pleasure, *you are not free*—have a *constitution*—an elected senate—extend the right of voting, to all
who possess one or two hundred francs—set the press free
from all shackles—& allow your people to meet & debate as they
wish—then may you say, the french are indeed free—the thousands who fell in *the three days have not perish'd in vain.*" [78]

Mrs. Custis' cure for what seemed to be ailing the French
body politic was a large dose of republicanism to offset monarchical elements in the system. Trusting Lafayette's judgment, she never suggested eliminating the throne entirely. Her
belief in the validity of the American example for France,
however simplistic, was modified to a certain extent by the
notion of relative progress. But other Americans, disillusioned
by Louis-Philippe's performance as Citizen King, repudiated
the monarchy altogether. One newspaper claimed to have
doubted the efficacy of the system of popular monarchy at
the very outset and criticized Lafayette for thinking it could
fulfill the objectives of the Revolution. [79] Another American
observed that the French had merely "exchanged one limited
monarchy for another limited monarchy, one Bourbon for an-

[78] Eliza P. Custis to Lafayette, March 28, 1831, and July 23, 1831, *ibid.*, X.
See also Custis to Lafayette, September 6, 1830, and September 25, 1830, *ibid.*;
James A. Washington to Lafayette, August 7, 1830, *ibid.*, XV.

[79] Clipping enclosed in letter of Morse to Lafayette, n.d. (probably from
a New York newspaper, circa 1832–33), *ibid.*, XI.

other Bourbon." [80] The implication of such statements was that only by totally abolishing the old government, whatever the risk such a move entailed, could revolutionaries gain the freedom and independence necessary to establish a republican form of government.

While some Americans repudiated the notion of relative progress, others denied the validity of the American example for France and criticized Lafayette for ignoring political realities and trying to establish republican institutions among a people unable to support them. A pamphlet published in August, 1831, addressed to Lafayette, and signed by "A North American," articulated this viewpoint. The occasion for the letter was probably Lafayette's manifesto to his constituents of Meaux defending the establishment of a "popular throne with republican institutions" and demanding, among other things, a widening of the suffrage. In support of such a measure Lafayette had cited "the illimitable suffrages of the United States." [81] The "North American" criticized Lafayette for urging his countrymen "to follow the political examples we afford," while ignoring the one factor distinguishing America from France: "different from any other country known to be civilized, the great majority of people here, voters or not, are holders of land, in their own right, or, which is the same in the matter in question, may be so of many acres too, at their own discretion." Ownership of land gave American citizens "an interest . . . in the maintenance of law and order" that was not necessarily shared by the landless. The conclusion seemed obvious. To enfranchise large numbers of unpropertied Frenchmen who lacked the "stake in society" ownership sup-

[80] A North American, *To General Lafayette, United States, August 10, 1831* ([New York?, 1831]), 3–4.
[81] Lafayette offered the declaration of principles on beginning his campaign for reelection to the Chamber of Deputies following its dissolution on May 31. The letter is published in full in B. Sarrans, *Memoirs of General Lafayette* (London, 1832), II, 247–62.

plied would be to risk a resurgence of mob rule such as had reigned during the Revolution of 1789.[82] In the view of the "North American" the American example of a broad suffrage was not applicable to France because of different economic and social conditions.

The debate over the French Revolution of 1830 reveals another contradiction within the American sense of mission, between the theory of revolution and the theory of government contained in the American example. Those Americans who called for elimination of the monarchy and establishment of a republican form of government—as opposed to a popular throne with republican institutions—were arguing from the theory of revolution enunciated in the Declaration of Independence. That theory set forth the absolute right of the people, regardless of past or present social, political, and economic conditions, to abolish despotism and to institute new government. According to the theory of revolution, only a government deriving its just power from the consent of the governed —a republic—could fulfill the purpose for which governments were established, that is, the protection of man's inalienable rights.[83] Yet other of Lafayette's correspondents based their prescriptions for France, not on this abstract and absolutist theory of revolution, but on a theory of government that was both realistic and relativistic. This was the political theory on which the American republic was based. Its primary characteristic was a sense of the tension between human nature and government. The Founding Fathers, no believers in the perfectibility of man, had looked to government as a check on his

[82] *To General Lafayette*, 3, 5, 7, 9. For nineteenth-century American attitudes toward the relationship between suffrage and property see Stow Persons, *American Minds: A History of Ideas* (New York, 1958), 149–50.

[83] As we have seen, even Thomas Jefferson, author of the American theory of revolution, had declined to apply it to France. In effect, his advice to compromise at constitutional monarchy was an admission that the American theory of revolution was not applicable to other countries.

evil impulses. This theory of government explains Madison's remarks about "the tendency of a premature experiment to confusion"; he feared that if a republican form of government were too hastily established in France, it would be unable to restrain the anarchic impulses of the populace. Madison's comment on "arbitrary Government," Gallatin's fear that a republic might have degenerated into a military government, and even the opposition of the "North American" to an extension of the suffrage also derived from the same theory of government, with its emphasis on the necessity of an enlightened populace as a check on the tendency of government to assume absolute power. In sum, the theory of government implied that revolutionaries should determine the form of their new government by referring to existing conditions rather than to the ideal situation described in the natural rights philosophy. Ideally, all men had an inalienable right to self-government; from a realistic point of view, not all men were competent to govern themselves.

Embracing both an idealistic theory of revolution and a realistic theory of government, the American example became a source of confusion and dissension. This, plus the aftermath of the July Revolution (which indicated that France was still unready for republican institutions, much less a completely republican form of government) resulted in eventual disillusionment. Looking over the French and European scene in 1832, Peter Jay was led to proclaim the futility of the Revolution of 1830, indeed of all revolutions. He observed "a spirit of discontent" pervading Europe but "mingled with so much rancor and malevolence" as to inspire fear as well as hope. The present governments of Europe were "bad enough." Still, he asked, "is there reason to expect that the revolutionary Governments which may succeed them will be better?" The tone of his concluding remarks recalls American disillusionment with the outcome of the Greek and South American revolutions. "Is it not strange," he wrote, "that from the time of Charlemagne till now France was never better governed than under Lewis 18 and Charles 10th? They did right to dethrone the latter for breaking the Charter, but if they mean to break it to pieces themselves and put to sea anew, without knowing where they shall land, they may find that they have gained little by the glorious three days. Be assured they are not yet prepared for a republican Govt; such a one may be set up, but cannot last." [84]

Just as American disillusionment with the first French Revolution had not extended to Lafayette's role in it, in the same way the reaction against the July Revolution hardly touched America's adopted son. Indeed, the part Lafayette played in the Revolution of 1830 was a source of much gratification to Americans; the notion that he was leading it was an important factor contributing to its popularity. [85] Much of the celebration of the Revolution was a celebration of the man who appeared to be the principal actor in the drama. "Everybody here says of Lafayette 'finis coronat opus,' " David Lee Child, editor of the *Massachusetts Journal,* reported. "What disinterestedness, & discretion he has displayed! What an instructive contrast does his life exhibit compared with that of Napoleon! He is indeed *the* Second Washington! Such are some of the exclamations I have heard in Boston in all parts and all classes of this city since we heard of your heroic Revolution." [86]

Lafayette's role in the Revolution was seen as the pinnacle of

[84] Peter Jay to James Fenimore Cooper, February 21, 1832, in James Fenimore Cooper (ed.), *Correspondence of James Fenimore Cooper* (New Haven, 1922), I, 260–61. See also Charles Wilkes to J. F. Cooper, March 9, 1831, *ibid.,* I, 204; Emma Willard to Lafayette, May 1, 1833, in Cornell Lafayette Collection, XI.

[85] Eugene N. Curtis, "American Opinion of the French Nineteenth Century Revolutions," *American Historical Review,* XXIX (1924), 250n, 263; White, *American Opinion of France,* 85. See also George Ticknor, "Lafayette in America," *North American Review,* XXX (1830), 233; and the letters to Lafayette cited in note 71 above.

[86] David Lee Child to Lafayette, September 27, 1830, in Cornell Lafayette Collection, XII.

his career as agent of the American mission, a glorious consummation and vindication of his steadfast devotion to the principles of liberty. The hero of two worlds had not only fulfilled the American mission but had emerged the "saviour" of France—the father of *his* country—a status entirely appropriate to the "friend of Washington." Indeed, the qualities Lafayette exhibited in the Revolution of 1830 entitled him to almost equal rank with Washington. "Your heroic conduct, your admired magnanimity, your Self devotion have established a name for yourself as imperishable, as that of the great and good Washington," wrote an admirer.[87] Once again, as during the Revolution of 1789, Lafayette's disinterestedness was the characteristic most frequently praised. As commander of the National Guard he had a second time held the reins of power, only to relinquish them to constitutional authority, the Duke of Orleans, the Citizen King. Had he desired, Americans believed, he might have retained power or even have established a republican form of government if he had thought it preferable to monarchy. "I firmly believe that he needed but to speak the word, to have constituted France a republic; and placed himself at its head, as easily as he placed the crown on the temples of the Duke of Orleans," wrote Edward Everett.[88]

To be sure, in 1831 Alexis de Tocqueville found that American opinion on Lafayette was divided. "The enlightened classes judge M. de Lafayette without any kind of infatuation," he observed. Tocqueville's companion, Gustave de Beaumont, echoed this observation, writing that Americans were not "as enthusiastic about our revolutionists as it is thought. In

[87] Thomas A. Bacot, Jr., to Lafayette, October 5, 1830, *ibid*. See also William C. Woodbridge to Lafayette, September 17, 1830, *ibid.*, XV.

[88] "Remarks of Everett," newspaper clipping enclosed in letter of E. Everett to Lafayette, October 29, 1830, *ibid.*, X. See also J. F. Cooper to his wife, August 21, 1830, and to Wilkes, August 24, 1830, in James Franklin Beard (ed.), *The Letters and Journals of James Fenimore Cooper* (Cambridge, Mass., 1960–68), II, 5, 7–8.

general they consider the hero of two worlds as a fine man who lacks judgment and who wants to apply political theories to a people whom they don't suit." According to Beaumont, Lafayette was "judged a *niais*" or "*Visionary*" in the United States. But both Beaumont and Tocqueville conceded that Lafayette was at the same time a very powerful and popular symbol of liberty.[89]

No doubt Tocqueville and Beaumont were correct in sensing a different opinion of Lafayette among upper-class Americans. But, as they admitted, it was also true that the majority of Americans—whom Tocqueville called "the middle classes, the masses"—idolized Lafayette and gave his actions unquestioning support. In their eyes, Lafayette emerged from the disappointing aftermath of the July Revolution untainted. His role as symbol of liberty and agent of the American mission remained untarnished, for, despite his bad judgment in putting Louis-Philippe on the throne, most Americans believed he had acted disinterestedly and with good intentions.[90] In a comment reminiscent of the rationalizations of Lafayette's flight from France in 1792, Emma Willard advised Lafayette not to regret too much what had happened after the "Three Days." "Much has been gained by your revolution, though not all you could have wished," she observed. Her chief concern was not France but Lafayette. "I rejoice that all which has happened, is of a nature to exalt your own fame, as it will go down to a future time, the great benefactor of your own." Lafayette might have assumed control of the government of France, Miss Willard admitted, implying that he might have thereby saved it from Louis-Philippe. "But if you had," she argued, "the selfish and the ambitious would have said—there is no such

[89] Quoted in Pierson, *Tocqueville and Beaumont*, 73, 146, 357, 360, 371, 371n.

[90] See, for example, Wilkes to J. F. Cooper, March 9, 1831, in Cooper (ed.), *Correspondence of Cooper*, I, 206.

thing as disinterested benevolence,—even Lafayette had yielded to the dictates of ambition." In giving up the power that might have been his, Lafayette had preserved his reputation as an exemplary figure. "Now," Miss Willard wrote, "I regard you as standing among individuals as America among nations, a refutation in yourself of the slanders against humanity." [91]

Lafayette's behavior in the Revolution of 1830 had also demonstrated his faithful adherence to the American example and his consistent attachment to American principles. At a Fourth of July celebration in Paris in 1832, Samuel F. B. Morse praised Lafayette as the dedicated agent of the American mission, "the staunch undeviating defender of . . . our principles, of American principles." Like Lafayette, Americans continued to believe in and support the American mission. Morse admitted that the outcome of the July Revolution had been a disappointment, reinforcing the desire of Americans to isolate themselves from France and Europe as a whole. But disappointment had not dampened their ardor for republican principles or their faith in the American example:

> With the mazes of European politics we have nothing to do; to the changing schemes of good or bad government we cannot make ourselves a party; with the success of this or that faction we can have no sympathy; but with the great principles of rational liberty, of civil and religious liberty . . . we do sympathize. . . . They are the principles of order and good government, of obedience to law; the principles under which Providence have made our country unparalleled in prosperity, principles which rest not in visionary theory, but are made palpable by the sure test of experiment and time.[92]

Morse's speech shows that in 1832 the conservative conception of the American mission remained dominant. The United States was to serve as a model of republican government—an

[91] Willard to Lafayette, May 1, 1833, in Cornell Lafayette Collection, XI.
[92] Quoted in *Niles' Weekly Register* (Baltimore), September 1, 1832, p. 6.

example to which other nations might look, if they chose, for inspiration and guidance. She would encourage the spread of republican principles by offering sympathy, not active support, for such efforts. But though Americans delineated their own role in the struggle for liberty in passive and restricted terms, they nevertheless continued to look to Lafayette as the defender of the American experiment and disseminator of republican principles abroad.[93] Untainted by the failure of the July Revolution, Lafayette remained to his death the agent of the American mission, the apostle of liberty in Europe.

[93] American newspapers quoted with approval Lafayette's speech before the Chamber of Deputies, January 15, 1832, in which he called the government of the United States "the *pattern Government*" and declared that "republican institutions . . . are suited to every country where the citizens are intelligent, and wish to be free." Philadelphia *National Gazette*, March 21, 1833; Washington *Daily National Intelligencer*, March 25, 1833.

5 The Enduring Image

> Gen. La Fayette, the revolutionist
> of two nations; the intrepid champion
> of liberty—his fame is not the diurnal
> excitement of popular gratitude or
> whim; it will last till all other human
> applause has ceased; it is found in the
> affections and rights of man.
>
> J. HOGE WAUGH, Esq.,
> Erie, Pennsylvania[1]

For Americans, the death of Lafayette in 1834 had a special poignancy and significance. "Lafayette was one of the chief benefactors, we might say founders, of our vast Republic," the Philadelphia *National Gazette* pointed out. "During the last fifteen years of his life, he was the only individual alive who had taken a leading part, and figures in a conspicuous manner, in the events of the first revolution." [2] The loss of Lafayette, less than a decade after the passing of Jefferson and Adams, intensified Americans' sense of the growing gulf between them and the Revolution. "One by one the lights of the American Revolution have become extinguished," William Easton lamented, "and now the last glorious star is blotted from the firmament for ever." [3] Nor did the "calamity" of Lafayette's death affect only the United States, jeopardizing the republican experiment.[4] "Whilst La Fayette remained," Easton noted, "the dark political horizon of his own country had something

[1] Erie *Gazette*, June 9, 1825, quoted in Brandon, *Pilgrimage*, 392.
[2] Philadelphia *National Gazette*, June 24 and 26, 1834.
[3] William C. Easton, *Eulogium on La Fayette* (Washington, 1834), 18.
[4] House of Representatives, June 21, 1834, *Register of Debates in Congress*, LXI, 4642.

in it whereon to gaze; the hopes of the people something upon which to concentrate; and the wayward political navigator, his cynosure, which, in the stormy period of his voyage, he might glance at, and when without chart or pilot, steer his course by!" [5] Americans lamented "the irreparable loss sustained not only by American liberty, but by the cause of freedom throughout the world" as a result of the death of the chief agent of the American mission.[6] At the same time they pledged never to forget Lafayette. "To the remotest generation will the free people of America bless the name of La FAYETTE," Easton declared.[7]

Easton's prediction was borne out. Lafayette was not forgotten. He continued to serve as a hero-symbol for later generations of Americans—in many of the same roles he had filled before 1834; and his name was frequently invoked during crises affecting the republican experiment and the American mission, just as it had been before his death.

I

The image of Lafayette in 1834 and after was not radically different from what it had been in the 1820's. Lafayette continued to be celebrated in his previous roles: benefactor of America, disciple of Washington, lover of liberty, friend of mankind, model patriot, agent of the American mission. Americans of the late nineteenth and twentieth centuries echoed earlier generations in attributing Lafayette's actions to an "ardent love of liberty." The Marquis was celebrated as "one of the greatest apostles of liberty," "liberty's incendiary," and "a flag of liberty." [8] Similarly, the two virtues most often cited

[5] Easton, *Eulogium*, 18.
[6] Francis H. Davidge, *An Oration* ([Baltimore, 1834]), 6.
[7] Easton, *Eulogium*, 18.
[8] *Pictorial Life of General Lafayette* (Philadelphia, 1847), 27; John D. Long, *Lafayette in America* (Boston, 1902), 7; letter of Governor Alva Adams, October 10, 1898, in Colorado Department of Public Instruction,

in descriptions of Lafayette were disinterestedness and constancy. Writers cited his participation in the American Revolution and his service in "the cause of humanity" as evidence of his "unbounded benevolence," his "spirit of self-sacrifice," his "purest, most disinterested philanthropy." [9] When critics (mostly foreign) revived the question of Lafayette's ambition, Americans replied with arguments similar to those Madison and Jefferson had employed in the late eighteenth century. Admitting that Lafayette "aspired to the praise of men," that

LaFayette Memorial Day, Denver, Colorado, October 19, 1898 (Denver, 1898), no pp.; Henry D. Estabrook, "Lafayette," in *"The Spirit of '76" by James Hulme Canfield; "La Fayette" by Henry D. Estabrook: Addresses Delivered Before the Quill Club of New York* ([New York?, 1907]), 30; John Simpson Penman, *Lafayette and Three Revolutions* (Boston, 1929), 341. See also Francis Baylies, *Eulogy on Lafayette* (Boston, 1834), 39; Ebenezer Mack, *The Life of Gilbert Motier de Lafayette* (Ithaca, N.Y., 1843), 17; "Reminiscences of a Tempest-tost Life," *Putnam's Monthly*, 1855, p. 423, in Toner Collection, Rare Book Room, Library of Congress; Esther Reed Vernet, "Lafayette," *Potter's American Monthly*, VI (1876), 272, 274; Lydia Hoyt Farmer, *The Life of La Fayette, the Knight of Liberty in Two Worlds and Two Centuries* (New York, 1888), 471; Charlton T. Lewis, "The Character of Lafayette," *Washington Association of New Jersey Publications*, I (1896), 9; Howard Meriwether Lovett, "General Lafayette and the Eighteenth Congress," *Confederate Veteran*, XXVI (1918), 386; *Lafayette Day, September 6, 1919* ([New York, 1919]), 16; William Mather Lewis, "The Lafayette Centennial and Memorial," *Legion d'Honneur*, IV (1934), 229.

[9] "Cloquet's Lafayette," *American Quarterly Review*, XXXIX (1836), 123–24; Cutter, *Life of General Lafayette*, 405; "Tuckerman's Lafayette," *Nation*, XLVIII (1889), 431; Davidge, *Oration*, 17. See also James A[braham] Hillhouse, *An Oration* (New Haven, 1834), 5, 8–10; Easton, *Eulogium*, 5; Andrew Wylie, D.D., *An Eulogy on Lafayette* (Cincinnati, 1835), 9; Mack, *Life of Lafayette*, 17; Rose Standish, "Recollections of Lafayette," *Knickerbocker*, XXXII (1848), 215; [Nathaniel Hervey], *The Memory of Washington* (Boston, 1852), 206; E. Cecil [pseud.], *Life of Lafayette, Written for Children* (Boston, 1860), preface; "Lafayette as a Patriot and Soldier," *National Quarterly Review*, XVI (1867), 82; *The Life and Services of Major-General the Marquis de Lafayette* (New York, 1870), 9; Bayard Tuckerman, *Life of General Lafayette* (London, 1889), I, 103, II, 257; "Tower's Lafayette," *Nation*, LX (1895), 223; William T. Headley, *Makers of American History* (New York, 1904), 241–42; Hugo A. Dubuque, *Lafayette* ([Fall River, Mass., 1916]), 5; *Lafayette Day Exercises . . . September 6th, 1917* ([New York, 1917]), 68; *Lafayette Day, 1919*, p. 125; George Morgan, *The True La Fayette* (Philadelphia, 1919), 63; Lucy Foster Madison, *Lafayette* (Philadelphia, 1921), 368, 372.

his actions were often prompted by "vanity," "ambition," even "egotism," they protested that the nature and object of his ambition rendered it unobjectionable. It was not the kind "which seeks personal aggrandizement," but rather of a "noble and disinterested character." It was "consecrated by the purest and most patriotic motives." Lafayette's "ambition was but a world-embracing benevolence," one biographer explained. He sought only "the liberty and happiness of mankind," others declared.[10] The notion of Lafayette's "virtuous ambition," a product of the Enlightenment pattern of thought, persisted well into the twentieth century despite the reaction against the view of human nature on which it was based. Americans also continued to praise Lafayette's "constant adherence to principles," his "remarkable" and "rare consistency," his "inflexible will" and "continuity of purpose." [11]

While the late nineteenth- and twentieth-century image of Lafayette remained substantially the same as that of the 1820's,

[10] Cutter, *Life of General Lafayette*, 406; Mack, *Life of Lafayette*, 373; "Reminiscences of a Tempest-tost Life," 423; "Cloquet's Lafayette," 124. See also Davidge, *Oration*, 18; William Mann, "Oration," in *Ceremonies on the Completion of the Monument* ([Philadelphia], 1869), 10–11; Farmer, *Life of La Fayette*, 453–54; Lewis, "The Character of Lafayette," 17; E. J. Hale, *Monsieur Le Marquis de La Fayette* (Raleigh, 1901), 30–31; Sedgwick, *La Fayette*, 415; Brand Whitlock, *La Fayette* (New York, 1929), I, ix.

[11] *Pictorial Life of Lafayette*, 208; Tuckerman, *Life of Lafayette*, II, 255; Michael de La Bedoyere, *Lafayette, a Revolutionary Gentleman* (London, 1933), 7; D. L. Shorey, "Lafayette in the American Revolution," *Dial*, XVIII (1895), 208; Whitlock, *La Fayette*, I, x. See also Jarvis Gregg, *Eulogy on Lafayette* (Hanover, N.H., 1834), 20; Wylie, *Eulogy*, 26; Philadelphia *National Gazette*, June 24, 1834; Baylies, *Eulogy*, 39; Davidge, *Oration*, 25; William H. Seward, "Lafayette," in George E. Baker (ed.), *The Works of William H. Seward* (Redfield, N.Y., 1853), III, 43; *Life and Services of Lafayette*, 10; John Bigelow, *La Fayette* (Boston, 1882), 11; "Tuckerman's Lafayette," 432; Headley, *Makers of American History*, 282; *Lafayette Day Exercises, 1917*, 68; Rupert Sargent Holland, *Lafayette, for Young Americans* (Philadelphia, 1922), 354–55; William MacDonald, "Lafayette, an Aristocrat Who Gave Much for Liberty," *New York Times Book Review*, October 13, 1929, p. 3; Charles Willis Thompson, "Lafayette, a Revolutionary Gentleman," *ibid.*, April 29, 1934, p. 6; Geoffrey Bruun, "The Apostle of Liberty," *ibid.*, September 30, 1956, p. 12.

later generations evaluated his character and career differently in certain significant respects. Lafayette's conduct in the French Revolution—a question with which his American friends had grappled before 1834—continued to be a controversial issue. Interpretations which had formed the consensus before 1834 were no longer wholly satisfying. The skepticism and sense of uneasiness which Lafayette's biographers of the 1820's had only dimly felt and which had been manifested in implicit criticism of the Marquis intensified after his death.

At the root of the controversy over Lafayette's conduct was a difference of opinion as to his political views. Did he favor a republican form of government for France or a constitutional monarchy? Most of the eulogists, recalling Lafayette's relationship with Washington and "his heroic apprenticeship in America," maintained that he was a republican by conviction. Indeed, James Hillhouse pointed out, "he was exposed among us to become fanatically republican—to confound the form with the essence." Fortunately, however, Lafayette "saw the real necessities of his country" and "justly appreciated the changes . . . suited to her genius." [12] As William Seward noted, "Lafayette, although a republican, seems to have been the first of the patriots who had the sagacity to discover that the French people were not yet prepared to sustain a purely democratic government. Acting on this conviction, in 1789, no less than in 1830, he averred that for France, the best form of government was a *limited monarchy surrounded by republican institutions.*" [13]

On the other hand, one of the eulogists, and some later writers, contended that Lafayette was a constitutional monarchist not merely in practice but by conviction. In 1834, recognizing his countrymen's "difficulty in understanding this and forgiving La Fayette for his attitude," Andrew Wylie, president of

[12] Hillhouse, *Oration*, 16, 17, 34.
[13] Seward, "Lafayette," 33.

Indiana College, sought to explain it by making a distinction between "constitutionalists" and "republicans" similar to that implied by Thomas Jefferson some years earlier. Lafayette attached himself to the "constitutionalists" rather than the "republicans" because "the party in France calling themselves republicans, were not the same in character and views with those so denominated here," Wylie explained. "They were, as a party, violent, visionary, extravagant in their notions, and too little under the influence of justice and humanity. They were, in short, but jacobins of a lighter complexion." But there was another reason why Lafayette favored a constitutional monarchy for his own country. Wylie implied that the Marquis knew that France did not contain "the proper materials" necessary to the establishment of a republic. "Republican simplicity does not suit the French taste," Wylie asserted.[14] It was this argument regarding the alleged difference between France and America that most later writers employed to explain Lafayette's support of constitutional monarchy. Lafayette "thought that France was not yet ready for the form of government that was succeeding in America," Martha Foote Crow wrote. "For France he believed the constitutional monarchy to be best." [15]

What is significant about the controversy over Lafayette's political convictions is that although Americans debated the nature of those convictions, they agreed that Lafayette recognized the different capacities of France and America for republican government. Those who argued that Lafayette was a republican by conviction maintained that he nevertheless saw the unsuitability of a republican form of government for his country. Those who claimed that he was a constitutional monarchist explained his preference as a consequence of his awareness that France was unready for popular government. Whatever political convictions were attributed to him, Lafayette

[14]Wylie, *Eulogy*, 19–23.
[15] Martha Foote Crow, *Lafayette* (New York, 1916), 141.

was portrayed as the exemplar of the conservative conception of the American mission.

The conservative conception of mission also influenced those who criticized Lafayette's role in the French Revolution. Bayard Tuckerman, writing in 1889, declared that "the fault to be found with Lafayette's political views is that they were too advanced for his country." The Marquis thought "only of establishing correct principles, regardless of the fitness of the people to practise them." He could not "understand the liberty which he had seen practised in Anglo-Saxon countries," Tuckerman explained. "He failed to see that a great many national characteristics besides freedom made up American prosperity. Liberty can only exist among a self-controlling, conservative people; and to enjoy it, a nation must be gradually educated." [16] Almost a century later, John Dos Passos voiced the same idea, describing Lafayette as one of a "generation that had gone to its doom in an effort to apply Anglo-Saxon methods to Continental politics." [17] Lafayette, like the natural rights philosophy with which he was identified, was a victim of late nineteenth- and twentieth-century pessimism about the capacity of men for self-government. "We no longer share the illusion" that possessed Lafayette, a reviewer for the *Nation* declared. "We know now that there is no magic in liberty or in equality to make mankind fit for free institutions." [18]

If the late nineteenth- and twentieth-century evaluation of Lafayette reveals the continuing influence of the conservative conception of the American mission, it also betrays the increasing dread with which many Americans came to view revolution and radicals. [19] Whether they approved or disapproved

[16] Tuckerman, *Life of Lafayette*, I, 196, 237, II, 256–57.

[17] John Dos Passos, "Lafayette's Two Revolutions," *American Heritage*, VIII (1956), 116.

[18] "Tuckerman's Lafayette," 432.

[19] In an article on European attitudes toward revolution and Lafayette, Bernard Fay suggested a plausible explanation of American views as well. Writing in 1934, Fay described Lafayette as "the great technician of revolu-

of Lafayette's activities as an agent of change, Americans usually portrayed him in terms that conveyed their own conservative view of the means and ends of change. As described by his admirers, Lafayette was a man of prudence, moderation, and discretion, governed less by principle than by practicality. His critics, influenced by the same conservative bias, charged him with naïveté, imprudence, and devotion to abstract ideals whose fulfillment was either undesirable or impossible.

The metamorphosis of the hero of three revolutions into "a reformer, not a revolutionist" began in 1834.[20] No doubt developments of the 1830's had something to do with the transformation of the Lafayette image. The war on the Second Bank of the United States, the rise of abolitionism and the beginnings of nativism, increasing party conflict between Democrats and newly emergent Whigs, sectional tensions producing premonitions of civil war—all fostered a belief in the virtue of moderation. Thus the eulogists portrayed Lafayette as a

---

tions." Though "preoccupied by revolutions" Europeans "find his revolutions decidedly out of fashion. They are dreaming of new kinds of revolutions, more efficient and more thorough. Each century has a different style of revolution. . . . Twentieth-century revolutions are getting less and less cheerful and more and more businesslike," Fay observed. "There is no wonder if Lafayette is out of fashion. Moreover, Lafayette the nobleman was the man who made revolutions attractive and decent for the middle class in Europe and the New World, but nowadays the middle classes are not so fond of revolutions." For most Europeans, Fay wrote, "Lafayette does not appear any more as a great prophet; the technique of revolution has changed. But he is still a great legend. He never succeeded, even in 1830, when it seemed to be so easy, in achieving the 'perfect revolution,' but he succeeded in being the perfect revolutionist. One may prefer the Lenin type as more up to date; the Lafayette type is still more cheerful, more picturesque—and maybe not less mysterious." Bernard Fay, "Honor to Lafayette—and to Revolution," *New York Times Magazine*, May 20, 1934, pp. 8–9. For writings justifying revolution and defending Lafayette's revolutionary activities see Hillhouse, *Oration*, 15; "Cloquet's Lafayette," 119, 121; "Reminiscences of a Tempest-tost Life," 416; Lewis, "The Character of Lafayette," 14; Penman, *Lafayette and Three Revolutions*, ii.

[20] Gregg, *Eulogy*, 14.

man who saw the necessity of gradual, not revolutionary change. He was always an "advocate of rational liberty," "a champion of temperate Freedom," opposed to license and anarchy.[21] He was a conservator, not a destroyer. "He sought to engraft the scions of liberty on the old stock of the state, rather than cut down the tree, and plant a young sapling in its stead." Standing between two systems, Lafayette sought "to preserve whatever is valuable in the old, for the benefit of the new." [22]

According to the eulogists, Lafayette was a conservator because he was a pragmatist. He was no visionary, "no idolatrous worshiper of mere abstractions." [23] Rather, Lafayette always tried to adapt his principles to existing conditions. He was "the apostle of liberty" but "he was no fanatic in the cause to which his life was devoted. He was not for giving to every people the utmost degree of liberty of which organized society is susceptible; but so much only as was adapted to their particular circumstances, as would conduce to their greatest happiness, and be most enduring." [24]

Writers of the late nineteenth and twentieth centuries echoed the themes of Lafayette's eulogists, depicting him as "a dedicated reformer," or, ambiguously, as "a revolutionary gentleman" who followed "the middle path" in times of social and political change.[25] Few biographers neglected to emphasize Lafayette's consistent support of "ordered liberty," citing his valiant attempts "to enforce 'the Washington formula of liberty within the law' " during the French Revolution.[26] "He believed in liberty and constitutional government, but he also believed

---

[21] Davidge, *Oration*, 21; Philadelphia *National Gazette*, June 24, 1834.

[22] Gregg, *Eulogy*, 14–15; Baylies, *Eulogy*, 19.

[23] Gregg, *Eulogy*, 9.

[24] Aaron Ogden Dayton, *Eulogy on La Fayette* (New York, 1835), 40–41.

[25] Dos Passos, "Lafayette's Two Revolutions," 106; Bedoyere, *Lafayette*, 7; Sedgwick, *La Fayette*, 225.

[26] Sedgwick, *La Fayette*, 225; Walter Phelps Hall, "Hero of Two Worlds," *New Republic*, LX (1929), 217.

in order," Rupert Holland explained in his biography "for Young Americans." [27] In the same vein, a reviewer for the *Nation* described Lafayette "as the advocate of constitutional government and progress, and at the same time as the determined enemy of revolutionary methods and of social disorder." [28] Such qualifications were apparently necessary, for it would seem from some of the descriptions of Lafayette that Americans unconsciously identified liberty and license, change and violence.

Not until the publication in 1889 of Bayard Tuckerman's *Life of General Lafayette, with a Critical Estimate of His Character and Public Acts* was the image of Lafayette as a gradualist reformer decisively challenged. Tuckerman termed Lafayette "noble-minded but unpractical" and charged him with "imprudent enthusiasm, which, in pursuit of an abstract good, overlooked the circumstances which made its immediate attainment undesirable." Lafayette, Tuckerman continued, "lacked the knowledge of human nature, which would have taught him that reforms must be gradual." [29] A reviewer of Tuckerman's book agreed, saying, "There is something perhaps a little painful in recalling in calm retrospect the sudden burst of self-devotion to an abstract idea with which Lafayette's life opens . . . . When we think of what was before him, . . . how everything was to be wrecked, including his own illusions . . . we cannot repress a feeling of doubt whether it was all worth while, a childish sigh that the story might be told in some other way, might be brought to some other conclusion." [30]

Perhaps Tuckerman's scorn for Lafayette and the reviewer's lament for his "wrecked illusions" were by-products of the widespread disillusionment with Reconstruction which marked

27 Holland, *Lafayette*, 247.
28 "Lafayette's Letters," *Nation*, LXXVI (1903), 514.
29 Tuckerman, *Life of Lafayette*, I, 196, 275, II, 254.
30 "Tuckerman's Lafayette," 431.

the post–Civil War period. Lafayette's reputation fared badly during periods of disillusionment with reform. In 1929, for example, a writer for the *New Republic* described the Marquis as "too much given to virtue." Like Tuckerman, Walter Phelps Hall argued that Lafayette "did not know how to deal with men." Consequently he was repeatedly "hood-winked . . . by the worldly-wise"—in the French Revolution "by pragmatic Jacobins" and in 1830 "by pragmatic bankers." Just as the failure of Reconstruction may have provoked Tuckerman's gibes against Lafayette's pursuit of an "abstract principle," the reaction against a war allegedly fought to make the world safe for democracy, but apparently engineered by bankers and munitions-makers, probably influenced Hall's unfavorable estimate of the French hero.[31]

Although the main charge against Lafayette was his ignorance of human nature, critics also condemned his "blind optimism" and his doctrinaire pursuit of "abstract political and social ideals." [32] To the extent that Lafayette had been made the embodiment of eighteenth- and early nineteenth-century ideas of progress and the perfectibility of man, he inevitably became the victim of the reaction against those ideas. Once heralded as a model for Americans to imitate, Lafayette's example seemed to later generations anachronistic and irrelevant. To be sure, many Americans continued to praise "his inherent unworldliness during an era when every one was, more or less,

[31] Hall, "Hero of Two Worlds," 217. Hall's evaluation of Lafayette was not completely unfavorable. He praised the Marquis for taking "the ignominious road, knowing what men would say," by fleeing from the French Revolution. "He would fight neither against the revolution nor for it," Hall continued. "He would neither support Bonaparte nor join in cabals against him. Instead, he calmly waited fifteen years for the Napoleonic storms to spend their force. La Fayette became a practising pacifist. One wonders if he was not intelligent in so doing?" Hall's laudatory picture of Lafayette as an uncommitted and pacifist spectator of events was as much a product of the 1920's as was his critique.

[32] Crow, *Lafayette*, 142; Bedoyere, *Lafayette*, 24. See also Tuckerman, *Life of Lafayette*, I, 204, II, 254; Madison, *Lafayette*, 301.

on the make," but for those who prided themselves on their own pragmatic realism, Lafayette was simply "out of touch with reality." [33]

Yet even the most unfriendly critics were often ambivalent toward Lafayette. Bayard Tuckerman, for example, argued that "the faults of Lafayette's character grew out of its virtues. The enthusiasm was too impulsive, the confidence in others too undiscriminating, the desire to do good too little modified by prudence." Still, Tuckerman admitted, "had he not been enthusiastic, confident, and benevolent, he would never have taken up the cause of liberty in the shadow of the old French monarchy." [34] Out of this kind of ambivalence developed the image of Lafayette as the knight of liberty.[35] Emerging in the late nineteenth century, the new image did not supersede the older portraits of the Marquis as disinterested patriot or agent of the American mission. Rather, the chivalric image of Lafayette was a highly romanticized version of earlier images.

Besides a love of adventure, the other traits emphasized as a part of Lafayette's chivalric image were generosity, "ardor," constancy, and idealism. The chivalric image had the effect of reconciling conflicting views of Lafayette through a metamorphosis of faults into virtues. Ambition, enthusiasm, impracticality, and naïveté—the traits for which Lafayette had frequently been criticized—when associated with knight-errantry seemed not only appropriate but worthy of praise. Besides being compared with Chaucer's knight, Lafayette was

[33] Henry Longan Stuart, "Lafayette Held to His Ideals Through Three Revolutions," *New York Times Book Review*, May 13, 1928, p. 3; Bedoyere, *Lafayette*, 204. See also John W. Thomason, Jr., "We've Paid Our Debt to Lafayette," *American Mercury*, XLVI (1939), 497; Geoffrey Bruun, "The Apostle of Liberty," 12.

[34] Tuckerman, *Life of Lafayette*, II, 255–56.

[35] The phrase "knight of liberty" is from Lydia Hoyt Farmer, *The Life of La Fayette, the Knight of Liberty in Two Worlds and Two Centuries*. "Knight-errant" was a more common term used by American speakers and writers to describe Lafayette.

also identified with the crusaders of the Middle Ages, with Sir
Galahad, Guesclin, and Bayard, with Dumas's musketeers, and
with Don Quixote.[36]

In many cases, the chivalric image implied a positive valuation of Lafayette. But, as the comparison with Don Quixote
suggests, the knightly image could also be ambiguous or even
negative in judgment. Lucy Madison, writing about Lafayette's
participation in the American Revolution, had General Washington say to the youthful soldier, "It was a chivalric thing to
leave your young wife, your child, and your friends to come
help a struggling people in their fight for liberty, Marquis. Perhaps it was unwise and imprudent, but it is the Quixotism that
one loves." [37] A reviewer for the *Nation* made the following
admission: "Judged dispassionately in the light of cold reason,
there never was a more hair-brained [*sic*] project." He added,
"But the world has always admired the spirit of adventure,
especially when it is successful, and it has admired La Fayette
ever since. . . . Throughout his life he was the true knight-
errant as he had been as a boy in the country, as a youth in the
American war, and as a national figure in France." [38]

Helen Nicolay reveals the ambivalent attitude underlying
the chivalric image of Lafayette. "Possibly no knight-errant,

[36] "Tuckerman's Lafayette," 432; "Honoring Lafayette," *Harper's Weekly*,
XXXVIII (1894), 1120; George H. Ford, "The Struggle for Liberty," *Connecticut Magazine*, VII (1902), 550; Headley, *Makers of American History*,
242; *Lafayette Day Exercises, 1917*, pp. 47–48; Henry van Dyke, "The Chivalry of Lafayette," *Outlook*, CXVII (September 19, 1917), 86–87; A. B. Hart,
"Lafayette," *Mentor–World Traveller*, V (January 15, 1918), 2; Lovett,
"Lafayette and the Eighteenth Congress," 386; James Mott Hallowell, *The
Spirit of Lafayette* (Garden City, N.Y., 1918), 43–44; *Lafayette Day, 1919*,
pp. 16–17, 23; Morgan, *The True La Fayette*, 62; Whitlock, *La Fayette*, II,
414; Tuckerman, *Life of Lafayette*, I, 194–95; New York *Times*, July 5, 1900,
p. 7; Marshall Putnam Thompson, "The Fifth Musketeer," *Bunker Hill Monument Association Proceedings*, June 17, 1914, pp. 33, 65; Sedgwick, *La Fayette*,
202, 214.

[37] Madison, *Lafayette*, 159.

[38] Ralph Volney Harlow, "A Great Adventurer," *Nation*, CXXIX (1929),
752–53.

ancient or modern, can seem altogether sane, much less prudent, to the average unimaginative dweller in this workaday world," she observed. "Yet what would the workaday world be without its knights-errant of the past; the good their knight-errantry has already accomplished; the courage it inspires for to-day; the promise it gives for the future?" On the one hand, in consigning knight-errantry to "the past," Nicolay seems to be suggesting its irrelevance in the present "workaday world," where sanity and prudence are emphasized. Yet her qualification bertays a certain nostalgia for the romance and idealism of knight-errantry. The negative judgment of "the average unimaginative dweller in this workaday world" is not sustained. Nicolay seems to urge the reader to transcend his mundane situation and recognize the positive aspects of knight-errantry.[39] The ambiguity of the chivalric image of Lafayette was in large measure a source of its appeal; at the same time the ambivalent attitude it reveals suggests the tension between idealism and realism in late nineteenth- and twentieth-century American thought.

II

Americans, Franklin Roosevelt observed on the centenary of Lafayette's death, cherished his memory "above that of any citizen of a foreign country." [40] Their demonstrations of perpetual love and reverence took many forms: monuments and statues, assorted celebrations, even a commemorative stamp.[41]

[39] Helen Nicolay, *The Boys' Life of Lafayette* (New York, 1920), 298.

[40] Quoted in New York *Times*, May 21, 1934, p. 1.

[41] Americans commemorated the anniversary of Lafayette's death; they also celebrated his birthday as a national holiday—Lafayette Day. During and after the First World War, Lafayette Day was also known as Lafayette-Marne Day, commemorating the anniversary of the Battle of the Marne, which coincided with the anniversary of Lafayette's birth. Celebrations of Lafayette also occurred on the following days: Washington's Birthday, the anniversaries of the battles of Brandywine and Yorktown, France Day, the Fourth of July. The last named holiday was the occasion of an annual ceremony at the tomb of Lafayette in Picpus cemetery. The United States Post Office issued a commemorative stamp on the bicentenary of Lafayette's birthday.

And, as was true before his death, veneration for Lafayette was prompted by various impulses, not alone that of love or admiration for the now legendary Frenchman. Similarly, the commemorative speeches and writings, along with other expressions relating to Lafayette, often reveal the thinking of Americans about themselves and their country. The response to Lafayette in the late nineteenth and twentieth centuries thus serves as an index to the continuing preoccupation with the republican experiment and the American mission, concerns with which Lafayette had been identified before 1834.

One impulse behind celebrations of Lafayette was the simple and sincere desire to show admiration and affection. Statues were erected "to recall the record of his imperishable deeds; to testify that his name is not a dead memory, but a living reality; to quicken our sense of appreciation and emphasize the fidelity of our affection." [42] Similarly, ceremonies honoring the French hero were occasions for demonstrating that, as Franklin Roosevelt declared on Lafayette-Marne Day, 1920, "there still lives, not as a shadowy incident of a distant past, but as a very real and present thing, deep in the hearts of every one of us, a personal love and admiration for Lafayette." [43] Celebrations also offered an opportunity to demonstrate American gratitude to Lafayette, proving "that Republics are not ungrateful to those who serve them both well and unselfishly." [44]

[42] New York *Times*, July 5, 1900, p. 7.
[43] Quoted in *Lafayette-Marne Day, September 6th, 1920* (n.p., n.d.), 15.
[44] Lafayette Day National Committee and Lafayette Day Citizens' Committee of New York, *Lafayette Day, 1916* ([New York, 1916]), 17. See also *ibid.*, 1; Easton, *Eulogium*, 18; Wylie, *Eulogy*, 5; Mack, *Life of Lafayette*, 375; "Our Debt to Lafayette," *American Church Monthly*, III (1858), 426; *Life and Services of Lafayette*, 19; "Honoring Lafayette," 1120; letter of Governor Adams, in Colorado Department of Public Instruction, *LaFayette Memorial Day, 1898*, no pp.; Joe Mitchell Chapple, "Tribute of American Youth to Lafayette," *National Magazine*, IX (1898), 198; Augustus E. Ingram, "America's Tribute to Lafayette," *Munsey's Magazine*, XXX (1903–1904), 226; "Lafayette Day . . . September 6, 1916," in *American Scenic and Historic Preservation Society Report*, XXII (1917), 681; Daniel Chester French, "The Lafayette Memorial," *Art World*, II (1917), 315; Hart, "La-

Indeed, as relations between France and the United States improved, and as Americans came to view Lafayette as the personification of his native country, celebrations of the French hero became more and more occasions for showing gratitude not only to Lafayette but to France as well.[45]

A more important function of Lafayette celebrations of the late nineteenth and twentieth centuries was the promotion of patriotism. Contemplation of Lafayette, of "the generous and exalted principles for which he fought and of which his name is significant," and of the important events of the past with which he was associated, recalled "the ideas and ideals" on which the republican experiment was founded.[46] Chief among these was the ideal of liberty, "with which the name of Lafayette was inseparably connected." [47] Thus celebrations of Lafayette offered Americans an opportunity to reaffirm their "sense of loyalty to freedom." [48] In Lafayette Day Exercises

---

fayette," 8; *Lafayette Day, 1919*, pp. 70, 124; James Hosmer Penniman, I, *Our Debt to France*; II, *What Lafayette Did for America: Dedicated to the Fatherless Children of France* ([Philadelphia, 1921]), 38; Lewis, "The Lafayette Centennial and Memorial," 229–30; Elbridge S. Brooks, *The True Story of Lafayette* (New York, 1940), preface; "Lafayette—Hero of Two Worlds," *Senior Scholastic*, LXXI (September 13, 1957), 11.

45 "The name of Lafayette brings to our hearts the name of France—it calls forever to our gratitude," declared Senator Warren G. Harding in 1920. Quoted in New York *Times*, September 7, 1920, p. 5. See also "Honoring Lafayette," 1120; U.S. State Department, *Report Respecting . . . the Statue of Lafayette* ([Washington, D.C., 1900]), no pp.; *Lafayette Day, 1916*, pp. 1, 19; Octavia Roberts, *With Lafayette in America* (Boston, 1919), xi; New York *Sun-Herald*, September 6, 1920, quoted in *Lafayette-Marne Day, 1920*, no pp.; John B. Kennedy, "A Historic Act of Friendship for France," *Current History*, XII (1920), 396; Penniman, *Our Debt to France*, 38–39; Alice Van Leer Carrick, "Let Us Remember Him," *Good Housekeeping*, LXXIX (September, 1924), 51; Henry Francis Du Pont Winterthur Museum, *Lafayette, the Nation's Guest* (Winterthur, Del., 1957), 4.

46 American Defense Society to governors of the U.S., quoted in New York *Times*, August 22, 1918, p. 10; Herbert Hoover, quoted *ibid.*, October 20, 1931, p. 1.

47 *Ibid.*, September 7, 1927, p. 20.

48 William Mather Lewis, "Our Centennial," in Lafayette College, *Lafayette College* (Easton, Pa., 1932), no pp.

at Hudson, New York, in 1917, the superintendent of schools exhorted citizens to "resolve to dedicate our own lives to the perpetuation of that same liberty for which Lafayette fought . . . that government of the people, by the people and for the people shall not perish from the earth." [49]

Lafayette celebrations also functioned as a proof or test of patriotism. As in the 1820's, so in the late nineteenth and twentieth centuries, love, gratitude, and admiration for the Marquis were regarded as evidence of loyalty to republican principles. Lafayette was revered by "every American to whom America's liberty, strength, and glory are dear," by "all . . . who love this great country, and who cherish the great memories of the days of the Revolution"—in short, by every "true-hearted American." [50] In particular, veneration for Lafayette demonstrated Americans' continuing love of liberty. [51] "There is no better proof that Americans will never forget or forsake the cause of liberty than our remembrance, undimmed and undiminished after a hundred years, of the great Marquis de Lafayette," Roosevelt declared in his 1920 Prospect Park speech. [52]

Just as during the Triumphal Tour certain "doubtful" groups had seized upon Lafayette's reception as an occasion for demonstrating their patriotism, so in the early twentieth century, when questions of loyalty arose again, other such groups availed themselves of a similar opportunity. Speaking before the statue of Lafayette in Union Square during Lafayette Day exercises in 1917, John Quinn, "an American of pure Irish descent," affirmed the loyalty of Irish-Americans. In response to the charges leveled against hyphenated Americans,

[49] Quoted in *Lafayette Day Exercises, 1917*, p. 88.

[50] Brooks, *True Story of Lafayette*, 260; Woodrow Wilson, quoted in New York *Times*, September 7, 1918, p. 3; Vernet, "Lafayette," 270. See also *Lafayette Day, 1919*, p. 6.

[51] Calvin Coolidge, quoted in New York *Times*, September 7, 1924, p. 30; Madison, *Lafayette*, 372.

[52] Quoted in *Lafayette-Marne Day, 1920*, p. 16.

Quinn declared "that Americans of Irish birth and descent generally are heart and soul loyal to the Flag in this war." [53] Perhaps Lafayette celebrations seemed a particularly appropriate occasion for American immigrants to prove their patriotism, since they honored a foreigner who had adopted America as his own and whose loyalty was unquestioned. During the early twenties, in the aftermath of postwar strikes and the Red Scare, the American Federation of Labor also chose Lafayette Day to affirm its fidelity to American principles. In 1920, in a message read at the West Point celebration of Lafayette-Marne Day, Samuel Gompers urged on "all of our people—especially the great masses of Liberty-loving working people—the fitting observance of Labor Day, Lafayette Day and Marne Day." [54]

Still another function of Lafayette celebrations was to hold the Frenchman up before the American people as an example of republican virtue and character. As "a patriot exemplar," a model of "pure philanthropy," "disinterested patriotism," "constancy," and "fidelity to the cause of liberty," Lafayette afforded an "undying incentive" to Americans, who were exhorted to "*be worthy, then, of our Lafayette*" by emulating "his transcendent virtues." [55] The French nobleman seemed a particularly appropriate model for the youth of America. As the New York *Times* noted, "The Lafayette who is best known and dearest to America is not [a] veteran figure, but a youth." [56] Convinced that the story of the nineteen-year-old

[53] Quoted in *Lafayette Day Exercises, 1917*, pp. 47–48.

[54] Quoted in *Lafayette-Marne Day, 1920*, p. 7. See also New York *Times*, September 8, 1921, p. 7. Previously, when the dates coincided, labor celebrated Labor Day and Lafayette-Marne Day simultaneously. See, for example, New York *Times*: Charles W. Eliot and others to the editor, August 29, 1915, II, 14; Joseph W. Mandart to the editor, September 6, 1915, p. 8; August 23, 1920, p. 16.

[55] New York *Times*, September 6, 1921, p. 14; Mack, *Life of Lafayette*, 17; *Lafayette Day Exercises, 1917*, p. 68; Secretary of State Cordell Hull, quoted in New York *Times*, May 6, 1934, II, 4; Ferdinand W. Peck, President, Lafayette Memorial Commission, quoted in New York *Times*, July 5, 1900, p. 7; *Life and Services of Lafayette*, 90.

[56] New York *Times*, September 6, 1921, p. 14.

who "dedicated himself to the cause of American liberty" provided "lessons of persistence, fidelity, unshaken loyalty to conviction, to truth, to honor, and to manly endeavor," elders urged the younger generation to follow Lafayette's example.[57] The purpose of the Lafayette monument in Paris, paid for by contributions of American schoolchildren and "dedicated in the name of the youth of the United States," was not simply to commemorate the virtues of the apostle of liberty. As the Denver, Colorado, superintendent of public instruction explained, "The lessons of the day, which open history at some of its most brilliant pages, will arouse a spirit of exalted enthusiasm and patriotism in the hearts of the children." [58]

As an example of "virtuous patriotism" Lafayette also served as a standard for judging America's "public men." Indeed, the impulse "to measure our public servants by the patterns of a purer time" was almost as strong after Lafayette's death as it had been during the Triumphal Tour.[59] Zachariah Allen's *Memorial of Lafayette*, published in 1861, suggests one way in which Lafayette's example was invoked during the Civil War. Writing during a "gloomy period in our national history," Allen was confident that the recollection of the revolutionary period would lead to a renewal of patriotism and union. "There never has been a time when the American people could more profitably study the history of the past perils of the cause of freedom, to learn what the prize cost; and to become aroused to

[57] Brooks, *True Story of Lafayette*, preface. See also Gregg, *Eulogy*, 28; Wylie, *Eulogy*, 5; Mann, "Oration," 14; Marshall S. Snow, *Lafayette, the Friend of Washington* (St. Louis, 1884), 4; letter of Governor Adams, in Colorado Department of Public Instruction, *LaFayette Memorial Day, 1898*, no pp.; Dubuque, *Lafayette*, 12; *Lafayette Day, 1916*, pp. 28–29; *Lafayette Day Exercises, 1917*, p. 68; Mildred Criss, *La Fayette: On the Heights of Freedom* (New York, 1954), vii; "Lafayette—Hero of Two Worlds," 11.

[58] Grace Espy Patton, Superintendent of Public Instruction, to the Teachers and Pupils of Colorado, October 10, 1898, in Colorado Department of Public Instruction, *LaFayette Memorial Day, 1898*, no pp.

[59] Willis Gaylord Clark, *An Address on the Characters of Lafayette and Washington* (Philadelphia, 1840), 3; Hillhouse, *Oration*, 36–37.

exert their energies and courage to preserve and defend what their forefathers fought for and won," he argued. A study of the "noble deeds" and virtuous character of the early patriots could not fail "to animate us all with fresh zeal for the discharge of this important duty"—preservation of the republic. "Such is the effect produced by studying the bright example of the character of Lafayette, distinguished alike for purity of moral excellence, for a generosity of purpose, a self sacrificing spirit, and an unwavering devotion to the great cause of human freedom," Allen concluded.

Americans also invoked Lafayette's example in discussing the slavery question during the Civil War. Allen hailed Lafayette as "the great champion of human rights" and Charles Sumner declared that the Frenchman's "opposition to African slavery" derived from "the same spirit which inspired him originally to enlist for us, the same instinctive love of Liberty, the same self-sacrifice, the same generosity, the same nobleness, expressed with affecting simplicity and frankness." [60] The implication was that loyalty to the American Revolution entailed opposition to slavery. But when it came to actual antislavery policy, Lafayette's example was as ambiguous in the 1860's as it had been during his last visit to the United States. Sumner maintained that the Marquis stood on the side of immediatism; his concern for the slave, Sumner declared, was based on the principle that "every slave . . . has a natural right to immediate emancipation, whether by concession or force; and this principle he declared above all question." [61] Yet other Americans

[60] Zachariah Allen, *Memorial of Lafayette* (Providence, 1861), 18–19; Charles Sumner, "Lafayette, the Faithful One: Address at the Cooper Institute, New York, November 30, 1860," in *The Works of Charles Sumner* (Boston, 1870–83), V, 393, 397.

[61] Sumner, "Lafayette," 425. Reporting Sumner's speech, the Philadelphia *Pennsylvanian* observed that "Sumner's nominal subject was 'Lafayette,' but he made his sketch of the noble Marquis a vehicle for the expression of the most ardent wishes and aspirations after negro equality." Quoted in Sumner, *Works*, V, 372.

portrayed Lafayette as a gradualist. The author of *Life of Lafayette, Written for Children*, published in 1860, explained that Lafayette "honestly desired that all men, not merely himself and his countrymen, should be free; but he had the common sense to see that some races of men require preparation even for freedom, and that a slave, who has all his life been fed and clothed by a master, does not know how to provide for himself in his old age." [62] Thus did some Americans apply the lessons taught by Lafayette's experiences in the French Revolution—moderation and the necessity of preparation for liberty—in handling the problem of an oppressed people within their own borders.

Lafayette's example proved to be as ambiguous in the realm of foreign as in domestic policy. As we have already seen, late nineteenth- and twentieth-century assessments of Lafayette's efforts in the French Revolution tended to reinforce the conservative conception of mission. On the other hand, the actions of the youthful warrior of the American Revolution were easily mustered in support of the radical conception of mission. In 1898, for example, a speaker at Barren Hill, Pennsylvania, rehearsed the legend of Lafayette's participation in the American Revolution. "This stranger saw oppression, and with pure disinterestedness went to the help of those in need," he observed, and noted with approval that "the example of Lafayette . . . has not been lost upon the American people." The same speaker added, "So now the American people as a mass see that another nation is laying waste a beautiful island, destroying its enterprise, murdering its men, starving its children, outraging its women, and in the name of humanity and righteousness it has arisen like our hero Lafayette, and will fight for the oppressed and downtrodden of Cuba." [63]

[62] Cecil [pseud.], *Life of Lafayette*, 79–80. See also "Cloquet's Lafayette," 126.

[63] Quoted in Ellwood Roberts (comp.), *Lafayette at Barren Hill* (Norristown, Pa., 1898), 17–18.

By far the most extensive use of the Lafayette image in support of the radical conception of mission occurred during the First World War, when commentators invoked Lafayette's name to justify and explain intervention. The most popular slogan of the war—"Lafayette, we are here"—compressed into four words the notion that Americans were responding to the appeal of their former benefactor and adopted son.[64] Seen in this light, American participation in the war became a kind of celebration of Lafayette, a concrete way of demonstrating the gratitude and veneration Americans felt for their former benefactor.

Americans also justified intervention by appealing to Lafayette's example. "Can we for a single moment be in any doubt as to what the brave Lafayette would do were he alive to face with us the present world crisis?" asked the Reverend St. Clair Hester.[65] To underscore the appropriateness of the Lafayette example, commentators stressed the similarity between the American Revolution and the World War. Frenchmen, they declared, were "fighting in defense of liberty, independence, and democratic freedom, which was, indeed, the fight of Washington and Lafayette."[66] American boys, explained one speaker, "go to urge just such a battle as their forefathers waged when they stood with Lafayette and conquered and gave to the world a lesson in what liberty, equality

[64] Roberts, *With Lafayette in America*, xi; Cassie Moncure Lyne, "When Lafayette Visited Arlington," *Confederate Veteran*, XXVI (1918), 386. See also *Lafayette Day Exercises, 1917*, p. 82; James Mott Hallowell, *The Spirit of Lafayette* (Garden City, N.Y., 1918), dedication and 55; New York *Times*, September 7, 1919, p. 3, and September 7, 1921, p. 17; Sedgwick, *La Fayette*, preface; Laurence Stallings, *The Doughboys: The Story of the AEF, 1917–1918* (New York, 1963), 16. Captain C. E. Stanton was the real author of the slogan, not General Pershing. For an amusing narrative of the ceremony at Picpus cemetery and Stanton's role in it, see *ibid.*, 15. See also "Lafayette, We Are Here" (Irving Brant to the editor), *Commonweal*, XIII (1931), 526.

[65] The Reverend St. Clair Hester, *Lafayette, the Apostle of Liberty* ([Brooklyn, 1917]), no pp.

[66] "Lafayette Day," *Outlook*, CXIV (September 20, 1916), 116.

and fraternity can be." [67] The war was thus no "foreign" conflict, from which the United States should remain aloof, but a "struggle . . . for our American ideals." [68] It was "a second war for independence and liberty." [69]

Confronting a situation similar to the one "the brave Lafayette" had faced in 1777, how could Americans fail to follow his example? In fact, as commentators never tired of pointing out, they *were* following Lafayette's example, intervening in the war from the same motives which had prompted the young Frenchman to join the American Revolution.[70] First, like Lafayette, they were motivated by a love of liberty and a concern for the welfare of mankind. "The same passion for human rights which drove Lafayette to America, is impelling the American youth today to take an important part in the battle against autocracy," explained the Hudson, New York, superintendent of schools. Second, and perhaps more important, Americans were following Lafayette's example of disinterested benevolence. "We have heard the call and in the same spirit in which Lafayette came to America, we are going across to battle unselfishly, to make the world safe for democracy," a Lafayette Day speaker declared in 1917.[71] As these quotations suggest, the appeal to Lafayette not only provided a way of justifying intervention, but of exalting and ennobling the motives behind intervention, of convincing public opinion at home and abroad that Americans had entered the war, as President Wilson maintained, as "one of the champions of the rights of mankind" and with "no selfish ends to serve." [72]

---

[67] J. P. K. Bryan, quoted in *Lafayette Day Exercises, 1917*, p. 84.

[68] Robert Bacon, quoted in *Lafayette Day, 1916*, p. 22.

[69] Judge Thomas Burke, quoted in *Lafayette Day Exercises, 1917*, p. 78.

[70] See, for example, *Lafayette Day, 1916*, p. 29; Hallowell, *Spirit of Lafayette*, 72, 101; *Lafayette Day, 1919*, p. 23.

[71] Charles W. Williams and the Reverend William B. Geogeghan, quoted in *Lafayette Day Exercises, 1917*, pp. 88, 82.

[72] Woodrow Wilson, "For Declaration of War Against Germany: Address . . . April 2, 1917," in Ray Stannard Baker and William E. Dodd (eds.), *War*

Referring to the President's speech asking for a declaration of war, John Finley observed, "Wilson is indeed today, in his message, our Lafayette to France." [73]

Though all Americans were said to be emulating Lafayette, the ones most often celebrated as "the Lafayettes of today" were the volunteers who served in the Lafayette Escadrille.[74] One of them, Kiffin Rockwell, was quoted as saying, "I pay my debt for Lafayette and Rochambeau." [75] Actually, the volunteers' desire for adventure, fame, and revenge was as much a motivation as idealism.[76] Indeed, in their reasons for joining the war, the young American fliers came closer to emulating the real Lafayette than the hero-symbol created by the American imagination. Nevertheless, they were celebrated as proof of American disinterestedness. Like the French nobleman, the New York *Times* observed, "the American Lafayettes . . . heard the call of endangered liberty in another land and went to risk their lives for it, without waiting, as he did not wait, for the slow processes of statesmanship." The voluntary nature of their actions particularly impressed American commentators. Asking "no official sanction," "mustered by enthusiasm and enrolled by devotion," the fliers "gave themselves as a true knight lays his gift at his lady's feet." Dr. Henry

---

and Peace: Presidential Messages, Addresses, and Public Papers (1917–1924) (New York, 1927), I, 14.

[73] Quoted in *Lafayette Day Exercises, 1917*, p. 25. See also *ibid.*, 21. Perhaps Wilson himself identified with Lafayette. The President twice laid a wreath on the tomb of the Marquis, each carrying a card with the following inscription: "To the Great Lafayette, from a Fellow-Servant of Liberty." New York *Times*, December 16, 1918, p. 1, June 8, 1919, II, 2.

[74] French Ambassador Jean Jusserand, quoted in New York *Times*, September 7, 1916, p. 7. See also Theodore Roosevelt, "Lafayettes of the Air," *Collier's*, LVII (July 29, 1916), 16.

[75] Quoted in James McConnell, "Flying for France," *World's Work*, XXXIII (1917), 506.

[76] On the formation of the Lafayette Escadrille see James Norman Hall and Charles Bernard Nordhoff (eds.), *The Lafayette Flying Corps* (Port Washington, N.Y., 1964), I, 3, 38; Edwin C. Parsons, *I Flew with the Lafayette Escadrille* (Indianapolis, 1963), v, vi, 8–10, 13, 15.

van Dyke proposed that the names of the young heroes should be written "in the roll of that order of chivalry which is headed by the name of Lafayette." [77]

Because the image of Lafayette was inextricably bound up with the arguments justifying American intervention, it was also a victim of the reaction against the war to make the world safe for democracy. Even during the war, battle-weary doughboys had returned from the front singing, "We've paid our debt to Lafayette; who the hell do we owe now?" [78] After the war, repudiation of American intervention, and of the reasons advanced in support of intervention, resulted in a certain amount of criticism of Lafayette. A book reviewer for the *American Mercury* questioned the extent of the American debt to Lafayette so "loudly raised by patriotic circles during the wartime" and concluded "that some substantial installments had already been applied to that debt before 1917." [79] A second article in the same magazine went even further in suggesting that Lafayette had been the recipient of undeserved gratitude, not only during World War I, but before. "Our country's founding fathers . . . were pushovers for a title, a spot of blue blood and a little plain and fancy hurrahing for liberty," the authors explained. "They fell all over themselves, decade after decade, to 'reward' the marquis 'suitably' for his services, though they let home-grown patriots go bankrupt, auction their belongings to stave off the world, and besiege Congress vainly for just recompense." While men like Jefferson and Monroe suffered financial difficulties, "Lafayette . . . lived in France off the fat of America." The implication of the article was that just as "Americans have always been suckers for title-sporting foreigners," forgetting that America and Americans

[77] New York *Times*, September 7, 1917, p. 8; Dr. Henry van Dyke, quoted *ibid.*, 3.

[78] Stallings, *Doughboys*, 16.

[79] Thomason, "We've Paid Our Debt to Lafayette," 493, 497–98.

come first, so too have they often been duped into fighting foreign battles that were none of their concern.[80]

To a considerable extent the reaction against American participation in the World War was a reaction against the fundamental assumption underlying intervention, the radical concept of mission. The effect of this on the Lafayette image is seen in the response generated by the news that some members of the Lafayette Escadrille had engaged to fly for the sultan of Morocco in his conflict with Riffian tribesmen. The New York *Times*, which had earlier hailed the fliers as "American Lafayettes" who, like their namesake, refused to wait "for the slow processes of statesmanship," now charged them with "impropriety." The *Times* explained that "the 'soldier of fortune,' once a figure of high romance, and still very useful in what may be described as costume novels, is now decidedly out of fashion. He was a man who went around looking for wars in which he could fight for pay or loot, or sometimes, though very rarely, from pure love of fighting. He probably had his uses and even his excuses, in other days . . . . Now things are different, and the man who takes part in any except his own country's wars must have exceptional explanations for his conduct." [81] Had the American fliers volunteered to aid the Riffians in their rebellion against the despotic sultan, would the *Times* and other Americans have responded differently? Probably not. The reaction against the radical version of the American mission was sweeping and total, resulting in an almost categorical dismissal of "the man who takes part in any except his own country's wars" as little more than a soldier of fortune, possibly dangerous to the welfare of his country, at the least "out of fashion," a romantic relic of "other days."

---

[80] Guy S. Allison and Doris McFerran, "Lafayette Hits the Jackpot," *American Mercury*, LIII (1941), 168, 170, and see also 172–73.

[81] New York *Times*, July 10, 1925, p. 5, September 22, 1925, p. 2, October 14, 1925, p. 24.

Because of its fundamental ambiguity, the Lafayette image did not become completely irrelevant as a result of the postwar reaction. The Lafayette of the American Revolution and the example he offered might be "out of fashion," like the radical conception of mission with which it was associated. But the lessons derived from Lafayette's experiences in the French Revolutions of 1789 and 1830 took on new significance after World War I. With the wave of postwar disillusionment and skepticism toward Europe—similar in cause and effect to an earlier generation's response to the failure of the American mission—Lafayette's example was once again invoked in support of the conservative view of mission. Speaking at a Lafayette-Marne Day celebration in 1924, Calvin Coolidge argued that the United States must pursue a foreign policy which avoided "political entanglements with other countries." The United States must play an essentially passive role in international affairs, aiding the attainment of world peace by setting "the example to the world, both in our domestic and foreign relations, of magnanimity." The President justified America's passive role by invoking the theory of relative progress underlying the conservative conception of mission. "We cannot make over the people of Europe," he warned. "We must help them as they are, if we are to help them at all." In such a course of action, Coolidge concluded, lay "the best guarantee of freedom" and "the greatest honor which we can bestow upon the memory of Lafayette." [82]

Though it survived the reaction against intervention, the Lafayette image played a steadily diminishing role during World War II and after. The revival of the radical concept of mission during the war meant a renewed emphasis on Lafayette as its symbol. Thus Raymond Moley, declaring that "the duty of the United States to teach the lessons of liberty is even more

[82] Quoted *ibid.*, September 7, 1924, pp. 1, 30. See also *ibid.*, September 7, 1925, p. 2.

imperative than it was 200 years ago," called upon "the ghost of Lafayette" to "come west to remind us of what we once did for Europe, and must do again." [83] The war also revived the American inclination to identify Lafayette with France. A resolution passed by the American Friends of Lafayette endorsed the Free French as "true successors of Lafayette" and asked the President and Congress "to recognize officially and extend immediately all possible aid and assistance to the Free French Forces of General de Gaulle." [84] During and after World War II Lafayette served as a symbol of Franco-American friendship; in the cold war some Americans enlisted him in support of the crusade against Communism.[85]

Since 1918, however, the appeal of the Lafayette image had been gradually narrowing. As Americans became more sophisticated and less inclined to the demonstrative patriotism of their grandparents, the inspirational appeal of the "patriot exemplar" declined. As the radical concept of mission lost influence, so did its chief symbol. By midcentury, invocation of Lafayette's name and example was confined primarily to children's literature and patriotic and Francophile organizations. Lafayette no longer served as a national hero-symbol.

[83] Raymond Moley, "The Star in the West," *Newsweek*, XXII (December 27, 1943), 88.

[84] New York *Times*, September 7, 1941, p. 29.

[85] *Ibid.*, September 7, 1939, p. 28, May 21, 1944, p. 6, May 22, 1951, p. 10. Beginning in 1961, the Order of Lafayette, an organization of officers who served in France and French possessions during the world wars, presented its annual Freedom Awards for "distinguished leadership in fighting Communism." *Ibid.*, May 20, 1961, p. 5, November 25, 1961, p. 47, December 4, 1962, p. 14, November 20, 1964, p. 26, November 28, 1965, p. 130, December 12, 1967, p. 53.

6 The Man
of Virtue

What, finally, explains the enduring appeal of the Lafayette image for the American people? A comparison with another hero-symbol, Thomas Jefferson, suggests a partial answer. As Merrill Peterson has demonstrated, the Jefferson image mirrored the "prodigality" of the man. "In the vast corpus of his mind anyone could find things to arouse anger or sympathy, invite ridicule or admiration. . . . He never had the occasion, probably never the desire, to work out a systematic statement of his philosophy. So he appeared before posterity with his rich intellectual garments dangling and disarrayed." Peterson concludes that "it was precisely because Jefferson lent himself to everyone that he had been so useful, that he had been for generations after his death a political watchword, that his reputation was carried forward until, indeed, he belonged to everyone and to no one." [1] Of course the image of Lafayette never possessed the political significance of the Jefferson image. But, like Jefferson, Lafayette "lent himself to everyone." Whereas the "political usefulness" of the Jefferson image was a consequence of the complexity and variety of the his-

[1] Peterson, *Jefferson Image*, 444–45.

torical man, the malleability of the Lafayette image derived from the fact that it was largely a creation of the imagination. For Americans Lafayette was primarily an image, a legend, rather than a real person. The vagueness and ambiguousness of the image allowed it to be used for many different, even contradictory, purposes.

There is another, more important reason for the enduring appeal of the Lafayette image: its representation of a man of virtue. The eulogists delineated this image of Lafayette as the embodiment of moral excellence, as a man whose entire life and conduct revealed the influence of moral principles. For example Jarvis Gregg admitted that Lafayette was not a "great man" as that term was commonly understood. He brought no "original genius, or profound philosophy, or commanding eloquence" to the world. Whether by choice or fate he attained no great seat of political power. "And yet," Gregg declared, "no man has impressed his opinions and sentiments more deeply on his own age, or is destined to send down a more pervading and controlling moral influence to future time." Lafayette was "an illustrious example of the *moral power of virtue.*" Herein lay the source of his considerable "influence and fame." Gregg explained,

> Lafayette was a star, not indeed of the first magnitude, but mild, beautiful and benign, shedding forth its genial "stellar virtue on all kinds that grow," and diffusing life, and beauty and delight. Lafayette's known virtue, his tried integrity, his uncompromising principles, gained him his influence and fame. It was this that made his name a spell to wake all the generous sympathies and noble sentiments in the bosoms of the human race. It was this that imparted a vitality, a living power to his opinions; that consecrated his character, and made him the oracle and embodied representative of freedom.[2]

---

[2] Gregg, *Eulogy*, 26–27. See also Baylies, *Eulogy*, 8, 43; John Quincy Adams, *Oration on the Life and Character of . . . Lafayette* (Washington, 1835), 68; Dayton, *Eulogy*, 39, 44; New York City Common Council, *Particulars of the Funeral Honours to . . . La Fayette* (New York, 1834), 33.

Indeed, for his eulogists, Lafayette was not only an example of virtue in the sense of being able to inspire virtue in others, but a proof of its very possibility. "That *political virtue* is not a phantom,—a mere phrase of cabala, for the use of demagogues, —but a *reality*, powerful, and, at last, *prevalent* in great affairs, is a truth emphatically taught by the life of Lafayette;—and forms its appropriate *moral*," declared James Hillhouse.[3]

The same quality that the eulogists pointed out as the source of Lafayette's influence in life, later Americans also singled out to explain his enduring appeal after death. Echoing Gregg, they admitted that Lafayette was not a great man in the ordinary sense of the word. He was not "a man of remarkable intellectual powers," nor was he a great orator, author, or soldier. "Least of all, was he a statesman, as that term is commonly understood." [4] But such qualifications only served to heighten the sense of Lafayette's uniqueness.[5]

Like the eulogists, writers and speakers of the late nineteenth and twentieth centuries emphasized Lafayette's character rather than his achievements. It was "not what he did but the way he did it that endeared him to his own age and to others," a reviewer for the *Nation* explained.[6] Martha Foote Crow admitted that Lafayette's "services to his own country and to ours were many and valuable," but she argued that "his personal example of character, integrity, and constancy was even more to us and to the world than his distinct services. What he *was*

---

[3] Hillhouse, *Oration*, 37.

[4] Headley, *Makers of American History*, 287; Sumner, "Lafayette," 429; "Reminiscences of a Tempest-tost Life," 424. See also "Cloquet's Lafayette," 116; Cutter, *Life of General Lafayette*, 407–408; Tuckerman, *Life of Lafayette*, II, 253-54; George P. Tilton, *An Account of the Life of . . . La Fayette* (Newburyport, Mass., 1907), 46; Thompson, "The Fifth Musketeer," 64–65.

[5] Mack, *Life of Lafayette*, 17, 373; *Pictorial Life of Lafayette*, iii, 136–37; W. W. H. Davis, "The Marquis de Lafayette," *Bucks County Historical Society Collections*, I (1880), 74; Sedgwick, *La Fayette*, 202.

[6] Harlow, "A Great Adventurer," 752.

endeared him to us, even more than the things he did." [7] A
writer for *Putnam's Monthly* summarized the typical portrait
of Lafayette: "his character was ennobled by unrivaled purity
of purpose, by disinterested and magnanimous aims, by in-
domitable courage and devotion to the highest interests of
humanity." [8] For later Americans, as for Lafayette's contemporaries, the Marquis was above all the man of virtue, the
embodiment of moral excellence.

The emphasis on character rather than achievements, on
what Lafayette was, rather than what he did, seems peculiar
for a people who were thought of and liked to think of themselves as basically pragmatic. But, as we have seen, a tendency
toward introspection and self-examination lay beneath the sur-
face of the American mind and emerged only occasionally into
full view. From the beginning of their nation to the twentieth
century, Americans were primarily concerned with carving a
nation out of the wilderness. But they were also periodically
anxious about the national character. Merrill Peterson has said
that "monuments to the great are symbolic acts. In them the
nation celebrates itself." [9] We have been dealing with the literary monument which Americans erected to Lafayette in the
course of their history. It would not be an exaggeration to say
that Americans created Lafayette in their own image, that they
made him the embodiment of the one quality they prized above
all others. In celebrating him as a man of virtue they celebrated
themselves—what they liked to think they were, or should or
could be.

The whole of the American tradition stressed the importance
of virtue as the bulwark of republican government, and the

[7] Crow, *Lafayette*, 199.

[8] "Reminiscences of a Tempest-tost Life," 424. See also Mack, *Life of Lafayette*, 17; Cecil [pseud.], *Life of Lafayette*, 218; Allen, *Memorial of Lafayette*, 19; Roberts, *Lafayette at Barren Hill*, 17; Headley, *Makers of American History*, 289; Sedgwick, *La Fayette*, preface, 415.

[9] Peterson, *Jefferson Image*, 429.

fact of inherent virtue as a guarantee of its possibility. American faith in the viability of republican government was at bottom a faith in man's inherent capacity for virtue, on which republican government depended. Montesquieu had named virtue the chief principle of a republic. The Founding Fathers, while not underestimating the function of self-interest in society, had also stressed the role of the moral sense as the source of public and private virtue. Indeed, the providential task assigned to the American people demanded virtue. On the one hand, in the absence of other sanctions such as those operating in monarchical forms of government, virtue was necessary as a means of holding republican society together. It was necessary to counterbalance self-interest, which, acting alone, might dissolve the bonds of society by elevating the interest of the individual over that of the general good. In addition, the peculiarly moral character of the American mission also suggested the necessity of virtue. America's serving as a model republic and spreading republican principles throughout the world depended on the virtue of her citizens.

Believing that virtue was necessary for the success of the republican experiment and the American mission, Americans made Lafayette their primary exemplar. That they found their image of the man of virtue in the person of a foreigner and an aristocrat is surely one of the ironies of American history.

Selected
Bibliography

PRIMARY SOURCES

MANUSCRIPT COLLECTIONS

Cornell Lafayette Collection. Rare Book Room, Cornell University Library, Ithaca, N.Y.

The Cornell Lafayette Collection, formerly housed at the Chateau de Chavaniac, consists of fifty-three cartons comprising approximately 10,000 pieces, most of them biographical material relating to Lafayette and his family. Seven of the cartons, used extensively in this study, deal with his American correspondence and "Triumphal Tour" through the United States in 1824–25. The American correspondence generally covers the period 1815–34, although some items are earlier. Cartons X and XI contain letters addressed to Lafayette by important or well-known Americans; cartons XII through XV include between 1,200 and 1,500 letters addressed to Lafayette by American friends from all classes and walks of life. They deal with a variety of subjects: thank-you letters from travelers who had visited Lafayette at La Grange, requests for employment or charity, letters transmitting gifts, testimonials or addresses, letters of congratulation for political speeches or actions. Cartons XVII and XVIII contain approximately 500 pieces relating to Lafayette's tour in 1824–25, the majority of them letters, as well as petitions, memorials, addresses, and poems he received during the journey.

Library of Congress, Washington, D.C.

Benjamin Thomas Hill Collection. "Lafayette in the United States, 1824–1825." 7 vols. This is a scrapbook of clippings with commentary, assembled in Worcester, Mass., in 1900–1901.

James Monroe Papers. Presidential Papers.

Lafayette Collection. Franklin D. Roosevelt, "Address of President

Roosevelt at Commemoration Ceremony in Honor of the One Hundredth Anniversary of the Death of La Fayette, at a Joint Session of Congress, May 20, 1934."

Rare Book Room. Scrapbook of newspaper clippings, 1824–25, relating to Lafayette's visit to America and his services in the Revolution.

United States Department of State. Diplomatic Despatches, France, The Hague, and Spain.

NEWSPAPERS

Connecticut Courant (Hartford). 1784–85, 1792–98.
New York *Times*. 1900–69.
Niles' Weekly Register (Baltimore). 1811–35.
Pennsylvania Gazette (Philadelphia). 1777–89.
Pennsylvania Journal and Weekly Advertiser (Philadelphia). 1784–85, 1791–93.
Pennsylvania Packet and Daily Advertiser (Philadelphia). 1788–90.
South Carolina and American General Gazette (Charleston). 1777–81.
Virginia Gazette (Richmond). 1777–80.
Washington *Daily National Intelligencer*. 1831–34.

ARTICLES

"Address to Gen. Lafayette, from 'The Slaves' in the Land of Freedom." *Columbian Centinel* (Boston), October 20, 1824.
Allison, Guy S., and McFerran, Doris. "Lafayette Hits the Jackpot." *American Mercury*, LIII (1941), 168–73.
Ayers, C. B. "When Fate Came to Dinner." *Coronet*, XXXIV (June, 1953), 168, 170.
Bacon, Robert. "Lafayette." *Outlook*, CXIV (September 20, 1916), 139–41.
Carrick, Alive Van Leer. "Let Us Remember Him." *Good Housekeeping*, LXXIX (September, 1924), 51, 187–93.
Chapple, Joe Mitchell. "Tribute of American Youth to Lafayette." *National Magazine*, IX (1898), 195–99.
"Charavay's Lafayette." *Nation*, LXVI (1898), 203–204, 221–22, 261–62.
"Cloquet's Lafayette." *American Quarterly Review*, XXXIX (1836), 102–29.
Davis, W. W. H. "The Marquis de Lafayette." *Bucks County Historical Society Collections*, I (1880), 66–76.
Desha, Joseph. "Extracts from the Messages of Governor Desha—Resolutions of the General Assembly, Reports of Committees, Etc. Relative to the Visit of General Lafayette to Frankfort, and to the Painting of Lafayette's Portrait by Jouett." *Kentucky Historical Society Register*, XI (1913), 69–77.

Dos Passos, John. "Lafayette's Two Revolutions." *American Heritage,* VIII (1956), 4–9, 104–16.

Elbrick, C. B. "Lafayette Bicentennial: Address, September 6, 1957." *U.S. Department of State Bulletin,* XXXVII (September 23, 1957), 489.

Estabrook, Henry D. "Lafayette." In *"The Spirit of '76" by James Hulme Canfield; "La Fayette" by Henry D. Estabrook: Addresses Delivered Before the Quill Club of New York at Its Meeting of February 19th, 1907.* [New York?: 1907].

Ford, George H. "The Struggle for Liberty." *Connecticut Magazine,* VII (1902), 549–52.

French, Daniel Chester. "The Lafayette Memorial." *Art World,* II (1917), 314–15.

Hall, Walter Phelps. "Hero of Two Worlds." *New Republic,* LX (1929), 217.

Harlow, Ralph Volney. "A Great Adventurer." *Nation,* CXXIX (1929), 752–53.

Hart, A. B. "Lafayette." *Mentor–World Traveller,* V (January 15, 1918), 1–11.

Histoire de l'Assemblée Constituante de France par M. Ch. Lacretelle, reviewed in *Quarterly Review,* XXVIII (1823), 286.

"Honoring Lafayette." *Harper's Weekly,* XXXVIII (1894), 1120.

Ingram, Augustus E. "America's Tribute to Lafayette." *Munsey's Magazine,* XXX (1903–1904), 225–28.

Johnson, Monroe. "The Prisoner of Olmutz." *National Republic,* XIX (July, 1931), 19–21.

Kennedy, John B. "A Historic Act of Friendship for France." *Current History, a Monthly Magazine of the New York Times,* XII (1920), 396–98.

Ladegast, Richard. "The Lafayette Monument." *Outlook,* LXIX (September 7, 1901), 56–57.

"La Fayette." *Saturday Review of Literature,* IV (1928), 753.

"Lafayette as a Patriot and Soldier." *National Quarterly Review,* XVI (1867), 71–95.

"Lafayette Day." *Outlook,* CXI (September 8, 1915), 117–18.

"Lafayette Day." *Outlook,* CXIV (September 20, 1916), 115–16.

"Lafayette Day." *Outlook,* CXIV (October 4, 1916), 240.

"Lafayette Day." *Outlook,* CXVII (September 19, 1917), 85–87.

"Lafayette Day. Official Account of the Ceremonies Held in the City Hall of New York City on September 6, 1916, Commemorating the 169th Anniversary of the Birth of the Marquis de Lafayette." *American Scenic and Historic Preservation Society Report,* XXII (1917), 669–700.

"Lafayette—Hero of Two Worlds." *Senior Scholastic,* LXXI (September 13, 1957), 11.

"Lafayette, We Are Here" (Irving Brant to the editor). *Commonweal,* XIII (1931), 526.

"Lafayette, We Are Here—Everywhere." *Life,* XLIII (September 23, 1957), 45–46, 48.

"Lafayette's Letters." *Nation,* LXXVI (1903), 513–14.

"The Lesson of Lafayette Day." *Outlook,* CXX (September 18, 1918), 85–86.

Lewis, Charlton T. "The Character of Lafayette, An Address Delivered Before the Washington Association of New Jersey at Their Meeting February 22, 1896." *Washington Association of New Jersey Publications,* I (1896), 3–18.

Lewis, William Mather. "The Lafayette Centennial and Memorial." *Legion d'Honneur,* IV (1934), 229–35.

Lovett, Howard Meriwether. "General Lafayette and the Eighteenth Congress." *Confederate Veteran,* XXVI (1918), 386–89.

Lyne, Cassie Moncure. "When Lafayette Visited Arlington." *Confederate Veteran,* XXVI (1918), 386.

McConnell, James. "Flying for France." *World's Work,* XXXIII (1916–17), 41–53, 497–509.

Moley, Raymond. "The Star in the West." *Newsweek,* XXII (December 27, 1943), 88.

"Our Debt to Lafayette." *American Church Monthly,* III (1858), 425–41.

"Pages from the Past." *Vermont Quarterly,* XIX (1951), 222–32.

Porter, Frank Gibson. "Lafayette as American." *National Republic,* XXIII (September, 1935), 6–7.

"Reminiscences of a Tempest-tost Life; I, Lafayette." *Putnam's Monthly,* VI (1855), 416–24, in Toner Collection, Rare Book Room, Library of Congress.

Roosevelt, Theodore. "Lafayettes of the Air: Young Americans Who Are Flying for France." *Collier's,* LVII (July 29, 1916), 16.

Shorey, D. L. "Lafayette in the American Revolution." *Dial,* XVIII (1895), 208–10.

Standish, Rose. "Recollections of Lafayette." *Knickerbocker,* XXXII (1848), 215–18.

Thomason, John W., Jr. "We've Paid Our Debt to Lafayette." *American Mercury,* XLVI (1939), 493–98.

Thompson, Marshall Putnam. "The Fifth Musketeer: The Marquis de La Fayette." *Bunker Hill Monument Association Proceedings,* June 17, 1914, pp. 31–65.

Ticknor, George. "Lafayette in America." *North American Review,* XXX (1830), 216–37.

"Tower's Lafayette." *Nation*, LX (1895), 222–23.

"Tuckerman's Lafayette." *Nation*, XLVIII (1889), 431–32.

Van Dyke, Henry. "The Chivalry of Lafayette." *Outlook*, CXVII (September 19, 1917), 86–87.

Vernet, Esther Reed. "Lafayette—The Nature of His Relations to America." *Potter's American Monthly*, VI (1876), 270–74.

BOOKS

Adams, John. *Diary and Autobiography*. Ed. Lyman H. Butterfield. 4 vols. Cambridge, Mass.: Harvard University Press, Belknap Press, 1961.

Adams, John Quincy. *An Address, Delivered at the Request of the Committee of Arrangements for Celebrating the Anniversary of Independence, at the City of Washington on the Fourth of July, 1821, upon the Occasion of Reading the Declaration of Independence.* Cambridge, Mass.: n.p., 1821.

————. *Memoirs of John Quincy Adams, Comprising Portions of His Diary from 1795 to 1848.* Ed. Charles F. Adams. 12 vols. Philadelphia: J. B. Lippincott and Co., 1874–77.

————. *Oration on the Life and Character of Gilbert Motier de Lafayette. Delivered at the Request of Both Houses of the Congress of the United States, Before Them, in the House of Representatives at Washington, on the 31st of December, 1834.* Washington: Duff Green, 1835.

Adams, Samuel. *The Writings of Samuel Adams*. Ed. Harry Alonzo Cushing. 4 vols. New York: G. P. Putnam's Sons, 1907.

Allen, Zachariah. *Memorial of Lafayette. Paper Read Before the Rhode Island Historical Society, February 4, 1861.* Providence: n.p., 1861.

American Military Biography; Containing the Lives, Characters, and Anecdotes of the Officers of the Revolution, Who Were Most Distinguished in Achieving Our National Independence. Also, the Life of Gilbert Motier La Fayette, Major-General in the Continental Army—Marshal of France, and Commander in Chief of the National Guards. [Cincinnati]: n.p., 1825.

The American Museum; or, Universal Magazine. For the Year 1792. Part II. From July to December. Philadelphia: n.p., 1792.

American Sketches; by a Native of the United States. London: n.p., 1827.

Annals of the Congress of the United States: The Debates and Proceedings in the Congress of the United States. 42 vols. Washington: Gales and Seaton, 1834–56.

An Authentic Biography of General La Fayette. In Which Many Errors and Deficiencies Existing in the Memoirs Heretofore Pub-

lished, Are Corrected and Supplied. Philadelphia: A. Sherman, 1824.

Bancroft, George. *The Life and Letters of George Bancroft*. Ed. Mark Antony De Wolfe Howe. 2 vols. New York: Charles Scribner's Sons, 1908.

Baylies, Francis. *Eulogy on Lafayette, Delivered in the Masonic Temple, Boston, October 9, 1834. At the Request of the Grand Lodge of Freemasons in Massachusetts*. Boston: n.p., 1834.

Bedoyere, Michael de La. *Lafayette, a Revolutionary Gentleman*. London: Jonathan Cape, 1933.

Benham, J. S. *An Oration on the Character and Services of General Lafayette, Delivered at the Celebration of His Visit to Cincinnati, May 20th, 1825; in the Presence of the "Nation's Guest," and an Immense Concourse of Citizens*. Cincinnati: n.p., 1825.

Béranger, P[ierre] J[ean] de. *Oeuvres Complètes de P. -J. de Béranger*. 2 vols. Paris: n.p., 1847.

Bernhard, [Karl], Duke of Saxe-Weimar Eisenach. *Travels Through North America, During the Years 1825 and 1826*. 2 vols. Philadelphia: n.p., 1828.

Bigelow, John. *La Fayette*. Boston: Little, Brown, and Co., 1882.

Biographical Notice of General Lafayette. Translated from Notice Biographique sur Le General Lafayette . . . . Paris, 1818. Accompanied with a Portrait, and the Original Work in French. Philadelphia: Benjamin Tanner, 1824.

Biographical Sketch of the Life of the Marquis de La Fayette, Late a Major General in the American Service. Together with an Account of His Embarkation at Havre, and Reception in the United States. Exeter, [N.H.?], n.p., 1824.

Biography of the Illustrious Citizen, General Lafayette, the Hero, the Statesman, the Philanthropist, the Early and Constant Friend of America, and the Champion of the Equal Rights of Mankind. By a Citizen of Washington, D.C. 2nd ed. Wilmington, Del.: n.p., 1824.

Brooks, Elbridge S. *The True Story of Lafayette*. Rev. ed. New York: Lothrop, Lee and Shepard Co., 1940.

Bryan, Daniel. *The Lay of Gratitude; Consisting of Poems Occasioned by the Recent Visit of Lafayette to the United States*. Philadelphia: Carey and Lea, 1826.

Butler, Frederick. *Memoirs of the Marquis de La Fayette, Major-general in the Revolutionary Army of the United States of America. Together with His Tour Through the United States*. Wethersfield, Conn.: Deming and Francis, 1825.

Calhoun, John C. *Correspondence of John C. Calhoun*. Ed. J. F. Jameson. Annual Report of the American Historical Association for the Year 1899, Vol. II. Washington: Government Printing Office, 1900.

Cappon, Lester J. (ed.). *The Adams-Jefferson Letters: The Complete Correspondence Between Thomas Jefferson and Abigail and John Adams.* 2 vols. Chapel Hill: University of North Carolina Press, 1959.

Cecil, E. [pseud.]. *Life of Lafayette, Written for Children.* Boston: n.p., 1860.

Ceremonies on the Completion of the Monument, to the Memory of Washington and Lafayette, in the Monument Cemetery of Philadelphia. [Philadelphia]: n.p., 1869.

Chinard, Gilbert (ed.). *The Letters of Lafayette and Jefferson.* Baltimore: Johns Hopkins Press, 1929.

Clark, Willis Gaylord. *An Address on the Characters of Lafayette and Washington: Pronounced Before the Washington Society of Lafayette College, Easton, Pa., on July 4, 1840.* Philadelphia: n.p., 1840.

Clay, Henry. *The Life and Speeches of Hon. Henry Clay.* Comp. and ed. Daniel Mallory. 2 vols. New York: Robert P. Bixby and Co., 1843.

————. *The Life, Correspondence, and Speeches of Henry Clay.* Ed. Calvin Colton. 6 vols. New York: n.p., 1864.

————. *The Papers of Henry Clay.* Ed. James F. Hopkins. 3 vols. Lexington: University of Kentucky Press, 1959–63.

[Coffin, Robert Stevenson]. *Oriental Harp: Poems of the Boston Bard.* Providence: Smith and Parmenter, 1826.

Colorado Department of Public Instruction. *LaFayette Memorial Day, Denver, Colorado, October 19, 1898.* Denver: n.p., 1898.

A Complete History of the Marquis de Lafayette, Major General in the Army of the United States of America, in the War of the Revolution. New York: Robert Lowry, 1826.

Cooper, James Fenimore. *Correspondence of James Fenimore Cooper.* Ed. James Fenimore Cooper. 2 vols. New Haven: Yale University Press, 1922.

————. *The Letters and Journals of James Fenimore Cooper.* Ed. James Franklin Beard. 6 vols. Cambridge, Mass.: Harvard University Press, Belknap Press, 1960–68.

[————]. *Notions of the Americans: Picked Up by a Travelling Bachelor.* 2 vols. London: Henry Colburn, 1828.

Criss, Mildred. *La Fayette: On the Heights of Freedom.* New York: Dodd, Mead and Co., 1954.

Crow, Martha Foote. *Lafayette.* New York: Macmillan, 1916.

Culbreth, John Hardcastle, Esq. *An Address, Delivered on the 4th of July, A.D. 1834; Being the 58th Anniversary of American Independence.* Annapolis: n.p., 1834.

Cumming, Hooper. *An Oration Commemorative of American Independence; Delivered July 5, 1824, in the Bowery Church, Before the Firemen of the City of New-York.* New York: n.p., 1824.

Cushing, Caleb. *A Eulogy on La Fayette, Pronounced at the Request of the Young Men of Dover, September 6, 1834.* Dover, N.H.: n.p., 1834.

Cutter, William. *The Life of General Lafayette.* 2nd ed. New York: Derby and Jackson, 1857.

Davidge, Francis H. *An Oration, Delivered at the Request of the Committee of Arrangements, on the Part of the Corporation of Baltimore, on the Tenth Day of July, 1834, in Commemoration of the Death of Lafayette.* [Baltimore]: Sands and Neilson, [1834].

Dayton, Aaron Ogden. *Eulogy on La Fayette, Pronounced Before the Society of Cincinnati of the State of New-Jersey, on the 4th of July, 1835.* New York: R. Curtis Brown, 1835.

Dubuque, Hugo A. *Lafayette. Address at the Dedication of the Equestrian Statue of General Lafayette, Fall River, Massachusetts, September 4, 1916.* [Fall River, Mass.: 1916].

Easton, William C. *Eulogium on La Fayette; Delivered in the First Baptist Church, Ninth Street, Washington City, by Appointment of the Union Literary Society, on the Evening of the 15th September, 1834.* Washington: Duff Green, 1834.

Elliott, Samuel. *Fayette in Prison; or, Misfortunes of the Great. A Modern Tragedy, by a Gentleman of Boston.* Worcester, Mass.: Printed for the Author, 1800.

————. *An Humble Tribute to My Country: Or Practical Essays, Political, Legal, Moral, and Miscellaneous, Including a Brief Account of the Life, Sufferings, and Memorable Visit of General Lafayette.* Boston: n.p., 1842.

Evenings in New England. Intended for Juvenile Amusement and Instruction. By an American Lady. Boston: Cummings, Hilliard and Co., 1824.

Everett, Edward. *Orations and Speeches, on Various Occasions.* Boston: American Stationers' Co., 1836.

————. *Orations and Speeches on Various Occasions.* 4 vols. Boston: Little, Brown and Co., 1879.

Farmer, Lydia Hoyt. *The Life of La Fayette, the Knight of Liberty in Two Worlds and Two Centuries.* New York: Thomas Y. Crowell and Co., 1888.

Ford, Worthington Chauncey (ed.). *Journals of the Continental Congress, 1774–1789.* 34 vols. Washington: Government Printing Office, 1904–37.

Foster, John. *A Sketch of the Tour of General Lafayette, on His Late Visit to the United States, 1824.* Portland, Maine: A. W. Thayer, 1824.

Foubert, Auguste. *A Patriotic Malediction, or Washington and La-*

fayette at Fairmount Park. Translated from the French. New York: n.p., [1876].

Franklin, Benjamin. *The Writings of Benjamin Franklin.* Ed. Albert Henry Smyth. 10 vols. New York: Macmillan Co., 1907.

Freneau, Philip. *The Poems of Philip Freneau, Poet of the American Revolution.* Ed. Fred Lewis Pattee. 3 vols. Princeton, N.J.: University Library, 1902–1907.

Frothingham, N. L. *A Sermon on the Death of General Lafayette, Preached to the First Church in Boston, on Sunday, the 29th of June, 1834.* Boston: n.p., 1834.

Gottschalk, Louis R. (ed.). *The Letters of Lafayette to Washington, 1777–1799.* New York: Helen Fahnestock Hubbard, 1944.

Gregg, Jarvis. *Eulogy on Lafayette, Delivered in the Chapel of Dartmouth College, July 4, 1834.* Hanover, N.H.: n.p., 1834.

Hale, E. J. *Monsieur Le Marquis de La Fayette.* North Carolina Booklet, I (December 10, 1901). Raleigh: Capital Printing Co., 1901.

Hall, James Norman, and Nordhoff, Charles Bernard (eds.). *The Lafayette Flying Corps.* 2nd ed. 2 vols. Port Washington, N.Y.: Kennikat Press, 1964.

Hallowell, James Mott. *The Spirit of Lafayette.* Garden City, N.Y.: Doubleday, Page and Co., 1918.

Hamilton, Alexander. *The Papers of Alexander Hamilton.* Ed. Harold C. Syrett. 15 vols. New York: Columbia University Press, 1961–.

Headley, William T. *Makers of American History.* New York: J. A. Hill and Co., 1904.

Henry Francis Du Pont Winterthur Museum. *Lafayette, the Nation's Guest: A Picture Book of Mementos Which Express the Respect and Affection of the American People for Lafayette.* Winterthur, Del.: n.p., 1957.

[Hervey, Nathaniel]. *The Memory of Washington; with Biographical Sketches of His Mother and Wife. Relations of Lafayette and Washington; with Incidents and Anecdotes in the Lives of the Two Patriots.* Boston: James Munroe and Co., 1852.

Hester, The Reverend St. Clair. *Lafayette, the Apostle of Liberty. Sermon Preached in the Church of the Messiah, Brooklyn-New York, Sunday, May 13, 1917, by the Rector.* [Brooklyn: 1917].

Hillhouse, James A[braham]. *An Oration Pronounced at New Haven, by Request of the Common Council, August 19, 1834, in Commemoration of the Life and Services of General Lafayette.* New Haven: H. Howe and Co., 1834.

Historical Sketches Illustrative of the Life of M. de Lafayette and the Leading Events of the American Revolution. By an American. New York: n.p., 1824.

Holland, Rupert Sargent. *Lafayette, for Young Americans.* Philadelphia: George W. Jacobs and Co., 1922.

Honour to the Brave. Merited Praise to the Disinterested. A Description of the Grand Fete Given at Washington Hall, by the Citizens of France, to Gen. La Fayette. New York: n.p., 1824.

Howe, Samuel Gridley. *Letters and Journals of Samuel Gridley Howe.* Ed. Laura E. Richards. 2 vols. Boston: Dana Estes and Co., 1906.

Ingersoll, Charles J[ared]. *A Communication on the Improvement of Government: Read Before the American Philosophical Society, at a Meeting Attended by General La Fayette, October 1st, 1824.* Philadelphia: Abraham Small, 1824.

Jay, John. *The Correspondence and Public Papers of John Jay.* Ed. Henry P. Johnston. 4 vols. New York: G. P. Putnam's Sons, 1890–93.

Jefferson, Thomas. *The Life and Selected Writings of Thomas Jefferson.* Ed. Adrienne Koch and William Peden. New York: Random House, 1944.

————. *Memoir, Correspondence, and Miscellanies, from the Papers of Thomas Jefferson.* Ed. Thomas Jefferson Randolph. 4 vols. Charlottesville, Va.: F. Carr, and Co., 1829.

————. *The Papers of Thomas Jefferson.* Ed. Julian P. Boyd. 17 vols. Princeton, N.J.: Princeton University Press, 1950–.

————. *The Works of Thomas Jefferson.* Ed. Paul Leicester Ford. 12 vols. New York: G. P. Putnam's Sons, 1904–1905.

————. *The Writings of Thomas Jefferson.* Ed. Andrew A. Lipscomb and Albert Ellery Bergh. Memorial ed. 20 vols. Washington: Thomas Jefferson Memorial Association of the United States, 1904.

[Knapp, Samuel Lorenzo]. *Memoirs of General Lafayette. With an Account of His Visit to America, and of His Reception by the People of the United States, from his Arrival, August 15th, to the Celebration at Yorktown, October 19th, 1824.* Boston: E. G. House, 1824.

The La Fayette Almanac, for the Year 1825. Philadelphia: n.p., [1825].

Lafayette College; a Book of the Centenary, 1832–1932. Easton, Pa.: Lafayette College, 1932.

Lafayette Day Exercises in Commemoration of the Double Anniversary of the Birth of Lafayette and the Battle of the Marne: September 6th, 1917. [New York: 1917].

Lafayette Day, Exposition Park, Los Angeles, September Sixth, One Thousand Nine Hundred and Seventeen at Three O'Clock P.M. [Los Angeles?]: n.p., 1917.

Lafayette Day National Committee and Lafayette Day Citizens' Committee of New York. *Lafayette Day, 1916.* [New York: 1916].

Lafayette Day, September 6, 1919. Call Issued by the Lafayette Day National Committee, and Report of the National Observance in the United States of the Double Anniversary, September 6, 1918, of the

Birth of Lafayette (1757) and the Battle of the Marne (1914). [New York: 1919].

Lafayette-Marne Day, September 6th, 1920. N.p.: n.d.

Lafayette, or Disinterested Benevolence. Boston: Office of the Christian Register, 1825.

Lee, Richard Henry. *The Letters of Richard Henry Lee*. Ed. James Curtis Ballagh. 2 vols. New York: Macmillan Co., 1911.

Lee, Walter. *Lafayette; or the Fortress of Olmutz. A Melo Drama in Three Acts. Founded on Events in the Life of General La Fayette*. Philadelphia: Thomas Town, 1824.

Letter on the President's Message; Supposed to Be Written by General Lafayette, to His Adopted Countrymen, on the Receipt of the President's Message, on the Opening of the Second Session of the Twenty-second Congress, December 4, 1832. New York: Peabody and Co., 1833.

Levasseur, A. *Lafayette in America in 1824 and 1825; or, Journal of a Voyage to the United States*. 2 vols. Philadelphia: Carey and Lea, 1829.

The Life and Services of Major-General the Marquis de Lafayette. New York: Beadle and Adams, 1870.

Life of Lafayette, Including an Account of the Memorable Revolution of the Three Days of 1830. Boston: Light and Horton, 1835.

Long, John D. *Lafayette in America*. Boston: Youth's Companion, 1902.

Mack, Ebenezer. *The Life of Gilbert Motier de Lafayette*. 2nd ed. Ithaca, N.Y.: n.p., 1843.

Madison, James. *Letters and Other Writings of James Madison, Fourth President of the United States*. 4 vols. Philadelphia: J. B. Lippincott and Co., 1865.

Madison, Lucy Foster. *Lafayette*. Philadelphia: Penn Publishing Co., 1921.

Memoirs of General La Fayette. New York: Russell Robins, 1825.

Memoirs of the Military Career of the Marquis de La Fayette, During the Revolutionary War, Down to the Present Time, Including His Reception in New-York, Boston, and the Principal Towns in New-England. Boston: n.p., 1824.

Monroe, James. *The Writings of James Monroe, Including a Collection of His Public and Private Papers and Correspondence Now for the First Time Printed*. Ed. Stanislaus Murray Hamilton. 7 vols. New York: G. P. Putnam's Sons, 1898–1903.

Montesquieu, Baron de. *The Spirit of the Laws*. Trans. Thomas Nugent. New York: Hafner Publishing Co., 1949.

Morgan, George. *The True La Fayette*. Philadelphia: J. B. Lippincott Co., 1919.

Morgan, Lady [Sydney Owenson]. *France [in 1816]*. 2 vols. New York: James Eastburn and Co., 1817.

Morris, Gouverneur. *The Diary and Letters of Gouverneur Morris.* Ed. Anne Cary Morris. 2 vols. London: Kegan Paul and Co., 1889.

Morse, Samuel F. B. *Samuel F. B. Morse, His Letters and Journals.* Ed. Edward Lind Morse. 2 vols. Boston: Houghton Mifflin Co., 1914.

Neilson, Peter. *Recollections of a Six Years' Residence in the United States of America, Interspersed with Original Anecdotes, Illustrating the Manners of the Inhabitants of the Great Western Republic.* Edinburgh: William Tate, 1830.

Nevin, Shirley. *LaFayette, the Patriot—the Soldier, the Man; an Essay; Awarded First Prize on the Occasion of the Dedication of the New Quarters of the Lafayette Trust Company, Easton, Pa., "Bastille Day," July 14, 1934.* [Easton, Pa.: Lafayette Trust Co., 1934].

New York City Common Council. *Particulars of the Funeral Honours to the Memory of General La Fayette, with the Eulogium Delivered by General James Tallmadge, June 26, 1834.* New York: n.p., 1834.

Nicolay, Helen. *The Boys' Life of Lafayette.* New York: Harper and Brothers, 1920.

A North American. *To General Lafayette, United States, August 10, 1831.* [New York?: 1831].

Outlines of the Life of General Lafayette: With an Account of the French Revolution of 1830, Until the Choice of Louis Philip as King. New York: Tappan, 1830.

Paine, Thomas. *The Writings of Thomas Paine.* Ed. Moncure Daniel Conway. 4 vols. New York: G. P. Putnam's Sons, 1894–96.

The Pamphlet, Containing a Description of the Grateful Manner in Which the Whole Population of the City of New-York Voluntarily with Open Arms Received General La Fayette on the 16th August 1824, and the Very Affectionate Manner in Which They Exhibited Their Farewell on the Memorable 14th July 1825; Together with a Description of the National Festival, Given by the Honourable The Corporation of the City of New-York, in Commemoration of the Glorious Fourth of July, 1776. Rendered Still More Interesting by the Presence of the "Nation's Guest." N.p.: n.d.

Parker, A[mos] A[ndrew], Esq. *Recollections of General Lafayette on His Visit to the United States, in 1824 and 1825; with the Most Remarkable Incidents of His Life, from His Birth to the Day of His Death.* Keene, N.H.: Sentinel Printing Co., 1879.

Parsons, Edwin C. *I Flew with the Lafayette Escadrille.* 2nd ed. Indianapolis: E. C. Seale and Co., 1963.

Paxton, John D. *Letters on Slavery; Addressed to the Cumberland Congregation, Virginia.* Lexington, Ky.: Abraham T. Skillman, 1833.

Penman, John Simpson. *Lafayette and Three Revolutions*. Boston: Stratford Co., 1929.

Penniman, James Hosmer. *I, Our Debt to France; II, What Lafayette Did for America: Dedicated to the Fatherless Children of France.* [Philadelphia: 1921].

Perkins, Samuel. *Historical Sketches of the United States from the Peace of 1815 to 1830*. New York: S. Converse, 1830.

Pictorial Life of General Lafayette; Embracing Anecdotes Illustrative of His Character. Embellished with Engravings. Philadelphia: Lindsay and Blakiston, 1847.

Quincy, Josiah. *Figures of the Past from the Leaves of Old Journals.* Boston: Roberts Brothers, 1883.

Register of Debates in Congress. 14 vols. Washington: Gales and Seaton, 1825–37.

Rice, Daniel T. *An Eulogium, on the Sublime Virtues of the Illustrious Hero and Philanthropist, Gen. Lafayette; with Sketches of the American and French Revolutions.* Enfield, [?]: n.p., 1832.

Roberts, Ellwood (comp.). *Lafayette at Barren Hill: Exercises at the Dedication of the Monument Erected by the Historical Society of Montgomery County, Pa., Saturday, May 21, 1898.* Norristown, Pa.: n.p., 1898.

Roberts, Octavia. *With Lafayette in America*. Boston: Houghton Mifflin Co., 1919.

Sarrans, B. *Memoirs of General Lafayette and of the French Revolution of 1830.* 2 vols. London: Richard Bentley, 1832.

Sedgwick, Henry Dwight. *La Fayette*. Indianapolis: Bobbs-Merrill, 1928.

Seward, William H. *The Works of William H. Seward.* Ed. George E. Baker. 3 vols. Redfield, N.Y.: n.p., 1853.

Sketch of the Life and Military Services of Gen. La Fayette, During the American Revolution. The Hero and Patriot, Who Abandoned His Home, His Family, His Rank, and a Princely Fortune, for the Sake of Fighting in the Cause of American Liberty. New York: n.p., 1824.

Snow, Marshall S. *Lafayette, the Friend of Washington. An Address Delivered in Memorial Hall, Friday Evening, February 22, 1884, in Commemoration of the One Hundredth and Fifty-Second Anniversary of the Birth of George Washington and the Thirty-First Birthday of Washington University.* St. Louis: n.p., 1884.

Sparks, Jared. *The Life and Writings of Jared Sparks, Comprising Selections from His Journals and Correspondence.* Ed. Herbert Baxter Adams. 2 vols. New York: Houghton, Mifflin and Co., 1893.

Sprague, William B[uell], D.D. *An Oration Commemorative of the*

Late General Lafayette, Pronounced Before the Military and Civic Societies of the City of Albany, in the South Dutch Church, July 24, 1834. Albany, N.Y.: Packard and Van Benthuysen, 1834.

Sumner, Charles. *The Works of Charles Sumner.* 15 vols. Boston: Lee and Shepard, 1870–83.

Ticknor, George. *Life, Letters and Journals of George Ticknor.* Ed. G. S. Hillard. 2 vols. Boston: James R. Osgood and Co., 1876.

[Ticknor, George]. *Outlines of the Principal Events in the Life of General Lafayette. From the North American Review.* Boston: Cummings, Hilliard and Co., 1825.

Tilton, George P. *An Account of the Life of Marie Joseph Paul Yves Roch Gilbert Dumotier Marquis de La Fayette, Major-General in the Service of America and Noblest Patriot of the French Revolution, with Illustrations of the La Fayette Pattern of Sterling Silver Tableware.* Newburyport, Mass.: Towle Manufacturing Co., 1907.

Tocqueville, Alexis de. *Democracy in America.* Ed. Phillips Bradley. 2 vols. New York: Vintage Books, 1954.

Tuckerman, Bayard. *Life of General Lafayette, with a Critical Estimate of His Character and Public Acts.* 2 vols. London: n.p., 1889.

United States State Department. *Report Respecting the Unveiling, at Paris, France, on July 4, 1900, of the Statue of Lafayette Provided by the Contributions of School Children of the United States.* [Washington: 1900].

Upham, Nathaniel G[ookin]. *Eulogy on Lafayette, Delivered at Concord, Agreeable to a Resolve of the New-Hampshire Legislature, on the 17th of June 1835.* Concord, Mass.: Cyrus Barton, 1835.

[Waln, Robert]. *An Account of the Visit of General Lafayette to the United States, from His Arrival in August, 1824, to His Embarkation on Board the Brandywine Frigate; Return to France, Reception, and Retirement to La Grange.* Philadelphia: J. P. Ayres, 1827.

————. *Life of the Marquis de Lafayette, Major General in the Service of the United States of America, in the War of the Revolution.* Philadelphia: J. P. Ayres, 1825.

Washington, George. *The Writings of George Washington: Being His Correspondence, Addresses, Messages, and Other Papers, Official and Private, Selected and Published from the Original Manuscripts; with a Life of the Author, Notes, and Illustrations.* Ed. Jared Sparks. 12 vols. Charleston, S.C.: A. Mygatt, 1837–39.

————. *The Writings of George Washington from the Original Manuscript Sources, 1745–1799.* Ed. John C. Fitzpatrick. 39 vols. Washington: Government Printing Office, 1931–44.

Webster, Daniel. *The Writings and Speeches of Daniel Webster.* National ed. 18 vols. Boston: Little, Brown and Co., 1903.

Wharton, Francis (ed.). *The Revolutionary Diplomatic Correspon-*

dence of the United States. 6 vols. Washington: Government Printing Office, 1889.

Whitlock, Brand. *La Fayette.* 2 vols. New York: D. Appleton and Co., 1929.

Wilcox, William A. *General Lafayette.* [Waterloo, N.Y.?: 1922].

Wilson, George. *Roosevelt's Insult to the Memory of Jackson and LaFayette.* Washington: n.p., 1903.

Wilson, Woodrow. *War and Peace: Presidential Messages, Addresses, and Public Papers (1917–1924).* Ed. Ray Stannard Baker and William E. Dodd. 2 vols. New York: Harper and Brothers Publishers, 1927.

Woodworth, Samuel. *LaFayette, or the Castle of Olmutz. A Drama, in Three Acts, as Performed at the New-York Park Theatre, with Unbounded Applause.* New York: Circulating Library and Dramatic Repository, 1824.

Wright, Frances. *Views of Society and Manners in America.* Ed. Paul R. Baker. Cambridge, Mass.: Harvard University Press, Belknap Press, 1963.

Wylie, Andrew, D.D. *An Eulogy on Lafayette, Delivered in Bloomington, Indiana, on the Ninth of May, 1835, at the Request of the Citizens and Students.* Cincinnati: Taylor and Tracy, 1835.

SECONDARY SOURCES

ARTICLES

Bergen, Frank. "Lafayette's Visit to New Jersey in 1824–'5." *New Jersey Historical Society Proceedings,* n.s., IX (1924), 209–22.

Butterfield, Lyman H. "The Jubilee of Independence, July 4, 1826." *Virginia Magazine of History and Biography,* LXI (1953), 119–40.

"Centennial of the Visit of General Lafayette to Shawneetown." *Illinois State Historical Society Journal,* XVIII (1925), 350–66.

Curti, Merle. "The Great Mr. Locke: America's Philosopher, 1783–1861." *Huntington Library Bulletin,* XI (1937), 107–51.

Curtis, Eugene N. "American Opinion of the French Nineteenth Century Revolutions." *American Historical Review,* XXIX (1924), 249–70.

Earle, Edward M. "American Interest in the Greek Cause, 1821–1827." *American Historical Review,* XXXIII (1927), 44–57.

Fishwick, Marshall W. "Giants on the Land." *Social Education,* XIV (1950), 16–20.

Galbreath, C. B. "Lafayette's Visit to Ohio Valley States." *Ohio Archaeological and Historical Quarterly,* XXIX (1920), 163–266.

Gillard, John T. "Lafayette, Friend of the Negro." *Journal of Negro History,* XIX (1934), 355–71.

Hume, Edgar Erskine. "Lafayette in Kentucky." *Kentucky Historical Society Register*, XXXIII (1935), 118–36, 234–51, 279–306, and XXXIV (1936), 42–76, 139–56.

Jones, Russell M. "The Flowering of a Legend: Lafayette and the Americans, 1825–1834." *French Historical Studies*, IV (1966), 384–410.

Klapp, Orrin E. "Creation of Popular Heroes." *American Journal of Sociology*, LIV (1948), 135–41.

———. "Hero Worship in America." *American Sociological Review*, XIV (1949), 53–62.

———. "Heroes, Villains and Fools, as Agents of Social Control." *American Sociological Review*, XIX (1954), 56–62.

"Lafayette in New Brunswick in 1824." *New Jersey Historical Society Proceedings*, n.s., V (1920), 112–16.

McCall, D. L. (ed.). "Lafayette's Visit to Alabama, April 1825." *Alabama Historical Quarterly*, XVII (1955), 33–77.

Meadows, P. "Some Notes on the Social Psychology of the Hero." *Southwestern Social Science Quarterly*, XXVI (1945), 239–47.

Quynn, Dorothy Mackay. "Lafayette's Visit in Frederick, 1824." *Maryland Historical Magazine*, XLIX (1954), 290–300.

Renshaw, James A. "Lafayette, His Visit to New Orleans, April, 1825, and the Centennial Celebration Thereof, April, 1925." *Louisiana Historical Quarterly*, IX (1926), 181–89.

BOOKS

Artz, Frederick B. *France Under the Bourbon Restoration, 1814–1830.* Cambridge, Mass.: Harvard University Press, 1931.

Bailyn, Bernard. *The Ideological Origins of the American Revolution.* Cambridge, Mass.: Harvard University Press, Belknap Press, 1967.

Beveridge, Albert J. *The Life of John Marshall.* 4 vols. Boston: Houghton Mifflin Co., 1916.

Boorstin, Daniel J. *The Americans: The National Experience.* New York: Random House, 1965.

———. *The Lost World of Thomas Jefferson.* Boston: Beacon Press, 1960.

Brandon, Edgar Ewing (comp. and ed.). *Lafayette, Guest of the Nation: A Contemporary Account of the Triumphal Tour of General Lafayette Through the United States in 1824–1825, as Reported by the Local Newspapers.* 3 vols. Oxford, Ohio: Oxford Historical Press, 1950–57.

———. *A Pilgrimage of Liberty: A Contemporary Account of the Triumphal Tour of General Lafayette Through the Southern and*

Western States in 1825, as Reported by the Local Newspapers. Athens, Ohio: Lawhead Press, 1944.

Bryan, William A. *George Washington in American Literature, 1775–1865.* New York: Columbia University Press, 1952.

Burns, Edward M. *The American Idea of Mission: Concepts of National Purpose and Destiny.* New Brunswick, N.J.: Rutgers University Press, 1957.

H. Trevor Colbourn. *The Lamp of Experience: Whig History and the Intellectual Origins of the American Revolution.* Chapel Hill, N.C.: University of North Carolina Press, 1965.

Conway, Moncure D. *The Life of Thomas Paine: With a History of His Literary, Political and Religious Career in America, France, and England. To Which Is Added a Sketch of Paine by William Cobbett.* 2 vols. New York: Putnam, 1892.

Cunliffe, Marcus. *George Washington, Man and Monument.* Boston: Little, Brown and Co., 1958.

Curti, Merle. *The Roots of American Loyalty.* New York: Columbia University Press, 1946.

Echeverria, Durand. *Mirage in the West: A History of the French Image of American Society to 1815.* Princeton, N.J.: Princeton University Press, 1957.

Fishwick, Marshall W. *American Heroes: Myth and Reality.* Washington: Public Affairs Press, 1954.

Forbes, Allan, and Cadman, Paul F. *France and New England. Wherein Is Related the Story of Lafayette's Visits to Boston and Other Places in New England Together with Facts Pertaining to His Life in France.* Vol. I. Boston: State Street Trust Co., 1925.

Gottschalk, Louis R. *Lafayette and the Close of the American Revolution.* Chicago: University of Chicago Press, 1942.

————. *Lafayette Between the American and the French Revolution, 1783–1789.* Chicago: University of Chicago Press, 1950.

————. *Lafayette Joins the American Army.* Chicago: University of Chicago Press, 1937.

————. *The United States and Lafayette.* Rock Island, Ill.: Augustana College Library, 1958.

Greene, George Washington. *The Life of Nathanael Greene, Major General in the Army of the Revolution.* 3 vols. New York: G. P. Putnam and Son, 1867–71.

Hazen, Charles Downer. *Contemporary American Opinion of the French Revolution.* Baltimore: Johns Hopkins Press, 1897.

Hudson, Nora E. *Ultra-Royalism and the French Restoration.* Cambridge: Cambridge University Press, 1936.

Hume, Edgar Erskine. *LaFayette and the Society of the Cincinnati.* Baltimore: Johns Hopkins Press, 1934.

Jones, Howard Mumford. *America and French Culture, 1750–1848.* Chapel Hill, N.C.: University of North Carolina Press, 1927.

Koch, Adrienne. *The Philosophy of Thomas Jefferson.* New York: Columbia University Press, 1943.

Larrabee, Stephen A. *Hellas Observed: The American Experience of Greece, 1775–1865.* New York: New York University Press, 1957.

Leys, M. D. R. *Between Two Empires: A History of French Politicians and People Between 1814 and 1848.* New York: Longmans, Green and Co., 1955.

Marshall, Thomas Maitland. *The Life and Papers of Frederick Bates.* 2 vols. St. Louis: Missouri Historical Society, 1926.

Marx, Leo. *The Machine in the Garden: Technology and the Pastoral Ideal in America.* New York: Oxford University Press, 1964.

Meyers, Marvin. *The Jacksonian Persuasion; Politics and Belief.* Stanford, Calif.: Stanford University Press, 1957.

Miller, Perry. *The Life of the Mind in America from the Revolution to the Civil War.* New York: Harcourt, Brace and World, 1965.

Nolan, J. Bennett. *Lafayette in America Day by Day.* Baltimore: Johns Hopkins Press, 1934.

Palmer, R. R. *The Age of the Democratic Revolution: A Political History of Europe and America, 1760–1800.* 2 vols. Princeton, N.J.: Princeton University Press, 1959–64.

Perkins, Dexter. *Hands Off: A History of the Monroe Doctrine.* Boston: Little, Brown and Co., 1943.

Persons, Stow. *American Minds: A History of Ideas.* New York: Holt, Rinehart and Winston, 1958.

Peterson, Merrill D. *The Jefferson Image in the American Mind.* New York: Oxford University Press, 1962.

Pierson, George Wilson. *Tocqueville and Beaumont in America.* New York: Oxford University Press, 1938.

Rozwenc, Edwin C. (ed.). *Ideology and Power in the Age of Jackson.* Garden City, N.Y.: Doubleday and Co., 1964.

Schouler, James. *History of the United States of America, Under the Constitution.* Rev. ed. 6 vols. New York: Dodd, Mead and Co., 1904.

Sears, Louis Martin. *George Washington and the French Revolution.* Detroit: Wayne State University Press, 1960.

Somkin, Fred. *Unquiet Eagle: Memory and Desire in the Idea of American Freedom, 1815–1860.* Ithaca, N.Y.: Cornell University Press, 1967.

Stallings, Laurence. *The Doughboys: The Story of the AEF, 1917–1918.* New York: Harper and Row, 1963.

Strout, Cushing. *The American Image of the Old World.* New York: Harper and Row, 1963.

Taylor, William R. *Cavalier and Yankee: The Old South and American National Character.* New York: George Braziller, 1961.

Ward, John William. *Andrew Jackson, Symbol for an Age.* New York: Oxford University Press, 1962.

Waterman, William Randall, *Frances Wright.* New York: Columbia University Press, 1924.

Wecter, Dixon. *The Hero in America: A Chronicle of Hero-Worship.* New York: Charles Scribner's Sons, 1941.

White, Elizabeth Brett. *American Opinion of France from Lafayette to Poincaré.* New York: Alfred A. Knopf, 1927.

Index

Short, William, 21*n*
Siders, Georgium, 40*n*
Slavery: and Lafayette, 67, 67*n*, 72–73, 152–53; and American Revolution, 68, 69–70, 74, 152; and visit of 1824–25, pp. 68–71; and Declaration of Independence, 70–71
Slaves, 68–70
South American republics, 104
South American revolutions: and American Revolution compared, 104; American response to, 104, 104*n*, 119, 127; and receptions for Lafayette, 104*n*; and Lafayette, 113
Stamp, commemorative, 146, 146*n*
Stanton, Captain C. E., 154*n*
Storrs, Henry R., 53
Story, Judge Joseph, 49–50
Sublimity, 56–59, 59*n*
Suffrage, 124, 125–26, 127
Sumner, Charles, 152, 152*n*

Tamerlane, 55
Tefft, J. K., 82
Temperance movement, 65
"Three Days." *See* Revolution of 1830
Ticknor, George: on Lafayette's role in French Revolution, 30; on visit of 1824–25, pp. 36, 42, 45, 46–47; on American Revolution, 46
Tocqueville, Alexis de, 64, 122, 129–30
Tolman, Thomas, 83*n*
Toomer, Judge John DeRossett, 28
Triumphal Tour. *See* Receptions for Lafayette; Visit of 1824–25
Tuckerman, Bayard, 139, 142–43, 144

Union: Lafayette on, 15–16, 75, 76, 79–80; Lafayette as symbol of, 16, 56, 72, 75, 75*n*, 77, 80, 81–82; and visit of 1824–25, pp. 75–77, 75*n*; and American Revolution, 80, 151; and American mission, 80–81; and nullification controversy, 82
Union Square, 149
Utilitarianism, 12

Veterans, 42–43, 53–54

Villeneuve, Jerome Petion de, 22
Virginia constitutional convention, 72
Virtue: and republican experiment, 10; American opinion of, 10*n*, 11, 34, 163; and Lafayette, 10, 12, 26–34, 42, 53, 55, 63, 143, 150, 152, 162–65; republican, 26, 33, 34, 53, 55, 63, 150; of Americans, 46, 55, 82; and republican government, 63, 164–65; of French revolutionists of 1830, p. 120; and American mission, 165
Virtues: of hero-symbols, 7; aristocratic, 10
Visit of 1784, pp. 11, 15, 16, 17*n*, 18–19
Visit of 1824–25; Lafayette on, 6, 6*n*, 76; and antislavery movement, 67–74; and slavery, 68, 70–71; and republicanism, 68, 118; and election of 1824, p. 75; and union, 75–77, 75*n*; and American mission, 97–118; European response to, 102; and Greek revolution, 113–16; mentioned, 83, 149, 151. *See also* Receptions for Lafayette

Waln, Robert, 96
Ware, Henry, 115
War of 1812, pp. 35, 44
Washington, George: tomb of, 3, 57–58, 58*n*; and Lafayette, 4, 17–18, 17*n*, 19, 30, 35, 44*n*, 83, 129, 134, 137, 145; as hero-symbol, 7; on union, 16; and Bastille, 16–17; and liberty, 16, 18, 141; on Lafayette, 16, 87*n*; and American Revolution, 18, 28, 59, 60, 154; and receptions for Lafayette, 44*n*; and nullification controversy, 79, 80; farewell address of, 83, 83n; and Greek revolution, 115; mentioned, 82, 96, 124
Washington, D.C., 113
Washington's Birthday, 45, 146*n*
Webster, Daniel: on American Revolution, 61; on death of Jefferson and Adams, 61; on liberty, 102–103, 109,